BASIC TRAINING

Equipping the Church in the Ministry of Healing

S A N D Y   B E L L

ISBN 978-1-0980-1697-5 (paperback)
ISBN 978-1-0980-1698-2 (digital)

Christian Faith Publishing, Inc.
832 Park Avenue
Meadville, PA 16335
www.christianfaithpublishing.com

This author uses may direct quotes and other materials by other authors or individuals which may not be noted directly within the pages. However, every resource is referenced on the resources pages at the end of this book.

Printed in the United States of America

CONTENTS

ACKNOWLEDGMENTS

I have to acknowledge and say thank you, to my husband, Jimmy Bell. You have been my greatest encourager and sideline warrior as I have walked through this adventure with our Lord. Thank you, for putting up with all the late night studies and research with out complaint! You are a great blessing from God!

I also want to say thank you to two very special editors, Kathy Gardner for taking this manuscript, many years ago and formatting it into a training manual, which I have used to training and equip the body of Christ for many years. I love you, my sister!

Eric Flore, thank you my friend and editor for taking this manual and re-editing all of my added works. Thank you Eric, for being that inspiration to seek publishing. I would never have done this without your encouragement! I love you my brother!

There is one other very special person that I want to thank. Deb Davis, you have walked along side of me and pulled on my gifts as you saw them growing and maturing. You my friend, have never ceased to call me out and encourage me to walk on water with Jesus! You have always encouraged me to be all that I am in Christ.

To everyone else who has believed in my giftings and ministry calling, Thank You! You know who you are!

The most important acknowledgement goes to my Lord, Jesus Christ! I would not be who I am today, without your transforming grace and amazing love. It is my pray that my life reflect my love for you and your love for me.

May all Glory and Honor be yours!

INTRODUCTION TO BIBLICAL
HEALING MINISTRY

Randy Clark says, and I quote, "*To properly understand healing, one must experience it! When it comes to healing, knowledge without experience is an inferior level of knowledge.*" Randy Clark is one of the many who have experienced the power of God in healing prayer. It is my belief that our God is Jehovah-Rophe, the Lord who heals! The Bible is full of scriptures that confirm Jesus is the Lord of all and that in His death and resurrection, we are alive in Him and healed in Him!

This manual was written for training of the church. It is a useful training in biblical healing ministry for any situation it is needed. It is not a set formula by any means because the key to all healing is not in anything that we can do, except to flow with what God is doing through our relationship with Him.

In the following pages, I hope to deliver a clear understanding of the why and how we minister to those in need of healing. I also hope to help you have a better understanding of what healing may or may not look like.

When I first heard the word *healing*, I remember thinking that it meant to be healed physically somehow, whether that was a disease cured, limbs grown out, eyesight and or hearing restored, or just an overall good bill of health. I have since learned that the way we see healing may not be the way God sees it. God has full knowledge of what needs to happen within each one of us, and He will accomplish what is needed to establish a relationship with us!

It will be essential that you, the reader, know the One who is the source of healing. I am talking about a knowing that goes far beyond a mere acquaintance with God, but a knowing that is the most intimate of all your relationships. That deep place in you calling out to that deep place in Him for more revelation of who He is and who you are in Him! It is only in this place of knowing Him that our faith grows because we learn to trust who He is—El Shaddai, God Almighty, the All Sufficient One! He is Immanuel (God with us) and "I Am." His promises never fail. When we are faithless, He is faithful. He never changes!

Our prayers are not too big for Him to handle. There are no circumstances in our lives that escape His fatherly awareness and care. El Roi (my God who sees me) knows us and our troubles!

It is my prayer that as you read the following pages, you will be enlightened to the heart of God as your Savior, Deliverer, and Healer. I pray that you will be blessed with a deeper level of wisdom, knowledge, and revelation to minister healing to others as the Holy Spirit leads you in the ministry of healing.

Shalom to you!

CHAPTER 1

A Good Servant, a Trained Minister

If you put these things before the brothers, you will be a good servant of Christ Jesus, being trained in the words of the faith and of the good doctrine that you have followed and have nothing to do with irreverent, silly myths. Rather, train yourself for godliness for while bodily training is of some value, godliness is of value in every way as it holds promise for the present life and also for the life to come. The saying is trustworthy and deserving of full acceptance. For to this end, we toil and strive because we have our hope set on the living God, who is the Savior of all people, especially of those who believe. Command and teach these things. Let no one despise you for your youth but set the believers an example in speech, in conduct, in love, in faith, and in purity. Until I come, devote yourself to the public reading of Scripture, to exhortation, and to teaching. Do

not neglect the gift you have, which was given
to you by prophecy when the council of elders
laid their hands on you. Practice these things
and immerse yourself in them so that all may see
your progress. Keep a close watch on yourself and
on the teaching. Persist in this for by so doing,
you will save both yourself and your hearers.

(1 Timothy 4:6–16)

A Good Minister

Truth: a good minister is one that remains positioned for personal refining! A true minister of God only ministers the truth in love and is without corruption. In other words, we should be as sold out for our own healing as we are sold out to minister. Another truth is that we cannot give away something we do not have. Sadly, we often do this!

The word of God is alive and active. It is powerful for pulling down of strongholds. What strongholds have been pulled down in your life?

Every day, a minister of the Lord needs to take a close-up evaluation of their own personal heart and life. Do I need to forgive someone? Does someone need to forgive me? Do I have proper accountability in my life? Am I submitted to the Lord? Do I respect authority? Where am I in my walk with the Lord? Do I have any open doors for the enemy to get in? Do I personally need to minister today?

In our evaluation of self, we must be honest! Is my house in order?

Here is the warning, our enemy prowls around like a roaring lion looking to destroy us! We can lie to ourselves and others, but we cannot lie to God nor the enemy. The enemy is always looking for an opportunity to gain access into our homes and destroy our identity as a son or a daughter.

We cannot take lightly the call and commissioning of a minister. It comes at a high cost. Have you counted the cost? Sin is sin, no matter what. Our means to justify our own personal sin is an open door. If we are aware of that sin and accountable to others for our confession and true repentance of that sin, then we should be walking swiftly toward freedom, not justification! If we are in denial and justification is an issue, then we are certainly compounding the consequences. We then give even more room for the enemy to get in and begin his subtle destruction. Don't forget the Lord will expose our sin if we do not humble ourselves and submit to God. He exposes it not to hurt us but because He does love us.

Remember that everything that we do or don't do has a potential to harm us and others if not handled properly. Our secret sin can hurt us, our family, even our church's reputation. Aside from that, what about the reputation of Jesus Christ! How are you representing Jesus?

I realize that all of this may sound harsh, but this is serious stuff! A life and death of a ministry lie in the balance, and who are we to take it lightly?

Christ never justified sin. He never made excuses for it! Jesus's response was always "*Go and sin no more!*" It was not a request or a "let me get back with you; we will deal with it later." It was a *command*!

Therefore, we as ministers of the Lord *must* receive the Word of the Lord and "*go* and *sin no more!*"

We cannot forget that we are representing the King of kings and the Lord of lords!

I am going to share some safety guidelines I firmly adhere to. These guidelines and values will only make us better ministers of the Lord Jesus Christ.

Guidelines for Ministry

The following are guidelines for anyone who chooses to be a minister of the Lord. The guidelines are also a safety measure for all volunteers, ministry team members, and staff and or leadership within any church or ministry organization. The word *guideline* should not be taken lightly.

Holy Spirit directs us to lead others in the image and likeness of Jesus Christ; therefore, we should never take lightly the safety of another person or ourselves. Although these are called guidelines, they can also be used to hold each individual accountable for their choices—good and bad!

Our mission as ministers with Jesus Christ should always be as follows:

- *Unity with the Holy Spirit.* He is our Leader, Guide, Director, and Teacher in every aspect of ministry.
- *Unity with our team (Hebrews 12:14–15).* Make every effort to live in peace with all men and to be holy. Without holiness, no man will see the Lord. See to it that no one misses the grace of God and that *no* bitter root grows up to cause trouble and defile many.

The bitter root that is spoken about here can cause harm to all persons in ministry. It gives the devil a foothold into our ministry time and creates an *unsafe* environment. *Disunity creates instability in our authority to minister*, leaving ourselves and the person we are ministering to be vulnerable to the demonic realm and greater bondage.

The keys to maintaining unity are the following:

- We hold nothing in our hearts toward anyone in leadership on ministry teams or that is a volunteer for the ministry of Jesus. This is especially true of anyone we are ministering to! Go immediately to the team member and work it out, forgive one another, pray together, and restore the unity between both parties.
- We will not hold secrets about each other. Sorry, hidden things are occult. We are the kingdom… We must refuse to be bound to secrecy by anyone on our team… *No secrets* (1 Timothy 5:17–20).

- If we hear a word of criticism about someone else, we will instruct the one with the issue to go *directly* to the other and talk about their criticism (Matthew 18:15–17)
- We should also warn that we are each accountable to God to report all gossip to leadership if it persists. Nor will we speak a word of criticism about any leader or about the ministry to anyone (Psalm 55:12–14).
- We will agree to pray for each other by name daily (Philippians 1:3–6).
- *Worship*—we should prepare our souls and spirits by entering into daily worship prior to ministry.
- We should be teachable and willing to attend all corporate training sessions as they are scheduled.
- We should be willing to attend all meetings as required by leadership.

The goal of a godly minister is not *to see a manifestation of some kind. The goal is an impartation of God's love through you and a release of power of the Holy Spirit in the name of Jesus for the person you are ministering to!*

- We are here to support the prayee (the person to whom we are ministering). *We are not to attempt to "fix" them. The person we are ministering to is our priority.* We must always be loving and compassionate, no matter the circumstances of the prayee.
- Anonymity and confidentiality are basic requirements. What's shared in ministry stays in the ministry. Anyone who talks about any of the ministry sessions outside of the facility and/or staff meetings without permission of the ministry director or overseer of the ministry should be given one warning only. The second time should result in a temporary suspension from ministry team. The purpose is to create and maintain a safe environment for healing. If we are ministering outside of a covering, we need this principle so that we become known as a trustworthy resource.

- Remember our Father, the Son Jesus Christ, and Holy Spirit are trustworthy. So must we be in Christlikeness!
- Honor and respect the person always... Remember, manifestations are not the person; it is the spirit! We will discuss this in deeper detail in a later chapter, but we never should allow a demon to abuse the person we are ministering to!

Same Gender Policy in Ministry—Safety First!

Women minister to women and men with men. Please do not minister alone with the opposite sex—always have accountability. In the case of deliverance, we should *almost* always have at least one of the same sexes on the team. This isn't always the case, so let the Holy Spirit lead you on this!

- Do not minister to the *opposite sex alone*!
- Do not counsel the *opposite sex alone* at the office.
- Do not counsel the *opposite sex* more than once without that person's spouse or mate. *Refer* them to whomever is in charge.
- Do not go to lunch alone with the *opposite sex* especially a ministry client. (Singles who are serving in the ministry are accountable to make dating known to the proper leadership. They should also honor and respect each other in public and private... Please use discretion while in ministry; professionalism is necessary.) Remember that we are leading by example!
- Do not hug (side hugs are acceptable) or kiss a ministry client, volunteer, or leadership of *opposite sex*. Please always use discretion and professionalism!
- Do not discuss detailed sexual problems with the *opposite sex* alone.
- Do not discuss *your* marital problems with your clients, especially the *opposite sex*, or any of your problems for that matter!

- Do *be careful* in answering e-mails (always cc someone in authority or any just for the accountability), cards, and letters from the *opposite sex*.
- Do make administrative support your ally!

Respect authority—always comply with the directions given by those in authority for the meeting or the place where ministry is to take place. This will usually be the pastor of the church where you are doing ministry, the ministry leader in charge, or the leader of the meeting where you are serving. If you are not sure, please ask. Do not assume (in corporate deliverance setting).

In a session of deliverance ministry, there is one leader and one assistant. The protocol in this setting is the lead minister has the authority in the session.

If you are the assistant and get a word of knowledge, question any leads, prophetic words, you should always bring them to the attention of the lead minister in the session. Never interrupt or override the authority of the lead minister. It creates confusion and sometimes disunity. It may lead any demonic to think that the lead minister does not know their authority and try to manifest or cause injury or conflict to the prayee or team members.

Remember, we are all about honor, unity, and covering. We must represent the kingdom of God, our own authority, and order of authority!

- In some settings, you may be asked to wear a name tag identifying you as a member of the ministry team. Please wear it.
- You should not minister without another ministry team member. Accountability is a must in a closed room; otherwise, someone on the staff needs to be notified and doors will always remain open.
- If you are not spiritually in the right frame of mind to minister, please let someone know so that we can pray with you and then decide if you should minister or not that day.

- Should the prayee need other community services please redirect them to any known resources that you have. If you tell them you're going to help them, be sure to follow through! Find out if your church or ministry offers other resources or has information about another resource center.

Laying on of hands—the appropriate places to lay hands on a person for prayer are hands, shoulders, and forehead but *never without permission*. Apply a soft touch, being sensitive to not offend. You may ask the person to place their hand on an injured area. If appropriate and with permission, you can place your hand or finger on top of theirs. Remember, it is important to touch a person in a way that they do not feel threatened, where they can retreat easily.

Remember to always use discernment when hugging someone during ministry. It is necessary because broken people who are love-starved can be misled by an innocent hug to mean more than you intended until they have worked through their issues.

Opposite sexes should not be embraced or kissed.

Hygiene—you as the minister should shower and use deodorant and keep breath mints handy, please!

Injuries—if a person is injured in any way, stop ministering and attend to their physical needs. Notify a supervisor or pastor as soon as possible. If you are injured, please seek a staff member and complete an injury report. If you need medical attention, make that a priority.

Complaints—we are working as a team. The ministry director or pastor handles any complaints about how you minister to an individual and or anyone that you are ministering with or to. Know what the protocol is in the place in which you are serving!

Quietness of ministry—always talk quietly during ministry. When you are through, please be aware of those around you who are still ministering and be soft-spoken in hallways. Remember that if we are always soft-spoken, it helps to calm and relax the prayee.

We do not need to draw attention to ourselves in ministry. That is flesh and not Holy Spirit! Always remember that Holy Spirit does not bring humiliation to a person by drawing unnecessary and negative attention to that person.

Training Guidelines to Minister

Qualities of a deliverance minister

Identity and authority. We must believe who God says we are. We are not of the world but the children of God. If we truly are walking as salt and light, every day keeping short accounts of our wrongs, taking captive our every thought, especially those thoughts that keep us bound to our old man, then we should know that we are in Christ!

We are a royal priesthood, holy and pleasing to God. We can enter the throne room with confidence that all that we ask shall be given. The Word says that we are seated in the throne room at the right hand of the Father. The Word does not lie, so all we need to do is look to the left and ask Abba Father!

We take for granted the expense that was paid for our salvation, healing, and deliverance. Therefore, to be holy and set apart does mean that we are to be *different*! A different breed of people! We are chosen for our laid-down lives to receive love and be transformed. Sin is in all people; however, we should be set apart to help those learn to walk without sin, not the justification of sin!

Walking in a calling to minister to others sets us at a higher standard to deal with and not deny or justify our sin. We should be constantly seeking to be changed, and change does happen! It is a part of our identity! A minister has a responsibility to pray and teach (disciple) those that they are encountering. We are accountable to show people how to walk this out. How can we do this if we are not doing it ourselves! James says in James 3:1 (AMP),

> Not many [of you] should become teach-
> ers [serving in an official teaching capacity], my

brothers and sisters, for you know that we [who
are teachers] will (*literally receive greater judgment*) be judged by a higher standard [because
we have assumed greater accountability and more
condemnation if we teach incorrectly]. (brackets
in original, italics mine)

Why? Because our words do carry power; our words should
line up with our actions. Otherwise, we are hypocrites in the eyes of
those that are watching! This scripture verse is a serious warning and
should not be taken lightly! We are representing Jesus!

The Living Word should be transforming us! If it is not, then
we are the one who need ministry, and we have no business trying
to give away something we do not have! Otherwise, we end up ministering from a place of our brokenness, perverted beliefs, and even
soulish prayers.

This may come as a hard word for some people, but we become
responsible for watering down the transforming *love* of God! Jesus
did not sacrifice His life so we could justify our sin. He did it to
transform us from the old to the new.

Therefore if anyone is in Christ [that is,
grafted in, joined to Him by faith in Him as
Savior], *he* is a new creature [reborn and renewed
by the Holy Spirit]; the old things [the previous
moral and spiritual condition] have passed away.
Behold, new things have come [because spiritual
awakening brings a new life]. (2 Corinthians
5:17, AMP)

Consecrate yourselves. Be holy for *HE is holy* (Leviticus 20:7)!

Skills and knowledge. These should be normal for a child of God;
after all, it is who we are. We belong, long before we believe (says Bill
Johnson). Our belief comes from our experience with Jesus or lack
of experience. We are discipled by the Holy Spirit. It is He who gives
us the revelation of the Word. It is also He who gives us ears to hear

so that we can become good listeners. The Holy Spirit is who teaches us to pray so that we can intercede and war on behalf of another. It is by the Spirit of God that we experience unconditional love, and it is He who guides us to learn to give it away to others. As we talk about skills and knowledge, please understand that we are to learn and apply. We must be willing to try and fail, trust that Holy Spirit is with us, always teaching and training us in every single situation. The Lord says,

> Be strong and courageous. Do not be afraid or terrified because of them, for the Lord your God goes with you; he will never leave you nor forsake you. The Lord himself goes before you and will be with you; he will never leave you nor forsake you. Do not be afraid; do not be discouraged. (Deuteronomy 31:6, 8, NIV)

It should be a comfort to know that the Lord Himself will go out in front of us and prepare the way for us to go in and plunder the enemy's camp. We should be able to go with all confidence because we know our Daddy's got our back.

I had to look up the word *forsaken* because I truly did not know what it meant, so let me share another word search with you because many of us have a fear of being forsaken and do not even realize it.

Forsake is to abandon, to give up on, or to renounce.

I had a major revelation on this one word. How many people in the world have been forsaken by their fathers? We have an epidemic of abandoned children, and in ministry, you will meet many of them. Remember, "iron sharpens iron," and we are to sharpen and get sharpened. Ministry is where we also experience the Lord.

Below is a practical list of knowledge and skills that leaders should be looking for as you build your ministry teams and release those to minister. Each of these are broken down in the following chapters that focus on inner healing and deliverance.

I feel that it is important to address what knowledge and skills means for ministers because often, we mix the holy and the profane. We do not want this to happen!

Let's look at what the Word says of knowledge.

> Desire without knowledge is not good, and whoever makes haste with his feet misses his way. (Proverbs 19:2, ESV)

> Two things can ruin your future success—ignorance and haste. We need to understand what we are doing before we do it. This means we must slow down for research first. We must know what is happening and what could happen before we take any action. Fools have no heart to learn (Pr 17:16); they are impulsive by nature (Pr 13:16). They rush decisions and actions without knowing the facts, and life punishes them. Wise men question everything (Pr 14:15); they do not rush decisions (Pr 14:29; 18:13; 25:8). They look ahead to see potential trouble and avoid it, but fools rush into pain (Pr 22:3; 27:12). The New Testament also teaches knowledge and caution. Paul condemned ignorance, for Christians are to prove all things (I Thes 5:21; Ac 17:11; Phil 1:9-11). Wise men examine in all directions and from all angles—they are circumspect (Eph 5:15-17). He warned against being "heady"—headstrong and impetuous actions hurried on by passion (II Tim 3:4). He listed "without understanding" as an inconvenient sin of reprobates (Rom 1:31) Letitbetrue.com/proverbs 19:2 commentary.

> The fear of the Lord is the beginning of wisdom, and the knowledge of the Holy One is insight. (Proverbs 9:10)

Personally, I like what Samuel says in his first book chapter 12, verses 14 and 15,

> If you will fear the Lord [with awe and pro-found reverence] and serve Him and listen to His voice and not rebel against His commandment, then both you and your king will follow the Lord your God [and it will be well]. But if you do not listen to the Lord's voice, but rebel against His command, then the hand of the Lord will be against you [to punish you], as it was against your fathers. (1 Samuel 12:14–15, AMP)

> For the Lord gives wisdom; from his mouth come knowledge and understanding. (Proverbs 2:6)

This proverb reminds us of the importance to seek the wisdom of God. It is He that has the only knowledge and understanding that we need!

There are so many other scriptures, and I encourage everyone to study this out, but I am going to share one more scripture.

> Then a Shoot (the Messiah) will spring from the stock of Jesse [David's father], And a Branch from his roots will bear fruit. And the Spirit of the Lord will rest on Him—The Spirit of wis-dom and understanding, The Spirit of counsel and strength, The Spirit of knowledge and of the [reverential and obedient] fear of the Lord—And He will delight in the fear of the Lord, And He will not judge by what His eyes see, Nor make decisions by what His ears hear; But with righ-teousness and justice He will judge the poor, And decide with fairness for the downtrodden of the earth; And He shall strike the earth with the rod

of His mouth, And with the breath of His lips
He shall slay the wicked. And righteousness will
be the belt around His loins, And faithfulness the
belt around His waist. (Isaiah 11:1–5, AMP)

We must never forget that this is Jesus we are
representing as ministers of the Lord!

Now that we have a better understanding of the knowledge we
must have as ministers, what does it mean to be skilled? It means to
have the ability and expertise that comes from knowledge and practice. It is a special training in which a person has competence and
experience.

Therefore, as ministers of God, we should be discipled (trained)
in the ministry of healing! After all, Jesus told every disciple to each
them all that I have taught you. *Teaching* means to educate, train,
and to impart!

As you minister in the body and in the world, you are going to
encounter many false beliefs, false teachings, watered down Gospels,
false religions, cultural beliefs, traumas of all types, and many demonic
and spiritual issues. We need the truth of God's Word, the revelation
to get people free. What is out there in the world is dark, and we need
Jesus and His Spirit to illuminate everything more than ever.

So let's look at a practical list of skill sets a minister will need to
know:

- In flow with the anointing of Holy Spirit (not a counterfeit)
- The Word of God
- Be an excellent listener
- Knowledge of inner healing and deliverance ministry and
  the spiritual realms (at least have a kingdom burden for
  deliverance and inner healing)
- Knowledge of intercession and spiritual warfare
- Unconditional love, honor, and respect for others
- Recognizing the difference in Holy Spirit manifestations
  and demonic manifestations

- Ministering to those with experience in the occult, New Age, witchcraft, and satanism
- Ministering to those with experience in cults and false religions
- Recognizing entry ways used by demonic to gain authority
- Tearing down strongholds
- Maturity in operation of the gifts of the Spirit
- Forgiveness and bitter root judgments
- Truth about godly sex and sexuality
- Breaking pronouncements and vows
- Inner healing and restoring the human spirit
- Minister freedom from fear and rejection
- Minister healing from accident and trauma
- Generational sin and curses
- Belief systems and thoughts
- Alignment with right relationships
- Understanding how to minister to children (requires special training not covered in this manual)

Please note that some of this feel like knowledge, but we should be skilled in our knowledge to lead deliverance. However, I do understand that we often must learn through the experience. An apprentice program is a safe way to train, educate, and impart before releasing anyone into this type of ministry. The ministry of inner healing and deliverance is a life or death ministry, both spiritually and in the natural, so training is essential.

I have heard the Lord say, "Many will be interested to be part of 'healing ministry' but not all will be called!"

We cannot go into a place that we have not been anointed to go! If you want this anointing, start asking Jesus for it! It is not just a gift it is an anointing!

Core Values and Team Protocol

Setting a standard: values of a minister

1. *God is love* (1 John 4:16). And so we know and rely on the love God has for us. Whoever lives in love, lives in God and God in Him! There is no fear in love, but perfect love drives out all fear. We are where we are today because of the *love* that is God! We must never forget what Jesus has done for us!

2. *Host the presence of God* (John 14–17). The spirit of truth, whom the world cannot receive, because it does not see him or know him. You know Him because He abides with you and is in you. Let me know your ways that I may know you! We do not move without the presence of God (Exodus 33:13).

   - *Baptism in Holy Spirit*—we need to model Christ at all times. God does not call for us to be perfect, but He does expect us to strive for excellence in all we do as His individual followers and as *family*, the children of God!

   - *We will be led by the Spirit of God on all matters concerning the ministry of healing and our lives!*

   - *Worship*—we will worship our Lord God Almighty, giving Him thanks and praise in *all* we say and do. We will have our corporate and individual worship daily. We demonstrate worship as a priority.

     I urge, then, first of all, that petitions, prayers, intercession, and thanksgiving be made for all people. (1 Timothy 2:1)

   - *Revelation from God*—hold true to your personal revelation from God. Do not waiver or be double-minded. Stand with the Holy Spirit!

- *Know the voice of God*—following the example of Jesus.

> I do nothing on my own but speak just what the Father has taught Me. The One who sent Me is with Me; He has not left me alone, for I always do what pleases Him. (John 8:28–29)

> I am telling you what I have seen in the Father's Presence, and you are doing what you have heard from your Father. (John 8:38)

3. *The Word of God* (1 Timothy 3:16). All scripture is God's breath and useful for teaching and rebuking.

> For the word of God is living and active sharper than any two-edged sword. (Hebrews 4:12)

4. *Supernatural lifestyle.* Signs wonders and miracles should be a daily part of our lives. We must become so accustomed to them that we walk with constant expectation.

> Very truly I tell you, whoever believes in me will do the works I have been doing, and they will do even greater things than these, because I am going to the Father. And I will do whatever you ask in my name, so that the Father may be glorified in the Son. You may ask me for anything in my name, and I will do it. (John 14:12–14)

5. *A culture of honor*
   - *Seek to be part of the solution, not the problem* (Hebrews 3:13).
   - *Seek to listen*—God has given us two ears and one mouth for a reason. We must communicate clearly, openly, and honestly and listen the same way (Proverbs 2:2).
   - *Pray for each other*—individually and as a *family* we need to pray continuously, asking God for help in keeping us surrendered.
   - *Zero gossip tolerance*—we will honor the safety of anonymity and confidentiality. Gossip will not be tolerated.
   - *Expects to make mistakes*—we must allow individuals to make honest mistakes without penalty or judgment. A healthy team will review what went wrong, why it went wrong, and what will make it right. We will work together with encouraging words, and from the same love and compassion, we will minister to our community.
   - *Seek accountability*—"Submit to one another out of reverence for Christ Jesus" (Ephesians 5:21). We all need to hold each other accountable for our lives, our relationships, and in our leadership as "Wilmington Healing Center" team members. We all will be held accountable by God and each other as to our actions and decisions regarding the ministry of healing and also in our personal lives.
   - *Honor the God-given gifts and authority in others we serve and serve with.*

   There are different kinds of gifts, but the same Spirit distributes them. There are different kinds of service, but the same Lord. There are different kinds of working, but in all of them and in everyone it is the same God at work. (1 Corinthians 12:46 NIV)

> But in fact God has placed the parts in the body, every one of them, just as he wanted them to be. (1 Corinthians 12:18)

- *Honor the call to unity*—let it begin here and overflow into our community.
- *Give everyone what you owe them.*

> This is also why you pay taxes, for the authorities are God's servants, who give their full time to governing. Give to everyone what you owe them: If you owe taxes, pay taxes; if revenue, then revenue; if respect, then respect; if honor, then honor. (Romans 13:6–7)

- *When we see a need, instead of judging, we intercede!*
6. *The true fast.* This is the example of the mission statement but must be considered a core value in order to succeed in our mission! This, like the other values, must not change (Isaiah 58:6–14)! This is God's heart for us as mature ministers:
   - Break the chains of injustice
   - Get rid of exploitation in the workplace
   - Free the oppressed
   - Cancel debts
   - Sharing your food with the hungry
   - Inviting the homeless and poor into your homes
   - Putting clothes on the shivering ill-clad
   - Being available to your own families
   - Get rid of unfair practices
   - Never blame victims
   - Do not gossip about other people's sins

- Restore old ruins, rebuild and renovate, make the community livable
- Treat the Sabbath as a day of joy, God's holy day as a celebration
- Be free to enjoy God

7. *Kingdom government.* The body of Christ fits together perfectly and functions properly when each individual discovers his/her significant assignment and operates in his/her unique gifting.

> God has put each part just where he wants it. (1 Corinthians 12:18, NLT)

> And God has appointed in the church, first apostles, second prophets, third teachers. (1 Corinthians 12:28, NASB)

> He makes the whole body fit together perfectly. As each part does its own special work, it helps the other parts grow, so that the whole body is healthy and growing and full of love. (Ephesians 4:16, NLT)

> Let everyone be subject to the governing authorities, for there is no authority except that which God has established. The authorities that exist have been established by God. Consequently, whoever rebels against the authority is rebelling against what God has instituted, and those who do so will bring judgment on themselves. (Romans 13:1–2)

8. *Kingdom family unity.*

- *The "I" became "we."*

This is how everyone will recognize that you are my disciples, when they see how you love each other. (John 13:35, MSG)

As a prisoner for the Lord, then, I urge you to live a life worthy of the calling you have received. Be completely humble and gentle; be patient, bearing with one another in love. Make every effort to keep the unity of the Spirit through the bond of peace. There is one body and one Spirit, just as you were called to one hope when you were called; one Lord, one faith, one baptism; one God and Father of all, who is over all and through all and in all. (Ephesians 4:1–6)

- *Embrace our differences*—we are each God's unique creation, each with different spiritual gifts and talents. This is what brings effectiveness and functionality to the *family*. We may not always agree with what every member of the *family* does or says but will still love them and embrace our differences.

Because of the privilege and authority God has given me, I give each of you this warning: Don't think you are better than you really are. Be honest in your evaluation of yourselves, measuring yourselves by the faith God has given us. Just as our bodies have many parts and each part has a special function, so it is with Christ's body. We are many parts of one body, and we all belong to each other. (Romans 12:3–5, NLT)

- *Be cooperative, not competitive*—when we are being cooperative we are committed to serving the *family* and others. We need to celebrate each other's victories and support one another's struggles.

> Live in peace with each other. Do not be proud but make friends with those who seem unimportant. Do not think how smart you are. (Romans 12:16, NCV)

> So Christ himself gave the apostles, the prophets, the evangelists, the pastors and teachers, to equip his people for works of service, so that the body of Christ may be built up until we all reach unity in the faith and in the knowledge of the Son of God and become mature, attaining to the whole measure of the fullness of Christ. (Ephesians 4:11–13)

CHAPTER 2

Biblical Foundation for Healing

*He said to them, "Go into all the world and
preach the gospel to all creation. Whoever believes
and is baptized will be saved, but whoever does
not believe will be condemned. And these signs
will accompany those who believe: In my name,
they will drive out demons; they will speak in
new tongues; they will pick up snakes with their
hands; and when they drink deadly poison, it
will not hurt them at all; they will place their
hands on sick people, and they will get well."
After the Lord Jesus had spoken to
them, he was taken up into heaven and
he sat at the right hand of God.*
—Mark 16:15–19

Biblical Foundation
Why We Are to Pray for the Sick,
Brokenhearted, and Tormented?

Why do we pray for those that are hurting physically, emotionally, and/or spiritually? It is simple: God wants to heal them! But not just to heal them but to bring a relationship through healing.

So why does God want to heal us? That's easy… *He loves us!*

> May you have the power to understand, as all God's people should, how wide, how long, how high, and how deep his love is. (Ephesians 3:18, NLT)

God's love for us is beyond our understanding. In *1 John 4:16*, it says *God is love.*

Paul gives us a clear picture of who God really is in *1 Corinthians 13:4–8 (NLT),*

> God (love) is patient and kind. God (love) is not jealous or boastful or proud or rude. God (it/ love) does not demand His (its) own way. God (it) is not irritable, and He (it) keeps no record of being wronged. God (it/love) does not rejoice about injustice but rejoices whenever the truth wins out. God (love) never gives up, never loses faith, is always hopeful, and endures through every circumstance. Prophecy and speaking in unknown languages and special knowledge will become useless. But God (love) will last forever!

Nothing can separate us from God's love because love is who He is!

Ask yourself if you have had this heart encounter with God. If you have, you will know. If you must, ask yourself, "Have I experienced this revelation of love/God?" It's okay. Ask God to fill you with a fresh baptism of His love and if possible, ask someone to pray with you!

New Covenant Promise

The New Covenant is essential to the foundation of any healing ministry. If we are not sure about the power and the authority of the New Covenant, then we are left with our own powerless works. It is only by the blood of Jesus that all our debts are paid, all sins are forgiven, and we are washed white as wool.

Before Christ, life in the Old Testament was about works, the work of the high priests going into the holy of holies to atone with the blood of the sacrificial animals to plead with God for the covering of the sins of man (Exodus 24). The Old Covenant only promised eternal life. Jesus entered into the holy of holies, and it was His blood that was sacrificed, not just a covering for mankind's sin but an actual cleansing of our sin, and in Him, the Old Covenant promise was fulfilled. In Christ, we all have received eternal life.

The Old Covenant was sealed with the blood of sacrificial animals and started with Abraham and God. The New Covenant is sealed with the blood of Jesus, God's very own Son.

In the Old Covenant, everything centered around the High Priest. If the High Priest failed, the people had no covering. In the New Covenant, everything is still centered around the High Priest; however, this High Priest is Jesus, the One who could never fail (Hebrews 8:1). Jesus is now the mediator between God and man.

Man is not in good standing with God except through Jesus Christ. Ephesians 2 says there is no hope for man without God. Jesus, who was without sin, became sin so we could enter a right standing before God our Father. In Christ, we are new creatures. The old is gone, and the new has come in Christ. In Christ, we are reconciled to God the Father, as the prodigal sons and daughters having returned home from squandering our inheritance only to be given a greater inheritance, one in which has no end. It is only by the blood of the

Lamb, Jesus Christ that we can enter our rightful place in the family of God, as sons and daughters.

Jesus had to come and be born as man to be the set-apart example for all men and women. His role as our savior, healer, and deliverer was the greatest part of His purpose for mankind's restoration to God. He also came to restore the purpose for which mankind was originally created—to rule, reign, and have dominion over all of God's creation (Genesis 1:24–31).

Jesus the Man

> For to us a child is born, to us a son is given; and the government shall be upon his shoulder, and his name shall be called Wonderful Counselor, Mighty God, Everlasting Father, Prince of Peace. (Isaiah 9:6)

We the children shared in flesh and blood while He became flesh and blood that through death, He might destroy the one who has the power of death, that is, the devil. For we do not have a high priest who is unable to sympathize with our weaknesses but one who, in every respect, has been tempted as we are yet without sin. The Word became flesh and dwelt among us, and we have seen His glory, glory as of the only Son from the Father, full of grace and truth.

> I have come that they might have life, and they might have it more abundantly! (John 10:10)

The following is found in Rodney Howard-Browne's book titled *Seeing Jesus as He Really Is*. Rodney credits Oral Roberts for this work and so will I. I added it because before we can know who we really are, we first must know whose we are.

I can honestly say that I know the Bible is all about Jesus and the family business, about a father's love for His precious family, but when I read this message, it really touched my heart. It really reached off the pages and grabbed me, and I heard clearly, "I *am* who I say I *am!*" Jesus was God manifested in the flesh (John 14:9)!

Jesus clearly is...

- Genesis—He is the Seed of the Woman.
- Exodus—He is the Passover Lamb.
- Leviticus—He is our High Priest.
- Numbers—He is our Pillar of Cloud by day and our Pillar of Fire by night.
- Deuteronomy—He is the Prophet like unto Moses
- Joshua—He is the Captain of our Salvation.
- Judges—He is our Lawgiver.
- Ruth—He is our Kinsman Redeemer.
- First & Second Samuel—He is our Trusted Prophet.
- Kings & Chronicles—He is our Reigning King.
- Ezra—He is our Faithful Scribe
- Nehemiah—He is the Rebuilder of the broken walls.
- Esther—He is our Advocate.
- Job—He is our Ever-Living Redeemer.
- Psalms—He is the Lord, our Shepherd, so we shall not want.
- Proverbs—He is our Wisdom.
- Ecclesiastes—He is our Goal.
- Song of Solomon—He is our Lover and our Bridegroom.
- Isaiah—He is the Prince of Peace.
- Jeremiah & Lamentations: He is the Weeping Prophet
- Ezekiel—He is the Wonderful Four-Faced Man.
- Daniel—He is the Fourth Man in the burning fiery furnace.
- Hosea—He is the Eternal Husband, forever married to the backslider.
- Joel—He is the Baptizer in the Holy Ghost!
- Amos—He is our Burden Bearer!
- Obadiah—He is our Savior!
- Jonah—He is the Great Foreign Missionary!
- Micah—He is the Messenger with beautiful feet!
- Nahum—He is our Avenger!

- Habakkuk—He is the Evangelist pleading for revival!
- Malachi—He is the Son of Righteousness, rising with healing in His wings!
- Matthew—He is the Messiah!
- Mark—He is the Wonder Worker!
- Luke—He is the Son of Man!
- John—He is the Son of God!
- Acts—He is the Holy Ghost, moving among men!
- Romans—He is the Justifier!
- 1st & 2nd Corinthians—He is the Sanctifier!
- Galatians—He is the Redeemer from the curse of the law!
- Ephesians—He is the Christ of unsearchable riches!
- Philippians—He is God who supplies all our needs, Jehovah Jireh!
- Colossians—He is the fullness of the Godhead bodily!
- 1st & 2nd Thessalonians—He is our soon-coming King!
- 1st & 2nd Timothy—He is the Mediator between God and man!
- Titus—He is the Faithful Pastor!
- Philemon—He is the Friend of the oppressed!
- Hebrews—He is the Blood of the everlasting Covenant!
- James—He is the Lord Who Heals the sick!
- 1st & 2nd Peter—He is the Chief Shepherd, who shall appear soon!
- 1st, 2nd & 3rd John—He is Love!
- Jude—He is the Lord coming with ten thousand of his saints!
- Revelation—He is King of kings and Lord of lords!

Jesus is Abel's sacrifice and Noah's rainbow! He is Abraham's ram and Isaac's well. He is Jacob's ladder and Ezekiel's burden. He is Judah's scepter, Moses' rod, David's slingshot and Hezekiah's sundial! He is the Church's head and is risen from the dead. He is the Husband to the widow and the Father to the orphan. To those traveling at night

He is the Bright and Morning Star. To those living in the valley He is the Lily of the Valley, the Rose of Sharon, the Honey in the Rock and the Staff of Life. He is the Pearl of Great Price, the Everlasting Father! The government is upon His shoulders. He is Peter's shadow and John's pearly white city. He is Jesus of Nazareth, Son of the Living God!

He is the One who owns the cattle on a thousand hills. He is the One who split the red sea. He is the One who took the children of Israel out of Egypt into the Promised Land. He is the one who humbled Himself, came to earth, healed the sick, raised the dead, cleansed the lepers, opened the eyes of the blind, and turned water into wine.

He is the One who fed five thousand, walked on water, and cast out devils. He is the one who humbled Himself again and became obedient unto death. He is the One who died on the cross, rose from the dead, ascended to the right hand of the Father, and ever lives to make intercession for us. He's coming back very, very soon. He is Jesus Christ of Nazareth, The King of kings and Lord of lords! Jesus Christ... The Alpha and Omega, the first and last! (Browne 1999)

As we study the scriptures, we begin to see Jesus as He really is. Rodney Howard-Browne shared Oral Roberts revelation of Jesus Christ, and what an eye-opening revelation it is. But even in this truth, there is greater truth that we have yet to see or understand. The Word of God is Jesus, but there are many more mysteries yet to be revealed.

Jesus Gave Authority

Jesus gave His disciples authority to drive out evil spirits (deliverance), to heal every sickness and disease (physical healing), and to baptize them and forgive their sins (inner healing).

> [The Great Commission] Jesus came to them and said, "All authority in heaven and on earth has been given to me. Therefore, go and make disciples of all nations, baptizing them in the name of the Father and of the Son and of the Holy Spirit, and teaching them to obey everything I have commanded you. And surely, I am with you always, to the very end of age." (Matthew 28:18–20)

> *He said to them, "Go into all the world and preach the good news to all creation. Whoever believes and is baptized will be saved, but whoever does not believe will be condemned. And these signs will accompany those who believe: In my name, they will drive out demons; they will speak in new tongues; they will pick up snakes with their hands and when they drink deadly poison, it will not hurt them at all; they will place their hands on the sick and they will get well. (Mark 16:15–18)*

In these two scripture passages, Jesus is not talking in parables, and He has some pretty specific instructions, not just to the twelve or the seventy-two but to all nations. I cannot remember where I heard this, "A nation is nothing more than a group of people," but it has really stuck with me. Every time I read this passage, I see groups of people everywhere. I especially see my mission field, here on the streets of my city, in my county, and my neighboring counties.

Jesus clearly says, "Go, depart, and leave this place. Go and make disciples, put into proper condition as for use, baptizing them and teaching them 'everything' I have commanded you."

Go, depart, and leave this place. Go into the world (every nation) and preach the good news to all creation (the world and everything in it). Whoever believes will drive out demons, speak in new tongues, pick up snakes, drink poison without harm, and "lay hands on the sick and they will be healed."

Of course, we cannot do this alone, in our own strength and power. But can we do this by co-laboring with Christ?

How Do We Co-Labor with Christ?

It is our responsibility to be obedient to the Word. Knowing the Word is great, but in order for us to be co-laborers with Christ, it is also a key that we not only hear but know the voice of the God to know someone is to have a relationship with them. The deeper the intimacy, the greater the knowledge. We should be able to identify everything about that person.

Co-laboring does not mean that Jesus is our servant to do as we expect. In fact, it is the opposite. We are under His rule. We must be very careful never to misalign ourselves in our co-laboring relationship. He is always the Head, and we are the body. The body does not function without the head. Cut the head off and the body dies!

Many of us pray soulishly, expecting Jesus to answer our prayers. And when He does not, we actually get angry at Him, as if He were the one out of line. Without the head, the body will die!

The New Covenant says that we are to continue *the works of Jesus*, especially in deliverance and healing.

> I tell you the truth, *anyone* who has faith in me *will do what I have been doing*. He will do even greater things than these, because I am going to the father. (John 14:12) italics added

Many New Testament scholars have pointed out that the Greek term *erga* used in this scripture of John, to mean "works," literally means miraculous works. So Jesus is saying that *anyone* who has faith in Him will do the same miraculous works that He did.

Paul says in 1 Corinthians 3:9 (HCSB), *"For we are God's coworkers"* (emphasis added). However, we do not always see ourselves this way.

We have seen in the first four books of the New Testament—Matthew, Mark, Luke, and John—many of the documented examples of the healing ministry of Jesus. If we are to co-labor with Christ, then we must see ourselves as co-laborers first. So how do we do that? Paul says,

> For Christ in all his fullness of the Deity lives in bodily form, and you have been given fullness in Christ, who is the head over every power and authority. (Colossians 2:9)

Jesus obviously was an exact representation of God and the fullness of deity lived in Jesus. So, I believe I can quote Randy Clark in saying that, "We saw Jesus do the will of the God. He revealed his heart, manifested God's power, and demonstrated God's love, especially through his ministry of healing and deliverance. And it was not just the apostles, but 'we' are also called to be God's coworkers, co-laboring with God."

> Because those who are led by the Spirit of God are sons of God. For you did not receive a spirit that makes you a slave again to fear, but you received the Spirit of sonship. And by him we cry, "Abba, Father." The Spirit himself testifies with our spirit that we are God's children. Now if we are children, then we are heirs—heirs of God and co-heirs with Christ, if indeed we share in his sufferings in order that we may also share in his glory. (Romans 8:14–17)

To co-labor with Christ, we must be submitted to His authority in our own lives. This means we should be submitted to His healing work in us first! If have not submitted to Him, we have no authority nor power, other than a counterfeit! In Jesus, we are made new.

Prayer: A Weapon of Warfare

John Wimber said, "Scripture teaches that we are called to warfare. It is critical, though that we understand the rules of war and what we are fighting against." Paul sheds much light on the nature of spiritual warfare in 2 Corinthians 10:3–6:

> For though we live in the world, we do not wage war as the world does. The weapons we fight with are not the weapons of the world. On the contrary, they have divine power to demolish strongholds. We demolish arguments and every pretension that sets itself up against the knowledge of God, and we take captive every thought to make it obedient to Christ. And we will be ready to punish every act of disobedience, once your obedience is complete.

Paul teaches that we don't wage warfare as the world does—lining up on opposite sides, fighting, killing one another. We have an alternative means of warfare; we employ different weapons that have "divine power to demolish strongholds," and we fight our battles on a different kind of battlefield.

Where does the battle take place? In the hearts and minds of men and women.

What can we learn about spiritual warfare from the Corinthian situation? There is a battle raging in the hearts and minds of men and women, and Satan knows that if we believe his lies, we will fail to love and serve God.

The word also teaches us there is power in the tongue; it can bring life or death (Proverbs 18:21). What we speak, what is spoken over us or others, what and how we pray does eventually affect us. Whether it is physically, mentally, emotionally, or spiritually, it does have either positive or negative effect.

Personal testimony: As a small girl, my father, who was a very verbally abusive alcoholic, would consistently bash my sister and I with the words "You will never amount to anything" and "Nobody will ever love you!" Well, guess what? I struggled most of my life being nothing—never good enough, always feeling that no matter how hard I tried to do the right thing, I was only good at screwing it up. At a very young age, I believed the lie that said I was a failure, a disappointment that could never be worthy of love. Relationship after relationship, broken marriage after broken marriage, I was a complete success at failure—the first thing I had ever done right. All because of the "power" in one tongue! (My dad was only repeating what he had been told as a child himself. I found out later that his motive was to push me into being the opposite but that is not how it unfolded in my life.)

I am here to tell you that words do carry power; they can create or destroy! Allow me to go on record to say that the Lord did restore my relationship with my earthly father. During the last eight years of his life, we were reconciled to each other through forgiveness, and I am happy to share that in the end, my dad was my best friend!

I hope this teaching will help you create faith for healing and at the same time, destroy the lies and schemes of Satan.

Learning to pray for the sick can be a challenge in our own strength, and it is important that we know it is okay to get it wrong or to be nervous. It is okay to make mistakes, and like me, it is especially helpful to know that I am not alone!

Getting out of our seat and obeying God is sometimes uncomfortable but well, worth the risk! I still get nervous and sometimes just downright scared! However, pressing through those feelings and being obedient is empowering because we know that our great and powerful God will meet us right there as we step off the cliff and into

His will and plans. We cannot learn to fly if we never jump! I want to encourage you to just take the risk.

Let's face it…some of us have trusted in a lot of lesser things than prayer. Some of us have taken much greater risks than just praying for someone.

Think about this for a moment. How many of you eat out in restaurants? I love to have someone else cook and be served sometimes! It is a special treat for us! Well, in doing so, we are taking a risk, right? We trust that the food will be of good quality and will not get us sick. We trust those preparing the food have taken proper steps to handle our food. Right? Isn't it safe to say that we are exercising faith in a lesser thing than God? Have any of you had to pass a slow-moving vehicle on a two-lane road, but you were blind to the oncoming traffic? You depended on the driver of that slow-moving vehicle to flag you around safely. I have and that was me exercising faith, trusting my life and those in my vehicle to a stranger.

God rewards those who are risk-takers in His kingdom. God will reward us for our faith. How do you spell *faith*? *Risk!*

John Wimber said, "Our job is to obey. God's job is to heal. So how can we fail!" (Wimber 1990).

Learning to heal the sick and minister the kingdom is not about the "how tos." It is about learning to walk on water. All the best methods will not keep you afloat but raw faith in God will! Jesus did what He did, was who He was through the indwelling presence of His Father by the power of the Holy Spirit.

There is no special formula to minister healing. It is a lifestyle, living your life by the fruit of the Spirit within you! It's by the Father. Jesus is our model; He also had to learn through discipline to live with the Father, just as we must. Jesus learned to see what the Father was doing, hear what the Father was saying, and feel what the Father was feeling in various situations. By taking risks and trusting, He learned to act on what He believed were the Father's thoughts, feelings, and actions. Thus, He increasingly lived, worked, and ministered in unison with the Father, changing the world.

Jesus simply abided in the vine.

God has more for us than we could ever imagine…

> What no eye has seen, what no ear has heard, and what no human mind has conceived the things God has prepared for those who love him. (1 Corinthian 2:9)

All the good that God wants to give us comes through the Holy Spirit. Many have struggled with knowing how Holy Spirit operates. Most Christians don't know! I went to churches that taught against the Holy Spirit. Some seminaries still teach that the Holy Spirit retired about AD 95.

I thought those who claimed to be filled with the Holy Spirit were practicing some sort of craft until I had my own encounter with the Holy Spirit.

My life-changing encounter happened on February 2, 2008. My husband, Jimmy, and I were enjoying a winter ride on our Harley-Davidson. It was a cool but bright and beautiful day. On our return from Myrtle Beach, as we traveled in the left lane toward our home in Wilmington, North Carolina, a car without any notice pulled out into our lane, directly on us. I watched in amazing slow motion as my husband tried to maneuver the Harley out of the side-swiping path of that fast-moving vehicle. I was whipped to the side as I was a passenger on the back, and my foot came off the peg and was dragging on the highway between the two wheels of our motorcycle. I was being pulled from my seat by the motion of the moving Harley. Barely holding on with the motorcycle still moving about fifty-five miles per hour, I tried with all my strength to pull myself back up. Miraculously, in an instant, a complete peace and trust come over me. In that moment, I felt the strongest hands tightly grip my shoulders (I did not understand), but I knew I had to release my grip from the motorcycle, and I was pulled from the moving bike. What took place in seconds felt more like thirty minutes of slow motion. I knew I was to expect the back tire to run over my leg, and I also knew I was going to live. I rolled across the highway in front of traffic behind us that was screeching to a halt. I could hear sounds, but they were all muffled, and then it all stopped as suddenly as it started.

I remember thinking, *Am I alive?* And then panic set in, and I couldn't breathe. I tried to reach for my helmet shield with my right arm, but the pain was unbearable. I was unable to move my arm. But a small still voice whispered in my ear, "Do not be afraid, breathe slowly, and reach with your left arm." I did, and my shield popped open. I felt the air, cool night air, and I began to breathe easy. The testimony does not end there, and I may refer to it in other parts of this book, but this is where my adventure with the Holy Spirit really began.

I shared this to encourage someone that it is okay to let go and trust your situation to the capable hands of the Holy Spirit. It may physically feel pretty rough and painful, but when we are at our weakest point, His hands are stronger. There, Jesus can and will bring glory to the Father in our weakness.

I was taken by ambulance to the local ER, and after a painful manipulation around the X-ray department, they sent me home saying, "Mrs. Bell, today is your lucky day. Nothing's broken. You're just badly bruised."

Well, I knew that didn't feel like the truth, but I also knew Jesus never left my side.

I couldn't sleep. I was in so much pain; Jesus was still by my side sitting next to me in the chair. After the third day of the worst pain I had ever experienced, I went to see my family doctor who sent me for an MRI. I had never had one before, and they offered me something to take to help me relax. I do not like tight spaces and the doctor feared I would have a panic attack and injured myself worse. I looked at him and said, "I'll be okay. Jesus is with me."

I cried on the way to the hospital, partly because of pain, and the rest because I was becoming fearful. Immediately, I felt that same peace I felt on the night of the accident. I knew Jesus was there!

My heart started to pound when they called my name. I remember clenching my fists as I got closer to that machine and how the pounding in my chest grew. I was placed on the table and told to lie flat and perfectly still. I began to cry, "You don't understand! I can't do this. I just cannot lie flat. The pain is too bad!" Then I felt my hand being squeeze again, and when I opened my eyes, He was standing there!

He whispered, "I am still here. I will not leave you, just close your eyes and look at me. Do not open your eyes until it's all over!"

The MRI was over, and suddenly, I realized two things—I had not been afraid but had experienced perfect peace, and in the presence of peace, I had no pain.

I learned a profound lesson about healing through my own experience. In the presence of Jesus, the Prince of Peace...there is no pain.

Today when I pray for someone in pain, whether it is physical, emotional, or spiritual, I call upon the Prince of Peace to impart His peace into this person and into me. I always wait on Him to come into the situation before I pray further.

> *The God of peace* be with you all. (Romans 15:33)

I always wait upon the Lord to set the atmosphere during prayer time. Sometimes, He calms the raging seas of anticipation, fear, doubt, and unbelief that sometimes arise during these times. The Lord is faithful, and when you ask the Father for peace in the name of Jesus, peace comes.

> Now may *the Lord of peace* himself give you peace at all times and in every way. The Lord be with all of you. (2 Thessalonians 3:16)

The Word tells us to ask the Father in the name of Jesus and we shall receive what we ask (John 15:16, 16:23). The divine order is that prayers are to be made to the Father, in Jesus's name, not to the Holy Spirit or Jesus. When you pray, say, "Our Father." Jesus stands between us and the Father in his high priestly ministry to make it good. E. W. Kenyon says, "Stand on your blood covenant rights. Dare to use the Name!"

Jesus is our surety. This is the most vital of all the ministries of Jesus. Under the Old Covenant, the High Priest was the surety. If he failed, it interrupted the relationship between God and Israel. The blood atonement lost its efficacy. Under the New Covenant, Jesus is the High Priest and the surety of the New Covenant. Our position before the Father is absolutely secure. We know that throughout our lifetime, Jesus is at the right hand of God, there for us. He is representing us before the Father. He is always standing with the Father. Always, regardless of our standing, we have one representing us before the Father. Our position is secure.

Faith Is a Relationship

It does not matter in what area we are ministering, whether it is inner healing, deliverance, or physical healing prayer. We must understand faith and how it operates in the healing process. Faith is critical in ministering and receiving healing. God is moved by faith. Our faith carries weight in the kingdom of God. Faith is the reality of Jesus and the language in which He speaks.

Hebrews 11:1 says, "Faith is being sure of what you hoped for and certain of what you do not see." Biblical faith is belief, reliance, confidence, and trust. It is to trust someone, not something! Faith is relational! It is an intimacy with someone that creates faith. Deeper levels of intimacy will create greater levels of faith.

God is moved by faith! Why? Because when we are intimate with Him and He feels our trust in Him and because He loves us, He moves through us to fulfill our prayers whether requests or declarations. Look at Hebrews 11:6 saying, "Without faith, it is impossible to please God." It displeases God to know that we do not believe in Him or his Son, Jesus. That verse also says that when we come to him, we must "believe" that He exists. If we do not believe, then we are wasting our time. If we believe, then He rewards those who earnestly seek Him. Mark says that all things are possible for those who believe.

God acts on behalf of those who believe in Him and who He is! Alexander Venter says that, "God does not disappoint... His integrity is at stake!" Faith is truly a verb; it is an action word. Faith is a decision, and it is an attitude of trust which we express in our actions.

The Lord said to Peter, "Come," and Peter trusted in the rhema word of Jesus and stepped out of his boat and walked on water. It was Peter's faith that released the rhema word, "Lord, if that is you, then tell me to come, and I will." Jesus did and Peter trusted and left the boat; however, there was a moment of doubt when Peter went into the water. During his moment of doubt, Peter cried out to the Lord for help because he knew the source of power and authority. It was not Jesus's faith that brought Peter out of the boat; it was Peter's. His faith was the key to unlocking all the power and authority in Jesus at that moment. Peter had a relationship with Jesus. He knew Him intimately because he had walked with Him and had witnessed Jesus's relationship to the Father. Peter had seen with his very own eyes the supernatural side of life in the kingdom of God. It was the same power of God that Moses and the Israelites had experienced in their exodus from Egypt in forty years in the wilderness. It was forty continuous years of supernatural encounters, one after another! The Bible is filled with testimonies of relationship, the love of a Father for his children. We are no different!

The Word tells us that with the faith the size of a mustard seed can move a mountain, but for most of us, when we do not see the mountain move, we begin to doubt God. The truth might be we never really believed. It may be possible that our motives were wrong. I ask myself regularly, "Am I having faith in what is God's will or mine?"

I know I have faith that every person I pray for will have an encounter with God through the name of Jesus! It may be the peace they did not have before prayer. I know their experience will bring glory to God, and a seed is planted in the ground of each person's spirit. How God uses that seed is up to Him, not me. He will see His perfect plan unfold, after all, He is God! He knows all things, and He knows what each person has need of. He also knows if that person will choose Him. He knows when and where His plan will unfold in that person's life! God knows what you and I need and if we are intimately involved with the Father, Son, and Holy Spirit. He knows if we will be able to flow with the Spirit of God to accomplish His will and purpose. If we are, we will see healing manifest itself in all areas—body, soul, and spirit!

I love this story from Bill Johnson. It is recorded in his book with Randy Clark, *The Essential Guide to Healing*. In chapter 7 entitled, "Creating a Faith Culture," Bill talks about an online e-mailing relationship that he had with a pastor from Utica, New York, Mike Servello. Eventually, they met and were at an all-day prayer event, and during worship, Mike leaned over to Bill and said, *"God is looking for a city that would belong entirely to Him, and once He gets that city, it will cause a domino effect across our nation."*

Bill expressed to Mike that he believed the city was Redding, California, and Mike told Bill he thought the city was Utica, New York. Bill is clear to write that they were two pastors expressing their faith for the big picture. Bill goes on to share that about thirty minutes later, in a different part of the sanctuary, a trusted friend came to him and said, "God is looking for a city that would belong entirely to Him, and once He gets that city, it will cause a domino effect across our nation. And I believe that city is Redding, California." Bill was stunned but he knew what God was saying. It was never about competition but about utilizing the resources that God had made available to complete the assignment. Bill says we are not in a race against each other but a race against time. He also states that the best way to create an atmosphere of faith is to start with an overwhelming awareness of need and realize the impossibility of our assignment from God.

So just to encourage anyone reading this manual, if the vision you have in your heart is much bigger and totally impossible for you to accomplish then just take a deep breath and then exhale. Smile big and give thanks and praise to God for He will accomplish His will and plan. Your job is to simply be obedient! This is how it was with the vision the Lord had given me for the Wilmington Healing Center. Some people were very encouraging. Others saw only me and what resources I lacked. I had to look past myself a lot of times, breath in deeply, exhale, and just smile big because I had faith that this was God's vision. I was called to be His hands and feet through my obedience in Jesus. The vision that the Lord gave me really isn't about a healing center. It is really about healing a city! The healing center was just a training ground for something bigger!

It is no different when we are asked by God to pray healing for someone or to spend the entire day in ministry. God's will is unfolding, whether we see a manifestation or not. Our faith will grow as we trust in God, who knows all things and created all things, to do what He promised He will do.

John G. Lake made the following statement in his sermon titled "Ministry of the Spirit" on November 24, 1916, which characterizes the real religion of Jesus Christ.

> Beloved, don't you see that this message and this quality of the Spirit contains the thing that confuses all philosophers and all the practices of philosophy in the world? It shows the clearest distinction which characterizes the real religion of Jesus Christ and makes it distinct from all other religions and all other ministries. The ministry of the Christian is the ministry of the *spirit*. He not only minister's words to another but he ministers the Spirit of God that inhabits the words, that speaks to the spirit of another and reveals Christ in and through Him. If a Christian cannot minister the Spirit of God, in the true sense he is not a Christian. If he has not the Spirit to minister in the real high sense, he has nothing to minister. Other men have intellectually, but the Christian is supposed to be the possessor of the Spirit. A minister of Jesus is far removed from above the realm of psychological influences as heaven is above the earth. He ministers God Himself into the very spirits and souls and bodies of men. Blessed be God!

Sozo = The Gospel of Salvation, Healing, and Deliverance

The Greek verb or action word *sozo*, depending on translation, is used between 108 to 110 times in the New Testament. Sozo, according to *Strong's Concordance*, means:

I.   to save, keep safe and sound, to rescue from danger or destruction
   A.   one (from injury or peril)
      i.   to save a suffering one (from perishing), i.e., one suffering from disease, to make well, heal, restore to health
      ii.   to preserve one who is in danger of destruction, to save or rescue
   B.   to save in the technical biblical sense
      i.   negatively
         A.   to deliver from the penalties of the Messianic judgment
         B.   to save from the evils which obstruct the reception of the Messianic deliverance

The following are scripture examples from the New International Version (NIV).

Salvation

Peter, preaching to the elders and rulers of Jerusalem, said, "Salvation is found in no one else, for there is no other name under heaven given men by which we must be [sozo] saved" (Acts 4:12).

Paul wrote to the Christians at Rome, "If you confess with your mouth, 'Jesus is Lord,' and believe in your heart that God raised him from the dead, you will be [sozo] saved" (Romans 10:9).

And to the Church at Ephesus: "For it is by grace you have been [sozo] saved, through faith, and this not from yourselves, it is the gift of God" (Ephesians 2:8).

Healing

Jesus turned and saw her. "Take heart, daughter," he said, "your faith has [sozo] healed you." And the woman was [sozo] healed from that moment. (Matthew 9:22)

And everywhere he went, into villages, towns of countryside, they placed the sick in the marketplaces. They begged him to let them touch even the edge of his cloak, and all who touched him were [sozo] healed. (Mark 6:56)

"Go," Jesus said. "Your faith has [sozo] healed you." Immediately he received his sight and followed Jesus along the road. (Mark 10:52)

Deliverance

Those that had seen it told the people how the demon-possessed man had been [sozo] cured. (Luke 8:36)

The Lord will [sozo] rescue me from every evil attack and will bring me safely to His heavenly kingdom. To Him be glory forever and ever. Amen. (2 Timothy 4:18)

Though you already know all this, I want to remind you that the Lord [sozo] delivered His people out of Egypt, but later destroyed those who did not believe. (Jude 1:5)

Salvation, healing, and deliverance

> Jesus said, "For the Son of Man came to seek
> and to save [sozo] what was lost." (Luke 19:9–10)

> Peace be with you! As the Father has sent
> me, I am sending you. (John 20:21)

When we pray and minister to others regarding eternal salvation, healing, or deliverance, we are sozoing them!

CHAPTER 3

Words of Knowledge, When God Speaks

*For I did not speak on my own, but
the Father who sent me commanded
me to say all that I have spoken.*
                              —John 12:49

Christians are instructed to seek answers for all types of situations through prayer, offered up to God the Father, in the name of Jesus Christ.

> Be still and know I am God. (Psalm 46:10)[1]

> If we have not, it is, because we ask not or we are asking with the wrong motives. (James 4:2) (Paraphrased)

These are common scriptures all Christians hear repeatedly in Bible studies, discipleship classes, our Sunday sermons, and in everyday conversation with our Christian family.

What I have found in my walk with the Lord is that some of the simplest scriptures are the hardest to follow. "Be still and know that I am God" can be sometimes the most difficult.

Life is very busy, and if you have not noticed, time doesn't seem to move as slowly as it did when we were children. I often ask myself, "How will I ever make time today?" Somehow by the very grace of God, I always manage.

I have learned that my walk with God is about relationship and allowing my Father to teach me His ways. I am learning daily to allow Him to organize my time. In order for my day to flow with the gracefulness of the kingdom, I must take time to really listen to my instructor, the Spirit of the Father and follow the example—Jesus.

Throughout scriptures, we see Jesus in constant communication with the Father. He always did exactly as He had seen and heard the Father do (John 12:49–50). Jesus is still doing exactly what He sees and hears the Father is doing. Jesus continues today to be the light unto our paths as we walk in His footsteps into the darkest of places in our lives.

We as Christians have been commanded to take up our cross daily and walk with Jesus (Luke 9:23). Just as Jesus sees and hears the

---

[1] New International Version of the Bible is used, unless noted.

Father, we are also to see and hear the Father and do as He does. We are to walk in complete surrender to the Father.

Jesus commanded us to,

> Go, and make disciples of all nations, baptizing them in the name of the Father, the Son and the Holy Spirit, and teaching them to do all that I have commanded you. And surely I am with you until the end of age. (Matthew 28:18–20)

> Go into the world and preach the good news to all creation. Whoever believes and is baptized will be saved, but whoever does not believe will be condemned. And these signs will accompany those who believe: In my name, they will drive out demons; they will speak in new tongues; they will pick up snakes with their hands; and when they drink deadly poison, it will not hurt them at all; they will place their hands on sick people, and they will get well. (Mark 16:15–18)

We must know the voice of our Father in order to fulfill our commissioning. Words of knowledge are simply a part of the Father's language.

What Are Words of Knowledge?

A word of knowledge is a supernatural revelation of information by the Holy Spirit of the divine will and plan of God. It is a supernatural insight or understanding of a circumstance, situation, problem, physical or emotional illness or trauma, and specific facts given by revelation that is without the assistance by any human resource but solely on divine aid. These facts can be about past or present. They are words from the Lord that the recipient would have no other way of knowing. Words of knowledge are instant for a particular person or time to accomplish a distinct purpose.

Definitions

Word came from the Greek word *logos*. It is the spoken word; the word spoken not written.

Knowledge came from the Greek word *gnosis*. It is knowing or understanding of a thing; an insight that manifests itself through understanding of the subject; knowledge of spiritual matters; acquaintance with facts, truths or principles; the fact or state of knowing; awareness as of a fact or circumstance.

Spoken word from God for knowledge of spiritual matters!

Biblical basis for words of knowledge

> There are different kinds of gifts but the same Spirit. There are different kinds of service but the same Lord. There are different types of working, but the same God works in all men. (1 Corinthians 12:4–6)

Verse 6 is a very important verse, so let's read it again. "There are different types of working, *but* the same God works in *all* men."

This verse is very clear about *all* men, not some, not a select few but same God works in *all* men.

The text clearly states: different gifts—same Spirit, different service—same Lord, and different workings—same God…*in all men*!

It is important to establish that the gifts are for today. The gifts of the spirit have not ceased; they are still in operation today and more active as we draw nearer to the second coming of our Lord Jesus Christ! But that is a lesson for another day!

> Now to each one a manifestation of the Spirit is given for the common good. (1 Corinthians 12:7)

Let us take a minute and look at the meaning of common good. First, let us look at the definition of *common*. It means

- belonging equally to or shared alike by two or more or all in question;
- pertaining or belonging equally to an entire community, nation, or culture—public;
- joint, united;
- widespread, general, ordinary; and
- of frequent occurrence—usual or familiar.

I believe that we have established that "common" is for *all*. So let us look at the meaning of *good*. It means

- morally excellent, virtuous, righteous;
- of high quality, excellent;
- right, proper, fit;
- (noun) advantage or profit, worth or benefit; and
- moral righteousness.

Let us better understand what this means and why it's important that the Spirit of God speak to us supernaturally giving "all men" revelations of information.

Why? For the common good, widespread united moral righteousness!

How does God accomplish this widespread united moral righteousness? He does this through salvation, healing, and deliverance. This is the purpose for the active gifts today!

Lastly, verse 8 says, "To one there is given through the Spirit the message of wisdom, to another the message of knowledge by means of same Spirit."

So it is with you. Since you are eager to have *spiritual gifts*, try to excel in *gifts* that build up the church. (1 Corinthians 14:12)

Follow the way of love and eagerly desire spiritual gifts, especially the gift of prophecy. For anyone who speaks in a tongue does not speak to men but to God. Indeed, no one understands him; he utters mysteries with his spirit. (1 Corinthians 14:1–2)

Jesus stepped into a boat, crossed over and came to his own town. Some men brought to him a paralytic, lying on a mat. When Jesus saw their faith, he said to the paralytic, "Take heart, son; your sins are forgiven." At this, some of the teachers of the law said to themselves, "This fellow is blaspheming!" *Knowing their thoughts*, Jesus said, "Why do you entertain evil thoughts in your hearts?" (Matthew 9:1–4)

How Would God Use a Word of Knowledge?

Healing

- Holy Spirit gives revelatory words of knowledge concerning a need for a person or persons for healing.
- Word of knowledge indicates that God wishes to heal the person or persons who have the condition revealed through the word of knowledge.
- Usually the healing will take place during the time that the word of knowledge is given, but this is not always the case.
- When healing occurs, it builds the faith of the person or persons receiving healing and the one who received the word.

Salvation

- When God reveals a word of knowledge in the form of a name or very specific incident and the person that God is calling out is unsaved, God becomes revealed to that person through undeniable supernatural circumstances and coupled with healing miracle, salvation usually occurs (John 5:15).

Deliverance

- Holy Spirit will sometimes reveal words of knowledge for emotional issues or certain spiritual bondage such as fear, anxiety, depression, oppression, rebellion, or one of the many spirits that can keep someone imprisoned. The one who receives this type of word should take authority over this spirit, bind it up, and cast it out, cutting the person or persons free "in the name of Jesus" and loose the opposite and the fruits of the Spirit.
- In Matthew 16:19 and 18:18, Jesus says these words two times, "Whatever you bind on earth will be bound in heaven, and whatever you loose on earth will be loosed in heaven." In chapter 16, He refers to the binding and loosing as the keys to the kingdom. And in chapter 18, Jesus says, "I tell you the truth."
- The one or the corporate body will be freed to receive their healing, whether it is physical, emotional, or spiritual.

How Does God Give a Word of Knowledge for Healing?

Feel it

- You may feel a very brief physical pain in your own body. It can be sharp pains, throbbing, or some other sensation. It could also be a strong emotion, for instance, panic or fear.
- God often chooses this way to reveal to us what He wants to do in a person's life at a certain moment. Feeling a word of knowledge releases faith in both or all parties involved.
- We must be careful that we are not feeling a condition in your own body. Example, if you often have pain in your left ear, you would not give that as a word of knowledge.

See it

- You may see a picture in your mind, a mental picture, like a snapshot.

    When Jesus saw Nathaniel approaching, he said of him, "Here is a true Israelite, in whom there is nothing false." How do you know me? Nathaniel asked. Jesus answered, "I saw you while you were still under the fig tree before Phillip called you." Then Nathaniel declared, Rabbi you are the Son of God; you are the King of Israel. Jesus said, "You believe because I saw you under a fig tree. You shall see greater things than that." (John 1:47–50)

- You may see body parts such as an ear, an eye, an ankle, or a kidney.
- You may see a person with a physical condition, like on crutches with a prosthetic arm. Maybe you'll envision a car accident or a house fire.

Example: I had snapshot picture of a right leg wearing light-colored blue jeans and a metal leg brace. I could tell that it was a man's leg.

Read it

- You may look at someone and see in your mind a word written on someone's forehead, chest, or back.
- You may even see it written in a banner over their head or like a newspaper headline, even a ticker tape like you see at the bottom of a TV program.
- It could be writing on the wall or in the carpet.

Think it

John 5 records the healing at the pool. This is a place where a great number of disabled people used to lie around. They were blind, some lame and even some were paralyzed. But there was one man who had been lying on his mat, and the Bible says that he had been an invalid for thirty-eight years. Jesus learned of his long-term condition and asked him if he wanted to get well.

The man was full of reasons why he could not get into the pool, but Jesus just said, "Get up, pick up your mat, and walk."

He was cured at once. The man left. Later, Jesus finds him at the temple. I find it interesting that Jesus "found" him and then said to him, "See, you are well again. Stop sinning or something worse will happen to you."

What is even more interesting is after being healed at the pool when this man was giving testimony to his healing, he did not know who Jesus was (verse 13). It was not until he received his word of knowledge about his sin; he then knew it was Jesus.

- We may get mental impressions, vague ideas, or a strong, favorable, or remarkable effect of the mind.
- Getting a word stuck in your head such as grief, bipolar, abortion, or hepatitis C.

Speak it

- Randy Clark calls this "Inspired Speech" when you do not think about saying it. It just comes out of your mouth abruptly while talking, praying, or just standing with someone. It could be related to a physical or emotional condition.
- An example is while praying with a young woman for favor on a job interview and for her acne to clear up before her interview, out of my mouth comes, "I believe you need to forgive your sister for stealing your date to the prom five years ago." I would have never known anything about this woman had it not been revealed by God.

Dream it

- You may have a vivid dream or vision in which you or someone else may have a new health problem.
- You may dream of a person or people talking about health issues.
- You may even see the event acted out like a movie, such as a hospital scene or an accident.
- Example: a few months back, I had a word of knowledge during worship where I actually visualized a white Jeep that was rolling over front to back and then on its side until it came to a complete stop on its wheels.

Experience it

- This is very similar to dreaming it because you almost feel as though you are part of the experience either as a witness or participant.
- Sometimes your senses are engaged, such as smelling an odor or a specific taste in your mouth.
- You may also experience strong emotion(s).

- It is important to keep in mind that you may experience several of these categories blending together.

There is a great biblical example of such an experience that Jesus had with the Canaanite woman who touched His garment in Matthew 15:21–28. Sensitivity to the Spirit will cause us to hear and feel certain cries of people and lead them to us or us to them.

Suggestions for Ministering a Word of Knowledge

Most of the time, a word of knowledge is given for someone who is present. However, this is not always true. It could be for someone who knows the person. For example, a word of knowledge is released for someone with ovarian cancer, and I am in that gathering. I hear the word and know that it is my neighbor who is diagnosed with this illness; therefore, I would come forward and receive prayer as a stand-in for my neighbor.

Words of knowledge can come anywhere at any time. You might get one at prayer meetings, Sunday morning worship services, or you may get one walking past someone in the supermarket or gas station. You may even get one while talking on the phone. You may or may not know who the revelation is for.

It is important to be specific in sharing the word of knowledge. If you receive the word through a feeling, be specific about exactly where it is located and describe how it felt.

Even more important, be careful not to add to it or remove any details. Speak it clearly just how you experienced it. Sometimes, we may think that a small detail is unimportant but to the person, that the word is for that small detail could be their deciding factor.

Here is a personal illustration that Randy Clark uses: the man and the green hose. He says, "I once had a mental picture of someone being injured by tripping over a green hose. The only hoses I had seen were garden hoses, so I said I had a picture of a person tripping over a garden hose. There was a man in the meeting that had tripped over a green pressure hose at work. He did not respond to the word at first because the hose he tripped over was not a garden hose. He would have responded more quickly if I had not assumed that the green hose was a garden hose and had given it just as I had seen" (Clark 2012).

Your delivery of a word of knowledge is just as important. You should speak out the word as soon as you receive it or at the next appropriate time.

If you are in church, be sure to check with your pastor about church protocol on giving words of knowledge. If you're not sure, write it down and hand it to your pastor or associate pastor.

If the person who has received the word of knowledge is open to a prayer, you should pray for them right there. If they want you to pray later then pray later. If someone is embarrassed, be encouraging and ask them lovingly to receive what God wants to do for them. Should they refuse, do not pressure them. Just bless them in Jesus's name.

Take the *risk* and follow the Spirit. We all have heard it said time and time again that *faith* is spelled *risk*! We must be willing to take the *risk* even if we are not sure. That's why it is called a risk. That is exactly what blind Bartimaeus did; he called out for Jesus! Even when he was rebuked by other people nearby, he called out even louder. "Jesus, Son of David, have mercy on me!"

Jesus stopped and told his disciples to "Call him!"

So they told Bartimaeus, "Cheer up! On your feet! *He* is calling you!"

This gave Bartimaeus great faith. He took off his cloak which was given to him by religious establishments to indicate that he was a legitimate beggar. He jumped to his feet, and I am sure he ran to Jesus.

Ask yourself these questions, "How would you feel if Jesus appeared right now, right in front of you? How would you feel if He told you He wanted to heal you this instant?" I believe you would be pretty excited. I know I would! Why? Because Jesus would be standing in front of me willing and ready to heal me! If Jesus was right in front of you, would you have any doubt that you would be healed? I do not think so; no doubt at all! Why? Because it is Jesus!

When we get words of knowledge, that's exactly what Jesus wants to do. He wants to heal somebody!

Insights for Growing in Words of Knowledge

Words of knowledge may come quickly, fluttering through your mind like a bird or a dancing butterfly.

Words of knowledge can be very vague, a gentle nudge of your spirit, and it could be tempting to miss it or ignore it all together.

Resist the thought that a word you have received is not important or that it's "just you." Remember, it builds faith in that other person to know God has revealed their condition to you. What seems vague to you may be screaming to someone else.

Do not be presumptuous! Do not say, "God just told me." Instead ask, "Do you have a pain or trouble?" Tell the person your experience and ask if it means anything to them!

Remember, honesty is the best policy!

It is okay to admit that you are nervous or to say that you had only a vague impression or a gentle nudge.

It is even okay to say that you have never prayed for anyone before!

The most important thing is that we are obedient to our Father and step out in faith that He will meet us. It is worth the risk to see someone healed, and it is in that risk taking that faith is built.

Remember: Activation began when you said yes to our Lord Jesus Christ! Press in and enjoy being used by God to bring healing to His children. You will never regret your choice!

CHAPTER 4

What Is Inner Healing?

*I am coming to you now, but I say these things
while I am still in the world, so that they may have
the full measure of my joy within them. I have
given them your word and the world has hated
them, for they are not of the world any more than
I am of the world. My prayer is not that you take
them out of the world but that you protect them
from the evil one. They are not of the world, even
as I am not of it. Sanctify them by the truth; your
word is truth. As you sent me into the world, I
have sent them into the world. For them I sanctify
myself, that they too may be truly sanctified.*
—John 17:13–19

*May God himself, the God of peace, sanctify
you through and through. May your whole
spirit, soul and body be kept blameless at
the coming of our Lord Jesus Christ.*
—1 Thessalonians 5:23

What is inner healing, and why is it important to us as believers? It is our sanctification and transformation process as believers in Christ. It is the body of Christ maturing into her fullness of her calling.

Have you ever experienced the difficulty of walking out your Christianity, especially as new believers? I know I have many times! I also am aware of all the times my "flesh" would rise up out of nowhere and take everybody by surprise. I questioned my salvation more times than I could count! Inner healing is like pulling up the weeds in the garden until all you can see is the beauty and colors. Inner healing is dealing with all the weeds that are growing within us, strangling out the beauty that God originally planted in us. We can pull out a weed, but if we do not get the root up, that weed will lie dormant until the next season. It will continue to grow deeper under the soil until it is strong enough to poke its little head above the surface. It takes time to find the weed in the denseness of the garden. Sometimes, we do not find it until it is big enough to stand out among the beautiful flowers. Have you ever noticed how certain weeds grow in the shadows of the garden and how others will just suddenly appear that weren't there a couple days before?

Much is the same about us and our beliefs, shortcomings, and character defects.

Let me explain what each of these mean so you have a better understanding as we discuss inner healing.

Beliefs are…

- *views*—to contemplate mentally, consider, to regard in a particular light;
- *tenet*—any opinion, principle, doctrine, dogma, etc., especially one held as true individuals or by members of a profession, group, or movement;
- *conclusions*—a reasoned deduction;
- *persuasion*—a deep conviction or belief, a form or system of belief, especially religious belief;

- *assurance*—belief, certainty, conviction, acceptance of or confidence in an alleged fact or body of facts as true or right without positive knowledge or proof; and
- *conviction*—settled, profound, or earnest belief that something is right, doctrine, dogma.

Belief is acceptance in general. Certainty indicates unquestioning belief and being positive in one's own mind that something is true (example: I know this for a certainty). Beliefs are learned and often passed down from one generation to the next. Beliefs become strongholds in our minds. They become our truth even if untrue! A belief will become our reality in which we put out trust...and a stronghold that will exalt itself above God. Here are some examples:

- *Shortcomings*—a weakness in someone's character, a personal fault or failing, a bad feature, a flaw or defect in something
- *Failures*—a subnormal quality, an insufficiency, proving unsuccessful
- *Defects*—lack or want, especially of something essential to perfection or wholeness
- *Deficiency*—areas of inadequacy in conduct, condition, thought, ability

In regard to *character defects*, *character* is defined as the set of qualities that make somebody or something distinctive, especially somebody's qualities of mind and feeling. It is somebody's public reputation, the combination of qualities or features that distinguishes one person, group, or thing from another. It is a distinguishing feature or attribute as of an individual, group, or category. *Defect* is defined as a flaw, a failing, blemish, especially one that still allows the affected thing to function, however imperfectly.

So *character defect* is a personal flaw, a personal failing, weakness, or shortcoming, especially in character. It is an imperfection, something that makes a person or thing less than perfect. The lack of something necessary or desirable for completion or perfection. It's a deficiency, a visual defect. It's an imperfection that causes inadequacy or failure, a shortcoming.

Lies and wrong belief systems create our worldviews, and the fruit of these wrong systems are character defects. These same defects then produce bad fruits. These shortcomings, our deficiency in conduct, condition, thought, ability, they just seem to pop up at the most inconvenient times.

Jesus tells us in *Luke 6:48* to dig deep and lay our foundation on the rock. In this, we see that digging deep is an inner healing term. We need to allow Jesus to dig deeply within our souls and within our hearts to build upon a solid foundation of the rock, which is truth of Jesus!

Conversion is not enough because in verse 46, Jesus says, "Why do you call me, 'Lord, Lord,' and do not do what I say?" Jesus is not speaking to those that are nonbelievers but to those that are believers. We as believers are required by God to clean up our temples. We are called to not just repair the outside of the house, but we must repair all the interior damage. Most of us try to repair the damage we have done to the exterior before we get to the interior structural damage and wonder why we cannot be successful.

You cannot restore freedom from something until you will admit it as an area of struggle.

John Sandford asks this question in his book on *Deliverance and Inner Healing*, "Why don't we do as Jesus says?" Here are some of the reasons that Johns states in his book:

- We have not dug deep to find those aspects of our "old man" that defile and undermine Jesus's character in us. Nor have we brought these defilements to death on the cross and rebuilt on the foundation of Jesus (rock).
- Our flesh refuses to stay dead. (Hebrews 12:15 says, "See to it that no one falls short of the grace of God and that no bitter root grows up to cause trouble and defile many.") Please note that "see to it," this is a command from God!
- Deep within our hearts still remains some unbelief. (Hebrews 3:12 says, "See to it, brothers and sisters, that

none of you has a sinful, unbelieving heart that turns away from the living God.") We all have to work out our salvation by bringing the truth of Jesus into those areas of unbelief so that they will cooperate with Christ! (Again, "see to it!")

- Our minds have not yet been renewed, and we have not yet been transformed. (Romans 12:2 says, "Do not conform to the pattern of this world but be transformed by the renewing of your mind. Then you will be able to test and approve what God's will is—his good, pleasing and perfect will.")

Christians cannot live the Gospel because they have believed only with their mind. Their faith has not yet totally conquered their heart. Thus, the work of inner healing is to evangelize the unbelieving heart of believers. It is the application of the blood and cross and resurrection life of our Lord Jesus Christ to those stubborn dimensions of believers' hearts that have so far refused the redemption their minds and spirits requested when they invited Jesus in.

Inner healing is a process of transformation by which we submit ourselves to be crucified in those areas which are blocking Christ's nature in us. *Transformation* is the process of sanctification, and inner healing is a very big part of this entire process.

Let's look at these two words for a minute—transformation and sanctification.

Transformation is

- a qualitative change, alteration, modification;
- an event that occurs when something passes from one state or phase to another;
- strengthening or becoming stronger;
- to undergo a change in form and condition, appearance, or character and nature; and
- to become transformed, *convert*, or be altered radically in form and function.

Transformation is a process by which Holy Spirit changes every wrong thing in us into blessing. Our deserts are transformed into gardens and our weaknesses into strengths, our degradations (disgrace) into glories.

> Do not conform to the pattern of this world but be *transformed* by the renewing of your mind. Then you will be able to test and approve what God's will is—his good, pleasing and perfect will. (Romans 12:2)

> The earth, from which food comes, is *transformed* below as by fire. (Job 28:5)

> And we all, who with unveiled faces contemplate the Lord's glory, are being *transformed* into his image with ever-increasing glory, which comes from the Lord, who is the Spirit. (2 Corinthians 3:18)

Sanctification means

- to set apart for sacred use, a process in which something is made holy, to consecrate;
- to make holy, purify;
- to make productive of holiness or spiritual blessing;
- to free from foreign, extraneous, or objectionable elements, to purify a language and our bodies;
- to free from guilt or evil;
- to clear or purge; and
- to make clean for ceremonial or ritual use.

Here are some other definitions for the purpose of gaining revelation of what it means to be sanctified. We cannot take lightly what the Word of God is really telling as ministers of God. I tell you the truth. You cannot give away some that you do not have!

We will minister from what we have—good or bad!

Consecration—a solemn commitment of your life or your time to some cherished purpose or to a service or a goal. The act of binding yourself intellectually or emotionally to a course of action.

Commitment—an obligation, promise that restricts one's freedom of action. The state of being bound emotionally or intellectually to a course of action or to another person or persons.

Loyalty—the state or quality of being loyal, fidelity. It's a feeling or attitude of devoted attachment and affection. It's a feeling of faithfulness or allegiance.

Dedication—a selfless devotion, complete and wholehearted devotion. It's a commitment affirmation or promise.

Religion—sanctification of something by setting it apart (usually with religious rites) as dedicated to God.

Purify—to make pure, free from anything that debases, pollutes, adulterates, or contaminates.

[Living to please God] As for other matters, brothers and sisters, we instructed you how-to live-in order to please God, as in fact you are living. Now we ask you and urge you in the Lord Jesus to do this more and more. For you know what instructions we gave you by the authority of the Lord Jesus. It is God's will that you should be *sanctified*: that you should avoid sexual immorality; that each of you should learn to control your own body in a way that is holy and honorable, not in passionate lust like the pagans, who do not know God; and that in this matter no one should wrong or take advantage of a brother or sister. The Lord will punish all those who commit such sins, as we told you and warned you before. For God did not call us to be impure, but to live a holy life. Therefore, anyone who rejects this instruction does not reject a human being but God, the very God who gives you his Holy Spirit. Now about your love for one another we do not need to write to you, for you yourselves have been taught by God to love each other. And in fact, you do love all of God's family throughout Macedonia. Yet we urge you, brothers and sisters, to do so more and more, and to make it your ambition to lead a quiet life: You should mind your own business and work with your hands, just as we told you, so that your daily life may win the respect of outsiders and so that you will not be dependent on anybody. (1 Thessalonians 4:1–12, NIV)

Sanctification is not striving to be holy but a process in which the Holy Spirit brings us more and more to death on the cross and to a new life in Jesus. Inner healing is a way of going through the process of sanctification and becoming what God says we are—free and forgiven! He wants to unlock more freedom. It is more than an experience; it is a lifetime of experiences that are changing as we are applying the truths of God's Word and making ourselves available to the grace of the Holy Spirit. *Grace is more than undeserved forgiveness; it is a divine enablement beyond our human capacity, the power to live differently! Grace is God's ability to do for us what we cannot do for ourselves!* But with grace, there needs a truth to come. Without the truth in our lives, a real understanding of the truth, it is harder for God to bring about His full transformation in us. Without that understanding, we actually believe the lie of the enemy rather than the truth of God.

John Sanford says that the greatest lack in the church is in not knowing how to transform our hearts at the deep levels. Without dealing with the roots, true sanctification and transformation cannot be fully accomplished in the body of Christ! Although every sinful deed was washed away when we received Christ as our Lord, not every part of our heart was immediately able to fully appropriate the good news of that fact.

> Since we have a great priest over the house of God, let us draw near to God with a sincere heart and with the full assurance that faith brings, having our hearts sprinkled to cleanse us from a guilty conscience and having our bodies washed with pure water. (Hebrews 10:20–21)

I want to share with you a bit of my inner healing experience. The Lord completely used others as tools to bring me into a deeper revelation of who I am—my true identity.

I want you to know that I am not good at remembering dates. My husband can attest to that as I always tell people we have been married longer than we actually have! So I will say with all honesty that I was saved as a born-again believer somewhere between 1991 and 1992.

Just to keep my very long testimony short, I will share that during this time, I was married for the second time to a very broken man who was extremely dangerous and very abusive. The abuse I suffered was terrifying and traumatic not only to me but especially to my children who could hear everything through our paper-thin walls in our mobile home.

I want to describe to you some of what I endured during those six long years because it is significant to my healing. It will also show how I developed certain beliefs and how lies became my identity.

I shared with you in the biblical foundation chapter about the power of words and the effect those words have on us. This is especially true when they come from the very people, we trust to take care of us and protect us from the rest of the bad world. I am talking about people like our families, parents, siblings, grandparents, aunts, and uncles. We wholly trust them. Not to mention the authority figures in the world who we are either taught to trust or not to trust. Teachers and police officers are just two examples I will talk about in my testimony.

There were many words that rang out with what I thought was truth during my years of abuse. For instance, "You will never be loved" made me feel such an impending doom during this time, and

I thought if this was love, I would rather die! I cried out to God so many times begging Him to end it all. "Please God, if you care at all about me, please just let me die. I cannot go through this one more minute!"

I began to believe God did not care about me. My logic said, "He would not let me die instead He chose for me to be beaten down daily, so how could He care?" I even believed that I somehow deserved this abuse. I remembered part of a verse I was taught in my Catholic after-school program as a child. It was Deuteronomy 5:9, and it says, "For I, the Lord your God, am a jealous God, punishing the children for the sin of the parents to the third and fourth generation of those who hate me."

Today I know there is much more to that scripture than what the enemy used to try to destroy me. I also know how that scripture, not in its full context, misrepresented the Lord my God! Nonetheless, it was a belief that nearly destroyed me. Not only me but all hope I had in a loving God that I had not experienced but heard others talk about. How many of you have experienced a similar totally out-of-context lie?

Because of that one belief and unanswered prayer, I stayed pinned under the weight of that lie, hating my parents, myself, my husband, and God! I lied to people who really cared about me because I believed no one cared. I was violated in all ways imaginable, and I had believed I was not worth saving.

Those words from my childhood tormented me. I even began to secretly question whether I really loved my children. I could not talk to anyone about what I was feeling or thinking because "children were to be seen and not heard" and "I was too young to feel like that." More tormenting words from childhood found a place to grow and became strongholds in my life. The roots grew deep from the foundation of the planting of those seeds.

I remember times over my young life when asked questions about my opinion either by my teachers or family members, my response would be "I don't know" or "I had not thought about it." In turn, I would ask them, "What is your opinion?"

The Lord later led me to look deeply at this area in my heart. Why had I not formed an opinion? Because I was taught at a very young age not to have an opinion, and this is why I would always respond asking, "What is your opinion?" I was taught other's opinions had more value than mine. Therefore, I just needed to agree!

I agreed with every negative structure that would construct itself in my mind and heart. After all, I believed that no one would ever love me.

Can any of you spell the word *rejection*? With rejection comes its strongman, "the bouncer"—*fear*. For those of you who do not know what a "bouncer" is, a bouncer is usually a very strong man who secures a bar or nightclub. The strongman is under the employment of the owner of that particular club. Usually, clubs have a few of them employed to maintain control by throwing out those causing problems in the club.

In my case, the strongman *fear* controlled me through fear and rejection. It would come against anything that tried to turn me from myself and point me toward God. Its obvious employer was Satan, and fear did not work alone.

Please don't be mistaken because fear is also an emotion. However, it can be an open door to demonic as well, and in my case, I know it was, and I was demonized. I was plagued with emotional fear and rejection and that strongman had taken up residence in my emotions! I believe this demon entered when I was very young and controlled me for about forty years. I remember when it left! (I will talk more about that later.)

Let us go back to my salvation experience in 1991–1992. A precious couple, a pastor and his wife, called me up to say they knew of a way out of my situation and wanted to come by to talk with me. I reluctantly agreed thinking that they meant they were going to take me and my two children far away from this evil man. That is not what they came for!

They asked me if I knew a man named Jesus, and I laughed inside and responded, "Yeah, I have heard of Him. Why?" The pastor's wife asked me what I had heard about Him, so I went on to say, "Well, I know that He is the Son of God, and I know I was taught that He died for mankind to be saved, but somehow I am not sure I believe that!"

She continued to ask just the right questions and rebutted my responses with scripture. Before I knew it, I was sobbing like a baby wanting to know Jesus the way His disciples did. I wanted to go into the Bible and become the Mary that went everywhere that Jesus did. Little did I know that was already His plan for me! I received Christ as my Savior that day, and salvation was mine. I started to attend their nondenominational church and thought it was kind of weird. But I felt the love of Jesus in that place, the people hugged me, and I felt the warmth of God. I was not afraid, and when I entered that building, I felt an overwhelming sense of peace. God was with me, and I was prophesied over and told I would help minister to many broken hearts. Of course, I did not know what any of that meant back then and had forgotten about it until recently. My life went on, and I would eventually find myself divorced from my abusive spouse but still completely tormented internally. I had moved away from my church family and began seeking to fill that emptiness with yet another relationship.

I was depending on another human to fill my void and not God. Eventually, I lost my way again causing my depression to deepen. Taking my focus off God allowed that strongman, fear, begin to show himself in even greater ways.

Years went by as I struggled through my life, isolated from people except my husband and children and a few friends in whom we had common recreational habits and/or children were friends.

Shame, guilt, and bitterness were my very close friends, and I knew them well. It seemed they were the only "friends" who cared to hang around! I was always wondering where Jesus was in all this. I truly believed I had blasphemed the Holy Spirit, and I would never get back into His grace.

Are you seeing the picture here? Those old thought patterns and beliefs were setting themselves up in the place of truth. After all, they did have greater roots than the new creation roots I received when I accepted the Lord Jesus as my Savior.

In order for me to receive any blessings in my salvation, I was going to have to experience a life-changing encounter with God.

When we receive Jesus as our Lord and Savior, we get everything at that very moment but just because we possess everything does not mean we know how to access everything. We must unpack it as needed. To have access to just all of it at once would overwhelm or destroy us. For this reason, it is a process, and we must learn to steward what God has given to us.

As a very small child, "death seeds" were planted in my little mind. I became what I was told. Like all of us, we are who we were led to believe we are; we are who we were told we were by those we were in relationships with. These relationships started with and still are influential by parents, grandparents, siblings, aunts and uncles, cousins, pastors, teachers, other students, our church family, and even our employers and coworkers. In our lives, we usually meet up with both the positive and negative influences. Some of us are blessed to have had a balance between both, but there are those in this world, and in your church, small groups, workplaces, and schools that do not receive balance in their identity.

Today, our children are faced with some of the worst bullying in the world. Bullying is a spirit. Did you know that? It's a spirit of intimidation. It is a preying spirit that preys on those who are weak in their identity. It is a mocker. It ridicules. It slanders. It is a violent spirit. A bully is a supremacy spirit. It thrives on control and power through extreme fear. A bullying spirit is aggressive, hostile, and has no respect for authority or rules.

It is known to travel the bloodline. A bully is usually taught to bully at home!

Why am I sharing this now since we are talking about inner healing and not deliverance? Because spirits can find access through the soul, which is our mind, will, and emotions! As you may already know, everything we do begins as a thought first.

Therefore, the Word of God commands us to *take captive of every thought*! We can stop the false truths that set up life in our mind and eventually turn our hearts away from God. We can stop any doors from opening into a realm of the demonic influence by taking captive of every thought!

Our minds can be mangled messes. Our thoughts evolved into beliefs, identities, and strongholds to protect ourselves.

The battlefield really is in the mind, and inner healing is all about bringing truth into the house.

Insanity has been defined as "doing the same thing and expecting a different result each time."

Sanity has been defined as "wholeness of mind, making decisions based on the truth."

The truth is that Jesus is the only One who offers the truth, the power, the way, and the life.

When we believe Jesus Christ has the power and will restore us to sanity, we receive these free gifts:

> *S*trength
> *A*cceptance
> *N*ew Life
> *I*ntegrity
> *T*rust
> *Y*our High Priest

Strength

> God is our refuge and strength, an ever-present help in trouble. Therefore, we will not fear, though the earth gives way and the mountains fall into the sea. (Psalm 46:1–2)

When we accept Jesus Christ as our Lord, we gain the strength to face the fears that, in the past, caused us to fight, flee, or freeze and become dependent on ourselves. We didn't believe we needed God for anything! When we turn our lives and over to God's care, we are plugged into the power source and our weaknesses become His strengths. Why? Because we have made a choice to plug into the only power source there is—God. Not our own limited power, weakness, and helplessness! This choice is our greatest source of *strength*! (Baker n.d.)

> My mind and my body may grow weak, but God is my strength; he is all I ever need. (Psalm 73:26, GNT)

Acceptance

> Accept one another, then, for the glory of God, as Christ has accepted you. (Romans 15:7)

We are accepted in Christ and we learn to pray and ask God to give us courage to accept the things that we cannot change. With acceptance comes responsibility to stop placing the blame on others for all our past actions and harms. We also learn to have realistic expectations of ourselves and others, learning not to relate to others the way we had in the past. We learn to accept others, right where they are and not where we think they should be. (Baker n.d.)

New life

> We were really crushed and overwhelmed and feared we would never live through it. We felt we were doomed to die and saw how powerless we were to help ourselves; but that was good, for then we put everything into the hands of God, who alone could save us, for he can even raise the dead. (2 Corinthians 1:8–9, TLB)

I love what I heard Bill Johnson say one time, "Because of Christ's crucifixion, we are indeed new creations (2 Corinthians 5:17). No longer sinners with a Band-Aid over the problem. When the Spirit of the Lord took residence in you, you lost all right to live as normal human beings!"

Integrity

We gain integrity when we follow through on our promises. Others will start trusting what you say. Men and women of integrity gain courage and are not afraid to tell the truth in love. The courage is not ours but Jesus Christ in us because He is the Way, the Truth, and the Life! Remember that a half truth is a whole lie! A lie is a result of weakness and fear. *Truth* fears nothing but concealment! Truth often hurts, but it is the lie that leaves scars!

> Nothing gives me greater joy than to hear that my children are following the way of truth. (3 John 1:4, NCV)

Trust

> It is dangerous to be concerned with what others think of you, but if you trust the Lord, you are safe. (Proverbs 29:25)

As we learn to trust God, we are learning to release our control to His care. By taking this action, we are admitting that we need His help. As we practice this in daily life, we are learning to trust ourselves and others. We are learning to make friends with our brothers and sisters in Christ, real relationships with people we can trust to walk alongside us and share with us in our journey advancing to God's kingdom! (Baker n.d.)

Your High Priest

> While we were still sinners Christ died for us! (Romans 5:8)

Jesus loves us just the way we are, He is faithful. He will not let us be tempted beyond what we can bare when we are, He will always provide us a way out (1 Corinthians 10:13). Also *He bears our burdens*

(Psalm 38:19). He is our protection and refuge in times of trouble. He cares for those that trust Him! (Nahum 1:7; paraphrased) (Baker n.d.)

To wrap up, I will leave you with this scripture. Romans 12:2 (PH) says this, "Don't let the world around you squeeze you into its own mold, but let God re-mold your minds from within, so that you may prove in practice that plan of God for you is good, meets all his demands and moves toward the goal of true maturity."

What Are Strongholds? (Godly and Ungodly)

You have heard me talk about strongholds, so let's discuss them a little.

Strongholds are "arguments and every pretension that sets itself up against the knowledge of God."

A stronghold is an area of our lives that is influenced/controlled by thought patterns and belief systems. They can be either godly or ungodly.

Ungodly strongholds are when a person's belief systems and thought patterns align with the world and are in agreement with Satan and his demons. Strongholds that are ungodly always pull us away from God and exalt themselves above the knowledge of God.

Godly strongholds on the other hand are thoughts and belief systems that exalt God and the kingdom of God. Our belief of His heavenly perspective will always remove the ungodly and replace it with righteous and holy thinking. How we think determines our behavior (actions and speech). Our thoughts always affect our identity as children of the Living God. We must tear down all ungodly strongholds and replace them by the renewing of our minds. After all, we do have the mind of Christ, and it is in doing this that we begin to walk in the reality of God.

World English Dictionary defines the words strong and hold in such a way that they suggest a mental strength that is resistant to attack.

Stronghold is

1. a defensible place, fortress; and
2. a major center or area of predominance.

Strong is

1. involving or possessing mental strength;
2. solid or robust in construction, not easily broken or injured;
3. having a resolute will or morally firm and incorruptible character;
4. intense in quality, not faint or feeble;
5. easily defensible, incontestable, or formidable;
6. concentrated, not weak or diluted;
7. having an extreme or drastic effect;
8. emphatic or immoderate;
9. having powerful means to resist attack, assault, or aggression;
10. decisively unyielding, firm, or uncompromising;
11. of great moral power, firmness, or courage, strong under temptation; and
12. powerful in influence, authority, resources, or means of prevailing or succeeding, a strong nation.

Hold is

1. the act or method of holding fast or grasping;
2. controlling force or influence;
3. the act or method of holding fast;
4. to support or bear;
5. to maintain or be maintained in a specified state or condition, hold firm;
6. to have the ownership, possession; and
7. to have the use of or responsibility for.

Within strongholds are lies and beliefs which all work against us. Here are a few of the lies I have heard...

Lie—people will think I am pushing my beliefs on them, and you know how that made you feel! *Truth*—speak the truth in *love,* and the Holy Spirit will do the rest!

Lie—don't do it. You will only make a fool out of yourself! *Truth*— Holy Spirit would not make a fool out of me!

Lie—there are many people more anointed/experienced at praying for the sick. *Truth*—the same Holy Spirit in them is in you. The same Holy Spirit is in you that came down and empowered Christ after baptism.

Lie—healing ministry is for the spiritually elite. *Truth*—God does not call the qualified. He qualifies the called.

Strongholds that are ungodly must be dealt with properly and by the leading of the Holy Spirit. As a minister, you may recognize a stronghold through behaviors, attitudes, and patterns. With strongholds usually come justifications, reasonings, and many excuses from the person that you are ministering too! A stronghold is truth to the one it affects. Those false truths known as strongholds must be torn down, and "true" repentance must happen for a person to get free!

The Key of Repentance

Repentance is one of the necessary ingredients for healing. On many occasions that Jesus healed people, he would say to the person, "Go and sin no more!" This is not a loving request. It is a command!

> Do not be deceived, God is not mocked [He will not allow Himself to be ridiculed, nor treated with contempt nor allow His precepts to be scornfully set aside]; for whatever a man sows, this and this only is what he will reap. For the one who sows to his flesh [his sinful capacity, his worldliness, his disgraceful impulses] will reap from the flesh ruin and destruction, but the one

who sows to the Spirit will from the Spirit reap
eternal life. (Galatians 6:7–8, AMP)

Repentance is not a feeling; it is an action! Repentance does not
affect much if we only "feel" sorry! Change only happens when we
turn from one thing toward something different!

Feelings of repentance could be defined as having deep sorrow, any
uneasiness or hesitation about the rightness of an action, or deeply
felt remorse for a past sin, wrongdoing, or the like. It is a regret for
any past action. *The action comes in* turning *away from.*

There are three Greek words used in the New Testament to
indicate repentance which are as follows:

1. The verb *metamelomai* (G 3338) meaning to care afterwards, to have regret. *Repent* (self) is used as a change of
   mind, such as to produce regret or even remorse on account
   of sin but not necessarily a change of heart. This word is
   used with reference to the repentance of Judas.

   When Judas, who had betrayed him, realized that Jesus had been condemned to die, he
   was filled with remorse. So, he took the thirty
   pieces of silver back to the leading priests and the
   elders. (Matthew 27:3)

2. *Metanoeo* (G3340) means to think differently or afterwards
   to reconsider (morally, feels compunction) to change one's
   mind and purpose as the result of after knowledge.
3. *Metanoia* (G3341) is a verb, with the cognate noun, used
   of true repentance, a change of mind and purpose and life,
   to which remission of sin is promised.

   Each of your commandments is right. That
   is why I hate every false way. (Psalm 119:128)

I had only heard about you before, but now I have seen you with my own eyes, I take back everything I said, and I sit in dust and ashes to show my repentance. (Job 42:5–6)

For the kind of sorrow God wants us to experience leads us away from sin and results in salvation. (2 Corinthians 7:10)

There's no regret for that kind of sorrow. But worldly sorrow, which lacks repentance, results in spiritual death.

True repentance consists of (1) a true sense of one's own guilt and sinfulness; (2) an apprehension of God's mercy in Christ; (3) an actual hatred of sin and turning from it to God; and (4) a persistent endeavor after a holy life in a walking with God in the way of His commandments. The true expression of sorrow or wrongdoing for sin is confession of guilt.

Against you, and you alone, have I sinned; I have done what is evil in your sight. You will be proved right in what you say, and your judgment against me is just.

Don't keep looking at my sins. Remove the stain of my guilt, *awareness of pollution.* For I was born a sinner—yes, from the moment my mother conceived me.

Purify me from my sins, and I will be clean; wash me, and I will be whiter than snow. Create in me a clean heart, O God. Renew a loyal spirit within me, *and of helplessness.*

Do not banish me from your presence, and don't take your Holy Spirit from me. (Psalm 51:4–5, 7, 9–11)

But deal well with me, O Sovereign Lord, for the sake of your own reputation! Rescue me

because you are so faithful and good. For I am
poor and needy, and my heart is full of pain.
(Psalm 109:21–22)

Thus, he apprehends himself to be just what God has always
seen him to be and declares him to be. But repentance comprehends
not only such a sense of sin but also an apprehension of mercy, without which there can be no true repentance (author n.d.).

Have mercy on me, O God, because of your
unfailing love. Because of your great compassion,
blot out the stain of my sins. (Psalm 51:1)

But with you there is forgiveness, so that we
can, with reverence, serve you. (Psalm 130:4)

We must turn from our sins and act on the glorious news!
Repentance is not self-loathing but God loving. When we do not
understand the importance of repentance, then we will end up
repenting out of fear of punishment rather than a true change of
heart! God is never looking to punish us; He is anticipating with
open arms on your turning toward Him. Repentance is learning how
to enjoy your freedom in the arms of a loving God.

Repent! Turn away from all your offenses;
then sin will not be your downfall. Rid yourselves
of all the offenses you have committed and get a
new heart and a new spirit. (Ezekiel 18:30–31)

True repentance is death to internal structures, those things that
set themselves up against God.
Look at Ephesians 4:17–32. Paul gave us a clear picture of a
heart and lifestyle of repentance especially starting in verse 20.

With the Lord's authority, I say this: Live no
longer as the Gentiles do, for they are hopelessly

confused. Their minds are full of darkness; they wander far from the life God gives because they have closed their minds and hardened their hearts against him. They have no sense of shame. They live for lustful pleasure and eagerly practice every kind of impurity. *But that isn't what you learned about Christ.* Since you have heard about Jesus and have learned the truth that comes from him, *throw off your old sinful nature* and your former way of life, which is corrupted by lust and deception. Instead, let the Spirit renew your thoughts and attitudes. Put on your new nature, created to be like God—truly righteous and holy. So, stop telling lies. Let us tell our neighbors the truth, for we are all parts of the same body. And "don't sin by letting anger control you." Don't let the sun go down while you are still angry, for anger gives a foothold to the devil. If you are a thief, quit stealing. Instead, use your hands for good hard work, and then give generously to others in need. Don't use foul or abusive language. Let everything you say be good and helpful, so that your words will be an encouragement to those who hear them. And do not bring sorrow to God's Holy Spirit by the way you live. Remember, he has identified you as his own, guaranteeing that you will be saved on the day of redemption. Get rid of all bitterness, rage, anger, harsh words, and slander, as well as all types of evil behavior. Instead, be kind to each other, tenderhearted, forgiving one another, just as God through Christ has forgiven you.

Here is a question: Why is it that when someone gets saved, we teach them that it is okay to justify their sin or some else's? The scriptures tell us otherwise! We are to bear fruit in keeping with repentance (Matthew 3:8).

The following scriptures are some of "what the Bible says about repentance." These scriptures were taken from the English Standard Version of the Holy Bible.

If my people who are called by my name humble themselves and pray and seek my face and turn from their wicked ways, then I will hear from heaven and will forgive their sin and heal their land. (2 Chronicles 7:14)

If we confess our sins, he is faithful and just to forgive us our sins and to cleanse us from all unrighteousness. (1 John 1)

Repent therefore, and turn again, that your sins may be blotted out. (Acts 3:19)

No, I tell you; but unless you repent, you will all likewise perish. (Luke 13:3)

But if a wicked person turns away from all his sins that he has committed and keeps all my statutes and does what is just and right, he shall surely live; he shall not die. None of the transgressions that he has committed shall be remembered against him; for the righteousness that he has done he shall live. Have I any pleasure in the death of the wicked, declares the Lord God, and not rather that he should turn from his way and live? (Ezekiel 18:21–23)

The times of ignorance God overlooked, but now he commands all people everywhere to repent. (Acts 17:30)

The Lord is not slow to fulfill his promise as some count slowness, but is patient toward you, not wishing that any should perish, but that all should reach repentance. (2 Peter 3:9)

Whoever conceals his transgressions will not prosper, but he who confesses and forsakes them will obtain mercy. (Proverbs 28:13)

Remember therefore from where you have fallen; repent and do the works you did at first. If not, I will come to you and remove your lampstand from its place, unless you repent. (Revelation 2:5)

Draw near to God, and he will draw near to you. Cleanse your hands, you sinners, and purify your hearts, you double-minded. Be wretched and mourn and weep. Let your laughter be turned to mourning and your joy to gloom. Humble yourselves before the Lord, and he will exalt you. (James 4:8–10)

And Peter said to them, "Repent and be baptized every one of you in the name of Jesus Christ for the forgiveness of your sins, and you will receive the gift of the Holy Spirit." (Acts 2:38)

As it is, I rejoice, not because you were grieved, but because you were grieved into repenting. For you felt a Godly grief so that you suffered no loss through us. For Godly grief produces a repentance that leads to salvation without regret, whereas worldly grief produces death. For see what earnestness this Godly grief has produced in you, but also what eagerness to clear yourselves, what indignation, what fear, what longing, what zeal, what punishment! At every point, you have proved yourselves innocent in the matter. (2 Corinthians 7:9–11)

Repent, therefore, of this wickedness of yours and pray to the Lord that, if possible, the intent of your heart may be forgiven you. (Acts 8:22)

And saying, "The time is fulfilled, and the kingdom of God is at hand; repent and believe in the gospel." (Mark 1:15)

Two men went up into the temple to pray, one a Pharisee and the other a tax collector. The Pharisee, standing by himself, prayed thus: "God, I thank you that I am not like other men, extortioners, unjust, adulterers, or even like this tax collector. I fast twice a week; I give tithes of all that I get." But the tax collector, standing far off, would not even lift up his eyes to heaven, but beat his breast, saying, "God, be merciful to me, a sinner!" I tell you, this man went down to his house justified, rather than the other. For everyone who exalts himself will be humbled, but the one who humbles himself will be exalted. (Luke 18:10–14)

Those whom I love, I reprove and discipline, so be zealous and repent. (Revelation 3:19)

And rend your hearts and not your garments. Return to the Lord your God, for he is gracious and merciful, slow to anger, and abounding in steadfast love; and he relents over disaster. (Joel 2:13)

Repent, for the kingdom of heaven is at hand. (Matthew 3:2)

Purge me with hyssop, and I shall be clean; wash me, and I shall be whiter than snow. Let me hear joy and gladness; let the bones that you have broken rejoice. Hide your face from my sins and blot out all my iniquities. Create in me a clean heart, O God, and renew a right spirit within me. Cast me not away from your presence and take not your Holy Spirit from me. (Psalm 51:7–17)

No, I tell you; but unless you repent, you will all likewise perish. (Luke 13:5)

I confess my iniquity; I am sorry for my sin. (Psalm 38:18)

And if that nation, concerning which I have spoken, turns from its evil, I will relent of the disaster that I intended to do to it. (Jeremiah 18:8)

This is the message we have heard from him and proclaim to you, that God is light, and in him is no darkness at all. If we say we have fellowship with him while we walk in darkness, we lie and do not practice the truth. But if we walk in the light, as he is in the light, we have fellowship with one another, and the blood of Jesus his Son cleanses us from all sin. If we say we have no sin, we deceive ourselves, and the truth is not in us. If we confess our sins, he is faithful and just to forgive us our sins and to cleanse us from all unrighteousness. (1 John 1:5–9)

From that time Jesus began to preach, saying, "Repent, for the kingdom of heaven is at hand." (Matthew 4:17)

I have not come to call the righteous but sinners to repentance. (Luke 5:32)

Again, though I say to the wicked, "You shall surely die," yet if he turns from his sin and does what is just and right, if the wicked restores the pledge, gives back what he has taken by robbery, and walks in the statutes of life, not doing injustice, he shall surely live; he shall not die. None of the sins that he has committed shall be remembered against him. He has done what is just and right; he shall surely live. (Ezekiel 33:14–16)

Testifying both to Jews and to Greeks of repentance toward God and of faith in our Lord Jesus Christ. (Acts 20:21)

When God saw what they did, how they turned from their evil way, God relented of the disaster that he had said he would do to them, and he did not do it. (Jonah 3:10)

Remember, then, what you received and heard. Keep it, and repent. If you will not wake up, I will come like a thief, and you will not know at what hour I will come against you. (Revelation 3:3)

Or do you presume on the riches of his kindness and forbearance and patience, not knowing that God's kindness is meant to lead you to repentance? (Romans 2:4)

Turn away from evil and do good; seek peace and pursue it. (Psalm 34:14)

It maybe they will listen, and everyone turn from his evil way, that I may relent of the disaster that I intend to do to them because of their evil deeds. (Jeremiah 26:3)

And then will I declare to them, "I never knew you; depart from me, you workers of lawlessness." (Matthew 7:23)

"Yet even now," declares the Lord, "return to me with all your heart, with fasting, with weeping, and with mourning." (Joel 2:12)

For you know that afterward, when he desired to inherit the blessing, he was rejected, for he found no chance to repent, though he sought it with tears. (Hebrews 12:17)

For Godly grief produces a repentance that leads to salvation without regret, whereas worldly grief produces death. (2 Corinthians 7:10)

He himself bore our sins in his body on the tree, that we might die to sin and live to righteousness. By his wounds you have been healed. (1 Peter 2:24)

Correcting his opponents with gentleness. God may perhaps grant them repentance leading to a knowledge of the truth. (2 Timothy 2:25)

Just so, I tell you, there will be more joy in heaven over one sinner who repents than over ninety-nine righteous persons who need no repentance. (Luke 15:7)

Again, when a wicked person turns away from the wickedness he has committed and does what is just and right, he shall save his life. (Ezekiel 18:27)

Leave your simple ways, and live, and walk in the way of insight. (Proverbs 9:6)

But declared first to those in Damascus, then in Jerusalem and throughout all the region of Judea, and also to the Gentiles, that they should repent and turn to God, performing deeds in keeping with their repentance. (Acts 26:20)

Truly, truly, I say to you, whoever hears my word and believes him who sent me has eternal life. He does not come into judgment but has passed from death to life. (John 5:24)

And there you shall remember your ways and all your deeds with which you have defiled yourselves, and you shall loathe yourselves for all the evils that you have committed. (Ezekiel 20:43)

God exalted him at his right hand as Leader and Savior, to give repentance to Israel and forgiveness of sins. (Acts 5:31)

Bear fruit in keeping with repentance. (Matthew 3:8)

Wake up, and strengthen what remains and is about to die, for I have not found your works complete in the sight of my God. (Revelation 3:2)

And even then, if they do not continue in their unbelief, will be grafted in, for God has the power to graft them in again. (Romans 11:23)

But when he came to himself, he said, "How many of my father's hired servants have more than enough bread, but I perish here with hunger! I will arise and go to my father, and I will say to him, 'Father, I have sinned against heaven and before you. I am no longer worthy to be called your son. Treat me as one of your hired servants.'" And he arose and came to his father. But while he was still a long way off, his father saw him and felt compassion, and ran and embraced him and kissed him. (Luke 15:17–20)

John appeared, baptizing in the wilderness and proclaiming a baptism of repentance for the forgiveness of sins. (Mark 1:4)

Therefore say to the house of Israel, thus says the Lord God: Repent and turn away from your idols and turn away your faces from all your abominations. (Ezekiel 14:6)

But let man and beast be covered with sack-cloth and let them call out mightily to God. Let everyone turn from his evil way and from the violence that is in his hands. (Jonah 3:8)

Come, let us return to the Lord; for he has torn us, that he may heal us; he has struck us down, and he will bind us up. (Hosea 6:1)

And you, son of man, say to the house of Israel, thus have you said: "Surely our transgressions and our sins are upon us, and we rot away because of them. How then can we live?" Say to them, "As I live, declares the Lord God, I have no pleasure in the death of the wicked, but that the wicked turn from his way and live; turn back, turn back from your evil ways, for why will you die, O house of Israel?" And you, son of man, say to your people, "The righteousness of the righteous shall not deliver him when he transgresses, and as for the wickedness of the wicked, he shall not fall by it when he turns from his wickedness, and the righteous shall not be able to live by his righteousness when he sins." (Ezekiel 33:10–12)

And when they come there, they will remove from it all its detestable things and all its abominations. And I will give them one heart, and a new spirit I will put within them. I will remove the heart of stone from their flesh and give them a heart of flesh, that they may walk in my statutes and keep my rules and obey them. And they shall be my people, and I will be their God. (Ezekiel 11:18–20)

Let us test and examine our ways and return to the Lord! (Lamentations 3:40)

I will give them a heart to know that I am the Lord, and they shall be my people and I will be their God, for they shall return to me with their whole heart. (Jeremiah 24:7)

As for me, I said, "O Lord, be gracious to me; heal me, for I have sinned against you!" (Psalm 41:4)

Therefore, O king, let my counsel be acceptable to you: break off your sins by practicing righteousness, and your iniquities by showing mercy to the oppressed, that there may perhaps be a lengthening of your prosperity. (Daniel 4:27)

For if you truly amend your ways and your deeds, if you truly execute justice one with another. (Jeremiah 7:5)

Seek the Lord while he may be found; call upon him while he is near. (Isaiah 55:6)

If you turn at my reproof, behold, I will pour out my spirit to you; I will make my words known to you. (Proverbs 1:23)

When I wept and humbled my soul with fasting, it became my reproach. (Psalm 69:10)

Though I am in the right, my own mouth would condemn me; though I am blameless, he would prove me perverse. (Job 9:20)

And to the one who does not work but believes in him who justifies the ungodly, his faith is counted as righteousness. (Romans 4:5)

And with many other words he bore witness and continued to exhort them, saying, "Save yourselves from this crooked generation." (Acts 2:40)

Thus says the Lord of hosts: Consider your ways. (Haggai 1:7)

Afterward Jesus found him in the temple and said to him, "See, you are well! Sin no more, that nothing worse may happen to you." (John 5:14)

And he went into all the region around the Jordan, proclaiming a baptism of repentance for the forgiveness of sins. (Luke 3:3)

The Key of Confession

The freedom of repentance comes with the confession of sins. One of the greatest tools Jesus gives us is *confession*. I learned several years ago through a Christ-centered program called Celebrate Recovery that I must openly examine and confess my faults to myself, to God, and to someone that I trust.

Therefore confess your sins to each other and pray for each other so that you may be healed. The prayer of a righteous person is powerful and effective. (James 5:16)

One of the most asked questions to any prayer minister, lay leader, leader or pastor is, "Why do I have to confess my sins to another person?"

The answer is...many of us have been keeping secrets for most of our lives. Those secrets keep us in bondage, we lose self-respect, and we become weighed down and tired. Were you aware that secrets and purposefully keeping things hidden are an occult practice? We will discuss this more in the next two chapters. Remember that our enemy comes only to steal, kill, and destroy (John 10:10)!

Did you know that keeping secrets is an inroad for depression, anxiety, and panic? Why is it that a physician normally recommends counseling along with medication as the treatment for depression? Because even science knows there are underlying truths about depression. Science does not see depression from a spiritual perspective, but they are very much aware that fear is the root cause of depression. However, they treat only the physical manifestations of depression. Science understands the value of confession and that dealing with the issues and traumas of our past are significant to treatment.

When we admit out loud those things that have tormented us, caused us fear, had control over us, we actually are stripping them of their power. It will, for the most part, cause them to loosen their grip on us, giving way for hope to come in. It is the light that pierces the darkness, not the other way around!

When we choose *not* to confess our sins, here are some consequences:

1. We lose freedom.
2. We become isolated, especially from the people who love us and most importantly, God!
3. We are prisoners to unforgiveness filled with resentment, bitterness, anger, rage, and hatred.
4. We become jealous and envious of others.
5. We often experience sickness and disease!
6. We are usually prideful and self-centered!
7. We lose joy and peace!
8. Our feelings are disabled!
9. We stop growing!

I know I could go on and on with this list, but I believe you are getting the point.

If we are to *overcome* these things, it is important that we bring all that is hidden in the darkness of our souls into the light.

Worrying about the past and dreading the future will make us unable to enjoy God's plans for us in the present! We let our fears and worries paralyze us, and the only lasting way to be free is to give them to God. Psalm 146:7–8 tells us, "The Lord frees the prisoners; He opens the eyes of the blind; He lifts the burdens from those bent down beneath their loads for the Lord loves good men."

Paul tells the church at Ephesus, "Stop lying to each other. Tell the truth for we are parts of each other and when we lie to each other we are hurting ourselves." Our denial only lengthens our pain and creates multiple problems in the long run. Remember, we are only as sick as our secrets! I personally learned in my Celebrate Recovery that God never wastes a hurt. God will never waste your darkness, but He can't use it until you step out of your denial and confess your hurt, your sin, and your secret darkness! Then and only then will God shine the light of His truth in your life! Jesus said, *"Know the truth, and the truth will set you free!"* (John 8:32). Being honest and confessing the truth is not easy. Taking off the mask we have become accustomed to living behind is hard, but God is love, and we must close our eyes and take that step of faith and fall into His unmeasurable grace.

Proverbs 28:13 tells us, "Whoever conceals their sins does not prosper, but the one who confesses and renounces them finds mercy."

Satan, the liar, would have us believe that we have dealt with those deep hidden things, and there is no need to dig them up again. The one thing I have heard the most in ministry is, "Oh, I am okay with that. I have dealt with it already!" In some cases, this is true. But in many cases, the hidden thing may have been touched on, but it is like a nasty splinter that has wiggled its way deeper into the skin, festering on the inside. You are only reminded of the pain when you accidentally touch it. The truth is, if we do not get that thing out, the wound only creates greater infection and eventually causes disease in other areas of our body.

So again, I remind you the importance of James 5:16. We must confess our sins to ourselves, to God, and to someone we trust! Pray for each other so that you may be healed.

The next step we must take in our "New Creation" lifestyles is forgiveness! So let's get started! But before we do, here are scriptures on confession:

> If we confess our sins, he is faithful and just to forgive us our sins and to cleanse us from all unrighteousness. (1 John 1:9)

> Therefore, confess your sins to one another and pray for one another, that you may be healed. The prayer of a righteous person has great power as it is working. (James 5:16)

> I acknowledged my sin to you, and I did not cover my iniquity; I said, "I will confess my transgressions to the Lord," and you forgave the iniquity of my sin. Selah. (Psalm 32:5)

> On the evening of that day, the first day of the week, the doors being locked where the disciples were for fear of the Jews, Jesus came and stood among them and said to them, "Peace be with you." When he had said this, he showed them his hands and his side. Then the disciples were glad when they saw the Lord. Jesus said to them again, "Peace be with you. As the Father has sent me, even so I am sending you." And when he had said this, he breathed on them and said to them, "Receive the Holy Spirit. If you forgive the sins of any, they are forgiven them; if you withhold forgiveness from any, it is withheld." (John 20:19–24)

> My little children, I am writing these things to you so that you may not sin. But if anyone

does sin, we have an advocate with the Father, Jesus Christ the righteous. (1 John 2:1)

If you forgive the sins of any, they are forgiven them; if you withhold forgiveness from any, it is withheld. (John 20:23)

Let us then with confidence draw near to the throne of grace, that we may receive mercy and find grace to help in time of need. (Hebrews 4:16)

For I do not understand my own actions. For I do not do what I want, but I do the very thing I hate. Now if I do what I do not want, I agree with the law, that it is good. So now it is no longer I who do it, but sin that dwells within me. For I know that nothing good dwells in me, that is, in my flesh. For I have the desire to do what is right, but not the ability to carry it out. For I do not do the good I want, but the evil I do not want is what I keep on doing. (Romans 7:15–25)

Whoever conceals his transgressions will not prosper, but he who confesses and forsakes them will obtain mercy. (Proverbs 28:13)

A Psalm of David, when Nathan the prophet went to him, after he had gone in to Bathsheba. Have mercy on me, O God, according to your steadfast love; according to your abundant mercy blot out my transgressions. Wash me thoroughly from my iniquity and cleanse me from my sin! For I know my transgressions, and my sin is ever before me. Against you, you only, have I sinned and done what is evil in your sight, so that you may be justified in your words and blameless in your judgment. Behold, I was brought forth in iniquity, and in sin did my mother conceive me. (Psalm 51:1–19)

David said to Nathan, "I have sinned against the Lord." And Nathan said to David, "The Lord also has put away your sin; you shall not die." (2 Samuel 12:13)

Also many of those who were now believers came, confessing and divulging their practices. (Acts 19:18)

But that you may know that the Son of Man has authority on earth to forgive sins—he then said to the paralytic—"Rise, pick up your bed and go home." And he rose and went home. When the crowds saw it, they were afraid, and they glorified God, who had given such authority to men. (Matthew 9:6–8)

Truly, I say to you, whatever you bind on earth shall be bound in heaven, and whatever you loose on earth shall be loosed in heaven. (Matthew 18:18)

If we say we have fellowship with him while we walk in darkness, we lie and do not practice the truth. But if we walk in the light, as he is in the light, we have fellowship with one another, and the blood of Jesus his Son cleanses us from all sin. (1 John 1:6–7)

Trust in the Lord with all your heart, and do not lean on your own understanding. In all your ways acknowledge him, and he will make straight your paths. (Proverbs 3:5–6)

All this is from God, who through Christ reconciled us to himself and gave us the ministry of reconciliation. (2 Corinthians 5:18)

As for me, I said, "O Lord, be gracious to me; heal me, for I have sinned against you!" (Psalm 41:4)

And they were baptized by him in the river Jordan, confessing their sins. (Matthew 3:6)

If my people who are called by my name humble themselves and pray and seek my face and turn from their wicked ways, then I will hear from heaven and will forgive their sin and heal their land. (2 Chronicles 7:14)

For we must all appear before the judgment seat of Christ, so that each one may receive what is due for what he has done in the body, whether good or evil. (2 Corinthians 5:10)

Behold, the Lord's hand is not shortened, that it cannot save, or his ear dull, that it cannot hear; but your iniquities have made a separation between you and your God, and your sins have hidden his face from you so that he does not hear. For your hands are defiled with blood and your fingers with iniquity; your lips have spoken lies; your tongue mutters wickedness. No one enters suit justly; no one goes to law honestly; they rely on empty pleas, they speak lies, they conceive mischief and give birth to iniquity. They hatch adders' eggs; they weave the spider's web; he who eats their eggs dies, and from one that is crushed a viper is hatched. (Isaiah 59:1–21)

If your brother sins against you, go and tell him his fault, between you and him alone. If he listens to you, you have gained your brother. But if he does not listen, take one or two others along with you, that every charge may be established by the evidence of two or three witnesses. If he refuses to listen to them, tell it to the church. And if he refuses to listen even to the church, let him be to you as a Gentile and a tax collector. (Matthew 18:15–17)

Since then we have a great high priest who has passed through the heavens, Jesus, the Son of God, let us hold fast our confession. For we do not have a high priest who is unable to sympathize with our weaknesses, but one who in every respect has been tempted as we are, yet without sin. (Hebrews 4:14–15)

And all the country of Judea and all Jerusalem were going out to him and were being baptized by him in the river Jordan, confessing their sins. (Mark 1:5)

I will give you the keys of the kingdom of heaven, and whatever you bind on earth shall be bound in heaven, and whatever you loose on earth shall be loosed in heaven. (Matthew 16:19)

Leave your gift there before the altar and go. First be reconciled to your brother, and then come and offer your gift. (Matthew 5:24)

The Key of Forgiveness

Heaven would be empty if God was not willing to forgive!

> I will cleanse them from all the sin they have committed against me and will forgive all their sins of rebellion against me. (Jeremiah 33:8)

> Who is a God like you, who pardons sin and forgives the transgression of the remnant of his inheritance? You do not stay angry forever but delight to show mercy. (Micah 7:18)

> Therefore, if you are offering your gift at the altar and there remember that your brother or sister has something against you; leave your gift there in front of the altar. First go and be reconciled to them; then come and offer your gift. (Matthew 5:23–24)

The Word of God is very clear about the importance of forgiveness. In Matthew 6, He says that if you forgive other people when they sin against you, your heavenly Father will also forgive you. But if you do not forgive others of their sins, your Father will not forgive your sins.

It doesn't sound like He will relent on this. I believe we are commanded to forgive unless we simply do not want to be forgiven in return. I somehow do not think this is what any person wants. I believe every man, woman, and child desires to be received by others.

Forgiveness is a great idea until we have to practice it in our own lives. But it is clearly God's prescription to those broken and wounded areas in our lives that keep us from receiving all that God has for us. No matter how great the offenses, along that path to healing lies forgiveness.

Jeremiah 6:14 says you cannot heal a wound by saying it's not there! The truth is, in our lives, we have been wounded and some of those wounds were caused by others! Those are sometimes the bitter roots that spring up and defile. God says to see to it that no one falls short of His grace. Therefore, we must initiate forgiveness; it will open up the way to God and destroy all bitterness that has kept us bound up and captive, imprisoned in darkness.

Forgiveness truly is a key that unlocks our shackles, and we can once and for all, walk in freedom of the work of Jesus on the cross.

Forgiveness is the crucifixion of bitterness, resentment, and judgement toward another human being!

It breaks the cycle. It does not settle all the questions of blame, justice, or fairness, but it does allow your relationship to heal and possibly start over.

Forgiveness doesn't remove or delete offenses from our lives. Forgiveness doesn't mean that you go into denial and forget this ever happened to you. It isn't that you are somehow wiping this event from your life, glossing over the wrongs others did. It is not developing a memory lapse of the pain you have suffered. Forgiveness will not erase your memory clean. What forgiveness does is to remove the power of that memory over your life.

Jesus exclaimed on the cross, "It is finished" (John 19:30). The grace of God is always sufficient for all people and all sin... Yes, I did say "all"! Unfortunately, not all will receive this great gift!

I know some who will read this may suggest that there is no way in heaven they could forgive someone who raped them or molested them as a child or severely abused them as a child or even as an adult. But I am here to tell you that you can forgive them! Forgiveness is a choice, a choice that opens the door to your prison cell.

Picture this: You are locked up in a cold, damp dark dungeon cell, crying out to God about how it isn't fair, how this should not have happened to you, and how you are the victim here and that you are the one who is locked up. The person who has done this to you is still out there walking around as if they have done nothing at all. Or maybe they are already in prison or have been in prison for what they have done. But you are also imprisoned! Now picture Jesus walking up to your prison door and handing you a key to your door. Jesus is looking at you and tells you He has given you the key to unlock the door so you can walk out with Him.

You look at the key in your hand and it says, "Forgive them for they know not what they have done!" What are you going to do? Some of you will forgive because of Jesus and His example for us… and some of you will choose to try to unlock the door with the key without forgiving only to find that the door won't open.

Some of you will hand Jesus the key back and say, "I can't forgive them because they don't deserve it." Some of us will try and bargain with Jesus to get out of jail free without forgiving your perpetrator(s)! *Which one of these people are you?*

I went through all these stages until I learned in my Celebrate Recovery group that I would forever remain a victim until I released my perpetrator into the hands of my mighty and just Judge, Jesus Christ! *Acts 10:42* says that He (Jesus) has been appointed the judge over the living and the dead. Never take your own revenge for it is written, "Vengeance is Mine. I will repay," says the Lord (Romans 12:19).

When I made a choice to let go and let God deal with punishment of my perpetrator, my prison door opened up and I walked out…free from the captivity of unforgiveness! I am here to tell you that you can also!

Forgiveness is a choice of letting go and letting God handle it! I want you to find comfort in knowing that forgiveness in no way excuses any person for the harm they have done to us and in the same. It does not excuse us from the harm we have done to others. What it does do is release us from the power it had over us. Forgiveness means, "You owe me, but I am not going to make you pay."

Most of the time, we are so consumed with our anger and bitterness that we do not even realize that the people who injured us have moved on with their lives without a care in the world. We are the only ones in pain! Then we wonder why there is so much disease in the world.

In order to be completely free from our resentment, anger, fear, shame, and guilt, we need to *give* and *accept* forgiveness in all areas of our life. If we don't, our lives and our journey with God will be stalled and incomplete.

Throughout history, God has always made a way for forgiveness. First, God gave the law, and then the law was broken. Then God set apart a priesthood, and it was up to the High Priest to make atonement for sin. Then it was the High Priest that stood in-between God and man. This remains the same today, only the High Priest is Jesus Christ, a man without sin who became sin so we could enter into a relationship with the Father. The first covenant atonement was meant "to cover," so all sin including unforgiveness would be "covered by the blood of the Lamb." In the New Covenant, with Jesus Christ as our High Priest, sin as well as unforgiveness is cleansed by His blood; therefore, His sacrifice has taken away the sin consciousness so that we stand un-condemned in God's presence. The key is our free will—we must choose to forgive.

We must remember that God first extended forgiveness to us. The question is, have you accepted it?

Peter came to Jesus and asked, "Lord, how many times shall I forgive my brother or sister who sins against me? Up to seven times? Jesus answered, "I tell you, not seven times, but seventy times seven." Therefore, the kingdom of heaven is like a king who wanted to settle accounts with his servants. As he began the settlement, a man who owed him ten thousand bags of gold was brought to him. Since he was not able to pay, the master ordered that he and his wife and his children and all that he had be sold to repay the debt. At this the servant fell on his knees before him. "Be patient with me," he begged, "and I will pay back everything." The servant's master took pity on him, canceled the debt and let him go. But when that servant went out, he found one of his fellow servants who owed him a hundred silver coins. He grabbed him and began to choke him. 'Pay back what you owe me!' he demanded.

His fellow servant fell to his knees and begged him, "Be patient with me, and I will pay it back." But he refused. Instead, he went off and had the man thrown into prison until he could pay the debt. When the other servants saw what had happened, they were outraged and went and told their master everything that had happened. Then the master called the servant in. "You wicked servant," he said, "I canceled all that debt of yours because you begged me to. Shouldn't you have had mercy on your fellow servant just as I had on you?" In anger, his master handed him over to the jailers to be tortured, until he should pay back all he owed. This is how my heavenly Father will treat each of you unless you forgive your brother or sister from your heart. (Matthew 19:21–35)

These are red letter words from the One who is the Word. I believe we should take it seriously, don't you?

It is also very important to understand that we must forgive ourselves. Honestly, this is where most of us will have the most difficult time. We are told to love our neighbor as ourselves, which means to love ourselves we first must forgive ourselves, right?

Self-forgiveness is not a matter of assigning the blame to someone else and letting yourself off the hook. It is not a license to irresponsibility. It is simply an acknowledgement that you are human like everyone else and that you have reached a stage in your life where you are able to give yourself greater respect.

Forgiveness is not a natural response to being hurt, but it certainly is a supernatural one that is empowered by our living God. Even though we may feel that we cannot forgive, God supplies us with enough power to forgive.

While forgiveness is always necessary, reconciliation is not. Forgiveness depends on the offended releasing the debt of the offender regardless of whether the relationship is restored. Forgiveness focuses on addressing the offense while reconciliation focuses on the relationship and requires both parties to be in agreement to be reconciled, choosing to work through the reconciliation process.

Boundaries are also necessary. Forgiveness does not mean that we have to allow people back into our lives to trample us all over again. We need to set healthy boundaries, not walls, by using our God-given wisdom. We are trying to become spiritually and emotionally healthy, but just because we are, this does not mean that those we have forgiven are doing the same. We must become wise as serpents and harmless as the doves (Matthew 10:16)!

In Conclusion

Inner healing is a lengthy subject and several authors have done tremendous jobs covering it. I have only touched the surface of what inner healing is and how we get there.

Confession is a great place to start after we ask Jesus into our hearts. Confession is like releasing the loads of baggage that we have been carrying around all our lives. With each instance of rejection, failure, trauma, hatred, sickness, etc., that we don't confess, we just added to the load that we already carried. Then we either collapse under the weight of it, or we choose to unpack those burdens and allow Jesus to be our baggage carrier.

When we see our transgressions, iniquities, and sins for what they are rooted in, then we are able to understand and repent for all the wrong we have done. This turns us from our wicked ways and allows us to be transformed into the likeness of Christ Jesus, who is our Model. Only then are we truly able to forgive others for the harm they have done to us. More importantly, we can forgive ourselves for all the harm we have done to ourselves, others, and God! This is the reality of the kingdom of God. Kingdom lifestyle begins here, right now, inside of each one of us!

Welcome home...to the Family you have never had!

Scriptures on forgiveness, forgive, and forgiven

But with you there is forgiveness, so that we can, with reverence, serve you. (Psalm 130:4)

This is my blood of the covenant, which is poured out for many for the forgiveness of sins. (Matthew 26:28)

And so John the Baptist appeared in the wilderness, preaching a baptism of repentance for the forgiveness of sins. (Mark 1:4)

To give his people the knowledge of salvation through the forgiveness of their sins. (Luke 1:77)

He went into all the country around the Jordan, preaching a baptism of repentance for the forgiveness of sins. (Luke 3:3)

And repentance for the forgiveness of sins will be preached in his name to all nations, beginning at Jerusalem. (Luke 24:47)

Peter replied, "Repent and be baptized, every one of you, in the name of Jesus Christ for the forgiveness of your sins. And you will receive the gift of the Holy Spirit." (Acts 2:38)

All the prophets testify about him that everyone who believes in him receives forgiveness of sins through his name. (Acts 10:43)

Therefore, my friends, I want you to know that through Jesus the forgiveness of sins is proclaimed to you. (Acts 13:38)

To open their eyes and turn them from darkness to light, and from the power of Satan to God, so that they may receive forgiveness of sins and a place among those who are sanctified by faith in me. (Acts 26:18)

[Forgiveness for the Offender] If anyone has caused grief, he has not so much grieved me as he has grieved all of you to some extent—not to put it too severely. (2 Corinthians 2:5)

In him we have redemption through his blood, the forgiveness of sins, in accordance with the riches of God's grace. (Ephesians 1:7)

In whom we have redemption, the forgiveness of sins. (Colossians 1:14)

In fact, the law requires that nearly everything be cleansed with blood, and without the shedding of blood there is no forgiveness. (Hebrews 9:22)

[Light and Darkness, Sin and Forgiveness] This is the message we have heard from him and declare to you: God is light; in him there is no darkness at all. (1 John 1:5)

But if you do not forgive others their sins, your Father will not forgive your sins. (Matthew 6:15)

This is what you are to say to Joseph: "I ask you to forgive your brothers the sins and the wrongs they committed in treating you so badly. Now please forgive the sins of the servants of the

God of your father." When their message came to him, Joseph wept. (Genesis 50:17)

Now forgive my sin once more and pray to the Lord your God to take this deadly plague away from me. (Exodus 10:17)

If my people, who are called by my name, will humble themselves and pray and seek my face and turn from their wicked ways, then I will hear from heaven, and I will forgive their sin and will heal their land. (2 Chronicles 7:14)

Why do you not pardon my offenses and forgive my sins? For I will soon lie down in the dust; you will search for me, but I will be no more. (Job 7:21)

But who can discern their own errors? Forgive my hidden faults. (Psalm 19:12)

For the sake of your name, Lord, forgive my iniquity, though it is great. (Psalm 25:11)

Blessed is the one whose transgressions are forgiven, whose sins are covered. (Psalm 32:1)

Help us, God our Savior, for the glory of your name; deliver us and forgive our sins for your name's sake. (Psalm 79:9)

Who forgives all your sins and heals all your diseases, but with you there is forgiveness, so that we can, with reverence, serve you. (Psalm 103:3–4)

And forgive us our debts, as we also have forgiven our debtors. For if you forgive other people when they sin against you, your heavenly Father will also forgive you. But if you do not forgive others their sins, your Father will not forgive your sins. (Matthew 6:12, 14–15)

[Jesus Forgives and Heals a Paralyzed Man] Jesus stepped into a boat, crossed over and came to his own town. Some men brought to him a paralyzed man, lying on a mat. When Jesus saw their faith, he said to the man, "Take heart, son; your sins are forgiven."

Which is easier: to say, "Your sins are forgiven," or to say, "Get up and walk"? But I want you to know that the Son of Man has authority on earth to forgive sins. So he said to the paralyzed man, "Get up, take your mat and go home." (Matthew 9:1–2, 5–6)

And so I tell you, every kind of sin and slander can be forgiven, but blasphemy against the Spirit will not be forgiven. Anyone who speaks a word against the Son of Man will be forgiven, but anyone who speaks against the Holy Spirit will not be forgiven, either in this age or in the age to come. (Matthew 12:31–32)

[The Parable of the Unmerciful Servant] Then Peter came to Jesus and asked, "Lord, how many times shall I forgive my brother or sister who sins against me? Up to seven times?"

This is how my heavenly Father will treat each of you unless you forgive your brother or sister from your heart. (Matthew 18:21, 35)

This is my blood of the covenant, which is poured out for many for the forgiveness of sins. (Matthew 26:28)

And so John the Baptist appeared in the wilderness, preaching a baptism of repentance for the forgiveness of sins. (Mark 1:4)

[Jesus Forgives and Heals a Paralyzed Man] A few days later, when Jesus again entered Capernaum, the people heard that he had come home.

When Jesus saw their faith, he said to the paralyzed man, "Son, your sins are forgiven."

Why does this fellow talk like that? He's blaspheming! Who can forgive sins but God alone?

Which is easier: to say to this paralyzed man, "Your sins are forgiven," or to say, "Get up, take your mat and walk"? But I want you to know that the Son of Man has authority on earth to forgive sins. So he said to the man. (Mark 2:1, 5, 7, 9–10)

Truly I tell you, people can be forgiven all their sins and every slander they utter, but whoever blasphemes against the Holy Spirit will never be forgiven; they are guilty of an eternal sin. (Mark 3:28–29)

So that, "they may be ever seeing but never perceiving, and ever hearing but never understanding; otherwise they might turn and be forgiven!" (Mark 4:12)

And when you stand praying, if you hold anything against anyone, forgive them, so that your Father in heaven may forgive you your sins. (Mark 11:25)

To give his people the knowledge of salvation through the forgiveness of their sins. (Luke 1:77)

He went into all the country around the Jordan, preaching a baptism of repentance for the forgiveness of sins. (Luke 3:3)

[Jesus Forgives and Heals a Paralyzed Man] One day Jesus was teaching, and Pharisees and teachers of the law were sitting there. They had come from every village of Galilee and from Judea and Jerusalem. And the power of the Lord was with Jesus to heal the sick.

When Jesus saw their faith, he said, "Friend, your sins are forgiven." The Pharisees and the teachers of the law began thinking to themselves, "Who is this fellow who speaks blasphemy? Who can forgive sins but God alone?"

Which is easier: to say, "Your sins are forgiven," or to say, "Get up and walk"? But I want you to know that the Son of Man has authority on earth to forgive sins. So he said to the paralyzed man, "I tell you, get up, take your mat and go home." (Luke 5:17, 20–21, 23–24)

[Judging Others] Do not judge, and you will not be judged. Do not condemn, and you will not be condemned. Forgive, and you will be forgiven. (Luke 6:37)

Simon replied, "I suppose the one who had the bigger debt forgiven." "You have judged correctly," Jesus said.

Therefore, I tell you, her many sins have been forgiven—as her great love has shown. But whoever has been forgiven little loves little. Then Jesus said to her, "Your sins are forgiven." The other guests began to say among themselves, "Who is this who even forgives sins?" (Luke 7:43, 47–49)

Forgive us our sins, for we also forgive everyone who sins against us. And lead us not into temptation. (Luke 11:4)

And everyone who speaks a word against the Son of Man will be forgiven, but anyone who blasphemes against the Holy Spirit will not be forgiven. (Luke 12:10)

So watch yourselves. "If your brother or sister sins against you, rebuke them; and if they repent, forgive them. Even if they sin against you seven times in a day and seven times come back to you saying 'I repent,' you must forgive them." (Luke 17:3–4)

Jesus said, "Father, forgive them, for they do not know what they are doing." And they divided up his clothes by casting lots. (Luke 23:34)

And repentance for the forgiveness of sins will be preached in his name to all nations, beginning at Jerusalem. (Luke 24:47)

If you forgive anyone's sins, their sins are forgiven; if you do not forgive them, they are not forgiven. (John 20:23)

Peter replied, "Repent and be baptized, every one of you, in the name of Jesus Christ for the forgiveness of your sins. And you will receive the gift of the Holy Spirit." (Acts 2:38)

God exalted him to his own right hand as Prince and Savior that he might bring Israel to repentance and forgive their sins. (Acts 5:31)

Repent of this wickedness and pray to the Lord in the hope that he may forgive you for having such a thought in your heart. (Acts 8:22)

All the prophets testify about him that everyone who believes in him receives forgiveness of sins through his name. (Acts 10:43)

Therefore, my friends, I want you to know that through Jesus the forgiveness of sins is proclaimed to you. (Acts 13:38)

To open their eyes and turn them from darkness to light, and from the power of Satan to God, so that they may receive forgiveness of sins and a place among those who are sanctified by faith in me. (Acts 26:18)

Blessed are those whose transgressions are forgiven, whose sins are covered. (Romans 4:7)

[Forgiveness for the Offender] If anyone has caused grief, he has not so much grieved me as he has grieved all of you to some extent—not to put it too severely.

Now instead, you ought to forgive and comfort him, so that he will not be overwhelmed by excessive sorrow.

Anyone you forgive, I also forgive. And what I have forgiven—if there was anything to forgive—I have forgiven in the sight of Christ for your sake. (2 Corinthians 2:5, 7, 10)

How were you inferior to the other churches, except that I was never a burden to you? Forgive me this wrong! (2 Corinthians 12:13)

In him we have redemption through his blood, the forgiveness of sins, in accordance with the riches of God's grace. (Ephesians 1:7)

In whom we have redemption, the forgiveness of sins. (Colossians 1:14)

Bear with each other and forgive one another if any of you has a grievance against someone. Forgive as the Lord forgave you. (Colossians 3:13)

For I will forgive their wickedness and will remember their sins no more. (Hebrews 8:12)

In fact, the law requires that nearly everything be cleansed with blood, and without the shedding of blood there is no forgiveness. (Hebrews 9:22)

And where these have been forgiven, sacrifice for sin is no longer necessary. (Hebrews 10:18)

And the prayer offered in faith will make the sick person well; the Lord will raise them up. If they have sinned, they will be forgiven. (James 5:15)

[Light and Darkness, Sin and Forgiveness] This is the message we have heard from him and declare to you: God is light; in him there is no darkness at all.

If we confess our sins, he is faithful and just and will forgive us our sins and purify us from all unrighteousness. (1 John 1:5, 9)

[Reasons for Writing] I am writing to you, dear children, because your sins have been forgiven on account of his name. (1 John 2:12)

CHAPTER 5

What Is Deliverance?

When Jesus had called the Twelve together, he gave
them power and authority to drive out all demons
and to cure diseases, and he sent them out to
proclaim the kingdom of God and to heal the sick.
—Luke 9:1–2

Deliverance (according to *Merriam-Webster's Dictionary* and Dictionary.com) is an act or instance of delivering someone or something, a salvation, a rescue from moral corruption or evil "action of setting free" in physical or spiritual senses, a liberation, a rescue.

- *Liberation*—the act or process of freeing someone or something from another's control.
- *Rescue*—to free or deliver from confinement, violence, danger, or evil.

Deliverance is a crucial part of the ministry of Jesus Christ. It is central to the Gospel and the commissioning of every disciple of Jesus Christ. It is Jesus cleansing the temple where He dwells of all trespassers, squatters, bad tenants and in this case, evil spirits and demons, often more than one. Deliverance is a valuable part of the healing ministry. All three areas must flow together to partake in a pure healing stream.

Jesus came into this world to be our living, breathing example. He taught us every aspect of His ministry as the Son of God. He came into this world born of man to save us and show us how we are to walk in our commissioning. He taught us everything in three years. So why are we taking our time learning how to work with precious tools in our toolbox?

We are going to look at the definitions of each of these later, so bear with me. So often we hear they are merely "trespassers," but I plan to show you why we often have trouble with those "trespassers" returning to squat on Jesus's property!

We also know from Chapter 2, "Biblical Foundation," that deliverance is part of the meaning of the Greek word sozo, which means healing, salvation, and deliverance! As a reminder sozo (G4982) from a primary *sos* (contraction for obsolete *saos*, "safe") meaning to save, deliver, or protect (literally or figuratively), heal, preserve, save, do well, be (make) whole.

In this instance of deliverance or casting out of demons, it was used, in various ways such as:

- "Those that had seen it told the people how the demon-possessed man had been [sozo] cured" (Luke 8:36).
- "The Lord will [sozo] rescue me from every evil attack and will bring me safely to His heavenly kingdom. To Him be glory forever and ever. Amen" (2 Timothy 4:18).
- "Though you already know all this, I want to remind you that the Lord [sozo] delivered His people out of Egypt, but later destroyed those who did not believe" (Jude 1:5).

Where Do Demons Come From?

Demons are not just ideas or indefinable forces that operate from within the mind of man. They are living, functioning spiritual beings with a mind, characteristics, and will of their own that are dedicated to the service of Satan. Jesus never treated a demon as anything but a living entity that was in opposition to the interests of God and man. Neither should we!

To understand where demons come from, we have to understand about Satan and his kingdom and how he got here, so let us look at this for a few minutes.

Satan is a created being who fell from his place in glory, but he tries to deceive people into thinking he is an alternative god.

Revelation 12:4 does say that Satan and one third of the angels (heavenly beings) rebelled against God and fell from heaven.

Revelation 5:11 describes the size of a heavenly host which surround the throne of God as thousands upon thousands and ten thousand times ten thousand.

Peter Horrobin says that what is clear is the angels involved are innumerable, and this is after one-third had been expelled, so now we are talking about a countless number of fallen angels that are serving Satan in rebellion against God and his ultimate creation—man.

We know that Satan has a hierarchy of demonic power.

> For we do not wrestle against flesh and blood, but against principalities, against powers, against the rulers of the darkness of this age, against spiritual hosts of wickedness in the heavenly places. (Ephesians 6:12, NKJV)

Let us examine the contrast between God and Satan because all too often people seem to fall into the belief that they are somehow equal or that Satan is bigger than God!

God is the *Creator*. Satan is a created being (Ezekiel 28:13–15).

God is *omnipresent*. God is present all the time, in all places. Satan is limited in both time and location. He can only carry out his work through the agency of demons and evil spirits (Job 1:6–7).

God is *omniscient*. There is nothing that God does not know! Satan and his forces are limited in knowledge (Acts 19:15).

God is *omnipotent*. God's power is *unlimited!* Satan's power is limited and restricted within the confines of what God allows (Job 1:6–12).

God is eternal. Satan's time is limited (Revelations 20:7–15).

Satan is the ruler or prince of demons (Matthew 25:41–46).

Matthew 12:24 tells us "it is only by Beelzebub, the prince of demons." Demons also have varying sizes, powers, and authority; therefore, in deliverance ministry, we see some lift with ease and others are sometimes stubborn because they are willfully rebellious.

Matthew 12:43–45 indicates demons are alive, and they choose where they want to live, further indicating they have a will of their own because they choose things to do of their own determination. They also have intelligence because they know where they have been, whether or not it is vacant or worth going back to. They also have wisdom to take with them others that are more wicked than themselves.

Demons do not have bodies of their own. They can exist outside a body as ruling territorial spirits. They express themselves most effectively through occupying the body of a human being (preferably) or animal.

We know that demons are able to speak. See Luke 4:33–34:

> In the synagogue there was a man possessed
> by a demon, an impure spirit. He cried out at the
> top of his voice, "Go away! What do you want with
> us, Jesus of Nazareth? Have you come to destroy
> us? I know who you are—the Holy One of God!"

Demons also have job functions and agendas; the main one is to worship Satan. They rejoice at Satan's works, execute his orders, and negatively affect the affairs of nations, regions, cities, and families. They undermined the work of the Church and more specifically attack believers. They torment Satan's enemies and perform extraordinary acts to achieve Satan's cause.

They also know the end of the story.

> "What do you want with us, Son of God?"
> they shouted. "Have you come here to torture us
> before the appointed time?" (Matthew 8:29)

Christ is in us, our hope of glory (Colossians 1:27)!

Difference between Demonized and Possession

The real question here is whether a Christian can be demon possessed or demonized!

The Bible is clear that a Christian cannot be possessed because God calls us His own possession (Ephesians 1:14). It also says demons can get a foothold through our anger.

> In our anger do not sin and do not let the
> sun go down on our anger this can give the devil
> a foot hold. (Ephesians 4:26–27)

The word here in Greek, *topos*, is the word used for foothold. It means physical place. It is our sin that gives authority to the kingdom of darkness to have access to physical places within us. For instance, where anger lives in us, we know that same anger secures a place for demonic occupancy—a right of squatting!

I want to say that many people choose to use the word *oppressed* rather that *demonized* because demonized is confusing and sometimes messy word. However, for my writings, I have chosen to compare demonization and possession. Some people believe that they are the same, but they are not. Allow me to show you the difference!

Demonized

I love to look at definitions of words, so let's do this!

Dictionary.com says that to be *demonized* is to be under the influence of or to be subject to demonic influence.

The key word here in the definition is *influence*. It's a power affecting a person, thing, or course, of events, especially one that operates without any direct or apparent effort.

- power to sway or affect based on authority, ability, or position;
- to produce an effect on by imperceptible or intangible means, to sway;
- to affect the nature, development, or condition of, to modify;
- to move or impel (a person) to some action;
- exerting shrewd or devious influence is manipulation, and manipulation is as witchcraft; and
- the act of influencing its enticement or temptation.

Demons use our sin or sin patterns to gain legal access to our body and soul; therefore, they gain the power to sway, to affect our nature and development. They gain the ability to condition and modify the way we think, act, and feel. Demons or evil spirits can impel or move a person to do something that they would not normally do. They are shrewd and devious, using manipulation to entice and tempt human beings into a life of deeper sin or disease, bringing death to us! Their main objective is to steal our identity as children of God and ultimately destroy who we are and all we have, and if allowed, they will kill us or ours. If they had their way, they would possess all that they could.

Let's look at the word and see the different scriptures and the effect of demonization. I am going to start with Matthew 17:14–20:

> When they came to the crowd, a man approached Jesus and knelt before him. "*Lord, have mercy on my son,*" he said. "He *has seizures* and is suffering greatly. *He often falls into the fire or into the water.* I brought him to your disciples, but they could not heal him."

Point number 1: the demonic seizures caused great harm to this boy, and if not (sozo) delivered of this demon, the boy could eventually be killed.

> "You unbelieving and perverse generation," Jesus replied, "How long shall I stay with you? How long shall I put up with you? Bring the boy here to me." *Jesus rebuked the demon*, and it came out of the boy, and he was healed at that moment. Then the disciples came to Jesus in private and asked, "*Why couldn't we drive it out?*" He replied, "*Because you have so little faith.*"

Here we can see that in desperation, a father had come first to some of the disciples who had not been able to sozo this little boy.

Point number 2: the Father asked for mercy. Jesus *rebuked* the demon which was the cause of seizures and suffering.

Point number 3: afterward, Jesus told His disciples that they had little faith, which really meant they didn't walk in their full authority due to lack of faith as disciples of Jesus.

Rebuke means to express sharp, stern disapproval of, reprove, reprimand, to express official disapproval of, and to condemn. *To rebuke in such a manner represents* authority!

In Luke 11:14, *Jesus was* driving out a demon *that was mute. When the demon left,* the man who had been mute spoke, *and the crowd was amazed.*

Possessed

To be possessed of a demon is to act under the control of a demon. Those who were thus afflicted expressed the mind and consciousness of the "demon" or "demons" indwelling them, as in Luke 8:28 (the demon-possessed man). The verb "demon possessed" is found chiefly in Matthew and Mark. In Matthew 4:24, 8:16, 28, 33, 9:32, 12:22, and 15:22 and in Mark 1:32, 5:15, 16, 18 and elsewhere in Luke 8:36 and John 10:21, "Him that hath a devil (demon)."

Daimonizomai (G1139) means to be exercised by a *dæmon* (G1142; demon/evil spirit) and have a (be vexed with, be possessed with) devil(s). It's a god, a goddess, an inferior deity, whether good or bad, in the New Testament. It's an evil spirit.

Dictionary.com's definition of *possession* is the act or fact of possessing.

1. The act or fact of *possessing* (of a spirit, especially an evil one) to occupy, dominate, or control (a person) from within.
   - *Occupy* means to take possession and control of, to take or fill up, to engage or employ the mind, energy, or attention of, and to be a resident or tenant of, dwell in.
   - *Dominate* means to rule, exercise control, and predominate. (To be the stronger or leading element or force.) To occupy a commanding or elevated position, to prevail over.
   - *Control* means to exercise restraint or direction over, dominate, command. It means to hold in check, to eliminate or prevent the flourishing, to command, direct, or rule, power to direct.

2. *Ownership* means to have legal right of possession, has the exclusive right or title to something.
3. *Law* is the actual holding or occupancy, either with or without rights of ownership.

Let's look at *Mark 5:1–20* (NIV). I believe everything that the Word of God says is important. The way each story is written and presented is there for a reason. Each word and each line has a degree of revelatory truth. So let us examine this scripture and seek God's wisdom on this subject!

Jesus restores a demon-possessed man

> They went across the lake to the region of the Gerasene's. When Jesus got out of the boat, a man with an evil spirit came from the tombs to meet him. This man lived in the tombs, and no one could bind him anymore, not even with a chain. (Mark 5:1–3)

It is interesting that the man with an evil spirit came to meet Jesus! Verse 3 indicates that he had been able to be bound before but not anymore!

> For he had often been chained hand and foot, but he tore the chains apart and broke the irons on his feet. No one was strong enough to subdue him. (Mark 5:4)

I think that it would be a fair statement to say that "he" had supernatural strength.

> Night and day among the tombs and in the hills, he would cry out and cut himself with stones. (Mark 5:5)

This behavior sounds to me as if he was tormented and not in his right mind! There is emphasis placed on his torment, and the purpose of demons' torment is to destroy the divine likeness in which human beings are created.

> When he saw Jesus from a distance, he ran
> and fell on his knees in front of him. (Mark 5:6)

Most people believe that the "he" mentioned here is the will of the man, but what if I were to tell you this is not the will of the man but the demon? I say this based only upon the facts that are presented for us. I want to suggest to you that the "evil spirits" here recognized Jesus and His superiority (they knew Jesus was the Son of God), and this act was one of the acknowledgement. Only a few verses away, they will plead for a place in the pigs for hosts.

Some teachers and pastors who believe in demons will suggest that demons flee in the presence of Jesus. For some, this is true; however, this is not the case with all. Those of us who are active in deliverance ministry will tell you that most demons will do all they can to remain hidden and keep their position of occupancy. Let's keep breaking down this story!

> He shouted at the top of his voice, "What
> do you want with me, Jesus, Son of the Most
> High God? In God's name don't torture me!"
> (Mark 5:7)

How would this tormented man know this was Jesus, the Son of God, as it is written that he was not in control of his body or mind?

> For Jesus had said to him, "Come out of
> this man, you evil spirit!" (Mark 5:8)

Look at the simplicity of Jesus command, "Come out!"

> Then Jesus asked him, "What is your
> name?" (Mark 5:9)

Did Jesus ask the demon his name? No, I think not! Jesus was demonstrating here in this verse that he cared for the person, and He was actually talking to the man! Jesus was speaking to the man as to establish expressed relationship and demonstrate compassion.

In ministry, the person's well-being should always be our primary concern. If we are asking demons their names, a couple of things will happen. First, we are giving them access and control of the person's vocal cords; and second, they are dishonest and will most likely lie to us anyway to send us on a wild goose chase. We must never allow the demon to humiliate the person we are ministering too!

> "My name is Legion," he replied, "for we are
> many." And he begged Jesus again and again not
> to send them out of the area. (Mark 5:9–10)

The demon prevented the man from responding and had control over his vocal cords. In this verse, we as disciples get a pretty clear picture of the state of the man. It is clear that the demon was speaking, after all, it told Jesus its name—Legion! Legion was not a name but a description. Let's look at this...

Here is an interesting fact to chew on. The word *legion* in the English and old-world dictionaries says the following: A legion is a military or semi-military unit comprised of three thousand to six thousand! It's any large military force, a picked body of soldiers.

Bible Dictionary says this. Legion is defined as a regiment of the Roman army, the number of men composing which differed at different times. It originally consisted of three thousand men, but in the time of Christ, it's consisted of six thousand, exclusive of horsemen, who were in number a tenth of the footmen.

Sounds more like a description instead of a name, and now we know how many!

It is demons numbering at least three thousand and with military rank with an order because no military is without rank and order.

> A large herd of pigs was feeding on the nearby hillside. The demons begged Jesus, "Send us among the pigs; allow us to go into them." (Mark 5:11–12)

It is certain in this verse that the Legion knew of Jesus's authority as the Son of God, and they did fear Him. That's why they were begging. The various translations of the same account in Luke (8:26–39) 31 says that they actually begged Jesus not to order them to the abyss or bottomless pit. I like Luke's version of this story as Luke was an educated man, and his depiction of this story has greater detail.

> He gave them permission, and the evil spirits came out and went into the pigs. The herd, about two thousand in number, rushed down the steep bank into the lake and was drowned. (Mark 5:13)

Now Jesus knew this would happen, right? Demons desire a host and that's why they wanted the pigs. When the pigs died, what happened to the evil spirits/demons? Some believe the scriptures do not say, but look at the next few verses!

> Those tending the pigs ran off and reported this in the town and countryside, and the people went out to see what had happened. When they came to Jesus, they saw the man who had been possessed by the legion of demons, sitting there, dressed and in his right mind; and they were afraid. (Mark 5:14–15)

Why were they afraid? They should be very happy and excited that Jesus the Son of God has entered their city, and the uncontrollable demon-possessed man who had tormented them was now free and healed. So why were they not happy with this situation?

> Those who had seen it told the people what had happened to the demon-possessed man and told about the pigs as well. Then the people began to plead with Jesus to leave their region. (Mark 5:16–17)

Why did they plead with Jesus to leave their region? Is it because their herd of two thousand pigs just got killed! I believe this is a great possibility! I also believe there is more to this story than is written. Look at Luke again…

> When those tending the pigs saw what had happened, they ran off and reported this in the town and countryside, and the people went out to see what had happened. When they came to Jesus, they found the man from whom the demons had gone out, sitting at Jesus' feet, dressed and in his right mind; and they were afraid. Those who had seen it told the people how the demon-possessed man had been cured. Then all the people of the region of the Gerasene's asked Jesus to leave them, because they were overcome with fear. So, he got into the boat and left. (Mark 5:34–37)

There are key factors within these verses, so let's look at them. First, there were witnesses, "those tending the pigs saw," and then they "ran off and reported what had happened," not just in their town but throughout the countryside. Luke then says the people came to see what had happened.

Here is what I am proposing about this situation. When those infested pigs drowned themselves, the evil spirits had to leave them and needed hosts. Now we have witnesses with open doors. Possibly, they are angry about losing their pigs because two thousand pigs were a big deal. Then their lack of faith and trust in Jesus as the Messiah, the Son of God, I believe, is a sin. Sin is an open door to the demonic, so where did those demons go? I believe they entered into the people! Verse 35 tells us they were afraid. Why? Because lack of trust in God creates "fear."

The evil spirits blinded their eyes from seeing Jesus and trusting Him! When those two thousand pigs drowned themselves, "a legion of demons" was unleashed on a region because they had occupancy rights because of sin (evil spirit over a region).

Now jump back to Mark 5.

> As Jesus was getting into the boat, the man who had been demon-possessed begged to go with him. Jesus did not let him, but said, "Go home to your own people and tell them how much the Lord has done for you, and how he has had mercy on you." So the man went away and began to tell all in Decapolis how much Jesus had done for him. And all the people were amazed. (Mark 5:18–20)

Now this last part is where God's plan is bigger than His enemy's plan because even though the new sozo man begged to go with Jesus, Jesus told him to go home. It is interesting that this man was from Decapolis, which is known as ten towns or cities.

He now had a larger territory to share his testimony of his encounter with love named Jesus Christ, the Son of God. This once demon-possessed man was now saved, set free, and healed carrying the testimony of the kingdom of God.

How Do You Know If a Person Needs Deliverance?

In this section, I have compiled a list of some various signs and symptoms that a deliverance minister should pay close attention to when evaluating the circumstances. Holy Spirit wisdom and your gift of discernment are essential in knowing what to do and how to move!

- Habitual sins, especially those that the person wants to be free from; pattern of consistent backsliding (addictions, compulsive behaviors)
- Seeking constant prayer especially for healing or break-through in an area that doesn't manifest; undiagnosable symptoms
- Restlessness exhibited during worship services
- Nightmares (occult, cult, and Satanic ritual involvement)
- Sleep disturbances, sudden sleepiness
- Feels compulsions for little or no reason
- Extreme behavior (highs and lows or compulsive also irrational)
- Feels commanded to do something unrealistic or will command others to do something unrealistic
- Chronic fear, anxiety, or hatred—for no apparent reason
- Heaviness in the chest
- Feels conditional forgiveness (performs for forgiveness)
- Makes unrealistic suggestions
- Dislike revealed for anything associated with religion and/or Christianity
- Not reading the scriptures (at all) or can't read scriptures for any length of time
- Not going to church and withdraws from church people
- Lives in isolation and or darkness
- Can't pray or doesn't want to pray
- Can't say the name of Jesus
- Feels something is inside of them controlling their actions and/or their speech

- Hearing voices in their mind speaking to them
- Exhibiting counterfeit spiritual gifts
- Having suicidal thoughts/tendencies
- Attempting suicide or frequent thoughts of suicide
- Cutting themselves
- Having glazed eyes or a vacant stare
- Speaking with an alternate voice that is not their own; there's evidence of a change of voice (or multiple voices) or they make animal sounds
- Sudden appearance of marks on the body
- Having conversation with unseen beings
- Unusual behavior: animal-like movements, the inability to sit still, unusual postures or gestures, including nearly-impossible contortions of the body
- Their eyes becoming white, unearthly, and vile; a stench or bad odor exists
- Objects begin to come out of the nose or mouth
- An unseen force throws the person
- Uncontrollable fits and foaming at the mouth
- Eyes that roll or twitch/flicker

The Generational Bloodline

Jesus said in Matthew 5:18, "For truly I tell you, until heaven and earth disappear, not the smallest letter, not the least stroke of a pen, will by any means disappear from the Law until everything is accomplished."

Well, heaven and earth have not disappeared; therefore, this statement must mean when Christ returns!

Now look at Exodus 20:5, which says, "You shall not bow down to them or worship them; for I, the Lord your God, am a jealous God, punishing the children for the sin of the parents to the third and fourth generation of those who hate me."

Children reap the consequences, not the guilt of the pre-generational sins of the fathers. For instance, a child of adultery can suffer unusual sexual temptation while another child whose grandfather was a murderer might suffer the loss of loved ones at an early age.

Sins which are not placed under the blood of Jesus through His work on the cross can give access to the demonic realm to influence and travel through our bloodlines until stopped by Jesus and the cross. Generational sin is just one way in which demons find agreement and entry into our beings.

Through deliverance ministry, we can find absolute freedom by confessing the sins of our forefathers by renouncing all agreements made that gave them access and authority and by asking Jesus to come and place His blood and the cross between that access point and you and all future generations. Those familiars can no longer trespass unto a property that fully belong to Jesus. Until this takes place, we have to understand there is authority for those evil spirits to be there.

Is God still punishing children for the sins of their fathers to the third and fourth generations? For the sin, yes, however the difference today from the days of Moses is Jesus Christ and the cross. We do live in the days of grace and that means the consequences of the fathers' sins have been dealt with through the cross. It is through Jesus that we can be healed. It does not happen automatically; we have to choose healing. Jesus knew we would not receive all that He had done instantaneously. We could never comprehend the fullness of His sacrifice. Jesus had to commission the church to "go" and heal the sick (physically and emotionally), deliver them and preach to them. Jesus knew people had demons and that we would have to cast them out; therefore, deliverance is a crucial part of the full ministry of Jesus.

Generational sins are open doors for access to demonic influences and those demons have authority and access to the future generations if not dealt with in deliverance. Transference can take place in many ways, for example at conception, at the death of a parent or at any time during those extremes.

The natural consequences of sins are usually sickness, abuse, poverty, violence, deprivation, and also spiritual (demonic). Dealing with demons that have come down the family line are also a curse (which we will discuss in next chapter). This is dealt with through the recognition of the sin as sin through confession and repenting on behalf of the family and forgiving of the generation or person where it began, seeking God's forgiveness.

God intended for the natural order of things to be that the children are covered, protected by their parents, and brought up in the Lord!

Hurts, Abuse, and Rejection

It is better to have a millstone tied around the neck and thrown into the sea than to harm a child! These are Jesus's words (Matthew 18:6), and He is pretty serious about this, and He intended children to be raised in loving homes with their moms and dads. This was His original plan and is still is His plan. Satan stole the identity of man through deception, and he continues to do so only because of lack of knowledge on our part and our abusing and asserting our free will.

No matter our age when we were abused or the type of abuse we have endured, the abuse and the abuser leave permanent scars. The scars may be physical and visible for only a short time, but the emotional and spiritual scars can last a lifetime if they are not dealt with thoroughly.

Who Can Minister Deliverance?

"Master," said John, "we saw someone driving out demons in your name and we tried to stop him, because he is not one of us." "Do not stop him," Jesus said, "for whoever is not against you is for you." (Luke 9:49–50)

Any born-again, spirit-filled Christian who is walking in Jesus's model can minister deliverance! It is part of the ministry of Jesus Christ and should be a part of every Christian's walk. After all, as born-again believers, we have been commissioned by Christ to His ministry. But one should take careful warning that deliverance can be a life or death ministry and not all persons are called to deliverance ministry. It does require some deep qualities on the part of the deliverance minister and the care of the person being ministered to is the most important objective.

What does The Bible Say about *Deliverance?*

These scripture are taken from English
Standard Version of the Holy Bible.

When the righteous cry for help, the Lord hears and delivers them out of all their troubles. (Psalm 34:17)

Then they cried to the Lord in their trouble, and he delivered them from their distress. (Psalm 107:6)

He said, "The Lord is my rock and my fortress and my deliverer." (2 Samuel 22:2)

And call upon me in the day of trouble; I will deliver you, and you shall glorify me. (Psalm 50:15)

Therefore, confess your sins to one another and pray for one another, that you may be healed. The prayer of a righteous person has great power as it is working. (James 5:16)

I sought the Lord, and he answered me and delivered me from all my fears. (Psalm 34:4)

But the Lord said to me, "Do not say, 'I am only a youth'; for to all to whom I send you, you shall go, and whatever I command you, you shall speak. Do not be afraid of them, for I am with you to deliver you, declares the Lord." (Jeremiah 1:7–8)

For sin will have no dominion over you, since you are not under law but under grace. What then? Are we to sin because we are not under law but under grace? By no means! Do you not know that if you present yourselves to anyone as obedient slaves, you are slaves of the one whom you obey, either of sin, which leads to death, or of obedience, which leads to righteousness? But thanks be to God, that you who were once slaves of sin have become obedient from the heart to the standard of teaching to which you were committed and, having been set free from sin, have become slaves of righteousness. (Romans 6:14–18)

For freedom Christ has set us free; stand firm therefore, and do not submit again to a yoke of slavery. (Galatians 5:1)

If you abide in me, and my words abide in you, ask whatever you wish, and it will be done for you. (John 15:7)

And you will know the truth, and the truth will set you free. (John 8:32)

I appeal to you therefore, brothers, by the mercies of God, to present your bodies as a living sacrifice, holy and acceptable to God, which is your spiritual worship. Do not be conformed to this world, but be transformed by the renewal of your mind, that by testing you may discern what is the will of God, what is good and acceptable and perfect. (Romans 12:1–2)

As for me, I am poor and needy, but the Lord takes thought for me. You are my help and my deliverer; do not delay, O my God! Be pleased, O Lord, to deliver me! O Lord, make haste to help me! (Psalm 40:17, 13)

And he called to him his twelve disciples and gave them authority over unclean spirits, to cast them out, and to heal every disease and every affliction. (Matthew 10:1)

I will restore to you the years that the swarming locust has eaten, the hopper, the destroyer, and the cutter, my great army, which I sent among you. You shall eat in plenty and be satisfied, and praise the name of the Lord your God, who has dealt wondrously with you. And my people shall never again be put to shame. You shall know that I am in the midst of Israel, and that I am the Lord your God and there is none else. And my people shall never again be put to shame. (Joel 2:25–27)

And David spoke to the Lord the words of this song on the day when the Lord delivered him from the hand of all his enemies, and from the hand of Saul. (2 Samuel 22:1)

For God so loved the world, that he gave his only Son, that whoever believes in him should not perish but have eternal life. (John 3:16)

O Lord, you are my God; I will exalt you; I will praise your name, for you have done wonderful things, plans formed of old, faithful and sure. For you have made the city a heap, the fortified city a ruin; the foreigners' palace is a city no more; it will never be rebuilt. Therefore, strong peoples will glorify you; cities of ruthless nations will fear you. For you have been a stronghold to the poor, a stronghold to the needy in his distress, a shelter from the storm and a shade from the heat; for the breath of the ruthless is like a storm against a wall, like heat in a dry place. You subdue the noise of the foreigners; as heat by the shade of a cloud, so the song of the ruthless is put down. (Isaiah 25:1–5)

For the Scripture says, "Everyone who believes in him will not be put to shame." For there is no distinction between Jew and Greek; for the same Lord is Lord of all, bestowing his riches on all who call on him. For "everyone who calls on the name of the Lord will be saved." (Romans 10:11–13)

I am the door. If anyone enters by me, he will be saved and will go in and out and find pasture. The thief comes only to steal and kill and destroy. I came that they may have life and have it abundantly. I am the good shepherd. The good shepherd lays down his life for the sheep. (John 10:9–11)

But Jesus rebuked him, saying, "Be silent, and come out of him!" (Mark 1:25)

But now thus says the Lord, he who created you, O Jacob, he who formed you, O Israel: "Fear not, for I have redeemed you; I have called you by name, you are mine. When you pass through the waters, I will be with you; and through the rivers, they shall not overwhelm you; when you walk through fire you shall not be burned, and the flame shall not consume you. For I am the Lord your God, the Holy One of Israel, your Savior. I give Egypt as your ransom, Cush and Seba in exchange for you. Because you are precious in my eyes, and honored, and I love you, I give men in return for you, peoples in exchange for your life. Fear not, for I am with you; I will bring your offspring from the east, and from the west I will gather you." (Isaiah 43:1–5)

He drew me up from the pit of destruction, out of the miry bog, and set my feet upon a rock, making my steps secure. (Psalm 40:2)

For I know that my Redeemer lives, and at the last he will stand upon the earth. And after my skin has been thus destroyed, yet in my flesh I shall see God, whom I shall see for myself, and my eyes shall behold, and not another. My heart faints within me! (Job 19:25–27)

And these signs will accompany those who believe: in my name they will cast out demons; they will speak in new tongues. (Mark 16:17)

For I delight in the law of God, in my inner being, but I see in my members another law waging war against the law of my mind and making me captive to the law of sin that dwells in my members. Wretched man that I am! Who will deliver me from this body of death? Thanks be to God through Jesus Christ our Lord! So then, I myself serve the law of God with my mind, but with my flesh I serve the law of sin. (Romans 7:22–25)

You have taken up my cause, O Lord; you have redeemed my life. You have seen the wrong done to me, O Lord; judge my cause. You have seen all their vengeance, all their plots against me. (Lamentations 3:58–60)

Remember not the former things, nor consider the things of old. Behold, I am doing a new thing; now it springs forth, do you not perceive it? I will make a way in the wilderness and rivers in the desert. (Isaiah 43:18–19)

For "everyone who calls on the name of the Lord will be saved." (Romans 10:13)

I have told the glad news of deliverance in the great congregation; behold, I have not restrained my lips, as you know, O Lord. I have not hidden your deliverance within my heart; I have spoken of your faithfulness and your salvation; I have not concealed your steadfast love and your faithfulness from the great congregation. (Psalm 40:9–10)

Then the Lord said, "I have surely seen the affliction of my people who are in Egypt and have heard their cry because of their taskmasters. I know their sufferings, and I have come down to deliver them out of the hand of the Egyptians and to bring them up out of that land to a good and broad land, a land flowing with milk and honey, to the place of the Canaanites, the Hittites, the Amorites, the Perizzites, the Hivites, and the Jebusites. And now, behold, the cry of the people of Israel has come to me, and I have also seen the oppression with which the Egyptians oppress them. Come I will send you to Pharaoh that you may bring my people, the children of Israel, out of Egypt." (Exodus 3:7–10)

The hand of the Lord was upon me, and he brought me out in the Spirit of the Lord and set me down in the middle of the valley; it was full of bones. And he led me around among them, and behold, there were very many on the surface of the valley, and behold, they were very dry. And he said to me, "Son of man, can these bones live?" And I answered, "O Lord God, you know." Then he said to me, "Prophesy over these bones, and say to them, O dry bones, hear the word of the Lord. Thus, says the Lord God to these bones: Behold, I will cause breath to enter you, and you shall live." (Ezekiel 37:1–14)

Fear not, for I am with you; be not dismayed, for I am your God; I will strengthen you, I will help you, I will uphold you with my righteous right hand. Behold, all who are incensed against you shall be put to shame and confounded; those who strive against you shall be as nothing and shall perish. You shall seek those who contend with you, but you shall not find them; those who war against you shall be as nothing at all. For I, the Lord your God, hold your right hand; it is I who say to you, "Fear not, I am the one who helps you. Fear not, you worm Jacob, you men of Israel! I am the one who helps you, declares the Lord; your Redeemer is the Holy One of Israel." (Isaiah 41:10–14)

The sacrifices of God are a broken spirit; a broken and contrite heart, O God, you will not despise. (Psalm 51:17)

When Abram was ninety-nine years old the Lord appeared to Abram and said to him, "I am God Almighty; walk before me, and be blameless." (Genesis 17:1)

For this reason God gave them up to dishonorable passions. For their women exchanged natural relations for those that are contrary to nature; and the men likewise gave up natural relations with women and were consumed with passion for one another, men committing shameless acts with men and receiving in themselves the due penalty for their error. (Romans 1:26–27)

All Scripture is breathed out by God and profitable for teaching, for reproof, for correction, and for training in righteousness. (2 Timothy 3:16)

For to set the mind on the flesh is death, but to set the mind on the Spirit is life and peace. (Romans 8:6)

And it shall come to pass that everyone who calls on the name of the Lord shall be saved. For in Mount Zion and in Jerusalem there shall be those who escape, as the Lord has said, and among the survivors shall be those whom the Lord calls. (Joel 2:32)

To grant to those who mourn in Zion—to give them a beautiful headdress instead of ashes, the oil of gladness instead of mourning, the garment of praise instead of a faint spirit; that they may be called oaks of righteousness, the planting of the Lord, that he may be glorified. (Isaiah 61:3)

He sent out his word and healed them, and delivered them from their destruction. (Psalm 107:20)

He who dwells in the shelter of the Most High will abide in the shadow of the Almighty. I will say to the Lord, "My refuge and my fortress, my God, in whom I trust." For he will deliver you from the snare of the fowler and from the deadly pestilence. He will cover you with his pinions, and under his wings you will find refuge; his faithfulness is a shield and buckler. You will not fear the terror of the night, nor the arrow that flies by day. (Psalm 91:1–5)

As for you also, because of the blood of my covenant with you, I will set your prisoners free from the waterless pit. (Zechariah 9:11)

Also henceforth I am he; there is none who can deliver from my hand; I work, and who can turn it back? (Isaiah 43:13)

Therefore I tell you, her sins, which are many, are forgiven—for she loved much. But he who is forgiven little, loves little. (Luke 7:47)

And I am sure of this, that he who began a good work in you will bring it to completion at the day of Jesus Christ. (Philippians 1:6)

Oh give thanks to the Lord, for he is good, for his steadfast love endures forever! Let the redeemed of the Lord say so, whom he has redeemed from trouble and gathered in from the lands, from the east and from the west, from the north and from the south. Some wandered in desert wastes, finding no way to a city to dwell in; hungry and thirsty, their soul fainted within them. (Psalm 107:1–5)

A Psalm of David. The Lord is my shepherd; I shall not want. He makes me lie down in green pastures. He leads me beside still waters. He restores my soul. He leads me in paths of righteousness for his name's sake. Even though I walk through the valley of the shadow of death, I will fear no evil, for you are with me; your rod and your staff, they comfort me. You prepare a table before me in the presence of my enemies; you anoint my head with oil; my cup overflows. (Psalm 23:1–5)

If my people who are called by my name humble themselves and pray and seek my face and turn from their wicked ways, then I will hear from heaven and will forgive their sin and heal their land. (2 Chronicles 7:14)

And Moses said to the people, "Fear not, stand firm, and see the salvation of the Lord, which he will work for you today. For the Egyptians whom you see today, you shall never see again." (Exodus 14:13)

But you have been anointed by the Holy One, and you all have knowledge. (1 John 2:20)

Whoever conceals his transgressions will not prosper, but he who confesses and forsakes them will obtain mercy. (Proverbs 28:13)

So that Christ may dwell in your hearts through faith—that you, being rooted and grounded in love, may have strength to comprehend with all the saints what is the breadth and length and height and depth, and to know the love of Christ that surpasses knowledge, that you may be filled with all the fullness of God. Now to him who is able to do far more abundantly than all that we ask or think, according to the power at work within us. (Ephesians 3:17–20)

But in Mount Zion there shall be those who escape, and it shall be holy, and the house of Jacob shall possess their own possessions. (Obadiah 1:17)

CHAPTER 6

Knowing the Enemy and the Realm of Darkness

For our struggle is not against flesh and blood,
but against the rulers, against the authorities,
against the powers of this dark world and against
the spiritual forces of evil in the heavenly realms.
                                              —Ephesians 6:12

How Can Demons/Evil Spirits Enter?

Personal Sin

An ongoing practice of sin that remains unconfessed and unforgiven will inevitably give rights to the demonic to enter and control a person in specific areas of the person's life. Sin is rebellion against God. It is a temptation from Satan to cause us to rebel against God. Yes, sin is personal! The nature of sin is through rebellion. When we choose sin, we choose to worship Satan. Like Jesus, we must overcome sin by way of the Holy Spirit, and in order to do that, we have to choose God! Demons have a legal right to enter in on our sin! The way we get rid of them is through confession and repentance. Confession is seeing the sin for what it really is. Repentance is seeing God's perspective on sin (in general and our particular sin) and turning away from it.

Occult Sin

The *occult* is a broad term that is given to practices, often of religious nature, whose power source is most definitely not of God. The word *occult* means "hidden," and this is exactly how Satan operates in the world—secretly and deceptively drawing people into offering worship to him, sometimes without their knowledge or even realizing that he exists. We must be wise to remember that there is no such thing as safe dabbling. Demons take occult involvement not only as an automatic invitation to demonize but as a legal contract to do so. Even if it is masked as scientific inquiry, one dabble is enough to open the door. Occult involvement does wound the personal spirit and requires both deliverance and inner healing. *Not only do we need to heal the effect of the sin but also the causes.*

All occult involvement is forbidden by God. Nowhere in the Bible will you find it written that it's acceptable for us to take a devilish, sinful practice and Christianize it. God is clear that these practices are *forbidden.*

In various religions, practices, and modalities, the word *occult* takes on a meaning to involve the supernatural in the nature of or pertaining to science. The end result of this lethal combination is theosophy as we talked about in the previous chapter, astrology, alchemy, and magic to name a few.

Magic in any form, other than the quickness of the hand and eye tricks, is employing a power either of your own or one outside of yourself to accomplish your own will.

Alternative Medical Practices

Alternative medicine is a big business and there are all sorts of practitioners out there who are willing to charge us for alternative remedies for healing at the cost of our soul and spirit. Again, these practices are using powers that are not of God, Jehovah-Rophe, the Great Physician but demonic medicine that will lead people to spiritual wilderness. After using such occult methods, the individual seems to lose a sense of trust and dependence on God and assumes an attitude of independence from the Lord. These practices are counterfeit to the work of God, and they do actually work. People find their symptoms are gone but not without a trade-off of far greater spiritual bondage. Upon deliverance, it is not unusual for the original symptom to return because it was masked by the demonic power; however, the exposure of it to the *true healer* often results in true healing.

Religious Sin

Rodney Hogue says, and I quote, "We make our experience our doctrine—what is normal for us becomes our doctrine!" We must remember that Satan is a religious being, and he will send religious spirits whose jobs are to simulate a form of Christian life that is *soulish* rather than spiritual. Cessationism, the belief that all spiritual gifts ended with the apostles, is a perfect example of this religious spirit.

Denominationalism is another example. When a denomination becomes more important than our relationship with the Lord and unity as the body of Christ, we have opened the door for agreement with a religious spirit through religious sin. As disciples of Christ, we should never embrace the sin but the Spirit of God that reveals the sin. Through repentance and forgiveness, we need to embrace the truth and each other in love to advance the kingdom of God.

More examples of religious spirits in operation are false religions, the abuse of the gifts of the Spirit, misinterpretation of scriptures, and universalism. A great book on this topic would be *Healing Through Deliverance* by Peter Horrobin.

Another religious sin is "abusing our spiritual gifts." Oftentimes, we abuse our gifts from God for personal gain. For example, a gift of discernment can be used as suspicion or judgment against someone. A gift of prophecy may be used as a word given to control the outcome of a situation for personal gain or to manipulate a person's thoughts or emotions. A seer gift used for the purpose of being a medium or psychic reading is witchcraft. Other examples are when we seek a gift rather than the Gift Giver when we publicly display a gift to draw attention to ourselves or use someone else's gift to draw attention to us or our ministry. Each of these abuses is an open door for the demonic to take control of that particular area of our lives!

Ungodly Soul Ties

In all of our relationships, we encounter people with whom we find ourselves tied to emotionally like our parents, siblings, a friend, pastors, teachers, spouses, and children. This list can go on and on. With some, we have godly soul ties, and then we have the ungodly. We are either rightfully bonded or unrightfully bonded. We have either healthy or unhealthy relationships. Let us look at an example of unhealthy, unrightfully bonded and ungodly soul ties. Children who are conceived out of wedlock usually react out of a place of rejection and escapism can become a way of life, hence, an open door. Peter Horrobin says this, "The extremes are total retreat into an externally passive personality (but inside there will usually be a cauldron of pain, ready to erupt like a dormant volcano without prior warning), and at the other end of the scale is the rebellion of teenage years that can manifest itself in drugs, violence, promiscuity, crime, running away, and a host of other rebellious activities. Within this hurt and pain, the demonic can have a field day."

Sexual partners other than our spouses are another way to open ourselves to demons. Sex is a physical, emotional, and spiritual union of two persons, and it was created for the union of marriage and anything outside of marriage is sin. Outside of marriage, a part of us remains with the other partner(s). This does cause us to feel incomplete and overwhelmed with guilt, not to mention all other sins that can be committed during such events like homosexuality, adultery, idolatry, perversion, abuse, masturbation, and rape. This list can go on and on, but I believe you understand.

Ungodly Soul Ties/Key scriptures

Do you not know that your bodies are members of Christ? Shall I then take away the members of Christ and make them members of a prostitute? May it never be! Or do you not know that the one who joins himself to a prostitute is one body with her? For He says, *"The two shall become one flesh."* But the one who joins himself to the Lord is one spirit with Him. Flee immorality. Every other sin that a man commits is outside the body, but the immoral man sins against his own body. Or do you not know that your body is a temple of the Holy Spirit who is in you, whom you have from God, and that you are not your own? For you have been bought with a price: therefore, glorify God in your body. (1 Corinthians 6:15–20)

For this is the will of God, your sanctification; that is, that you abstain from sexual immorality; that each of you know how to possess his own vessel in sanctification and honor, not in lustful passion, like the Gentiles who do not know God; and that no man transgress and defraud his brother in the matter because the Lord is the avenger in all these things, just as we also told you before and solemnly warned you. For God has not called us for impurity, but in sanctification. So, he who rejects this is not rejecting man but the God who gives His Holy Spirit to you. (1 Thessalonians 4:3–8)

Two becoming one, your body as a temple of God. God's will in this is your body is not your own and the concept of defrauding another. Biblically, soul ties are often referred to as "joined." *Joined* translated from its original context as *kollao*. *Strong's Concordance* Greek word *kollao* (G2853) taken from root word *kolla* means "glue." Meaning to glue, to glue together, cement, fasten together. To join or fasten firmly together. To join oneself to, cleave to.

According to Dictionary.com, *joined* means to participate within some act or activity. To come into the company of. To bring together in a particular relation or for a specific purpose. Unite. To incorporate as to form a whole. To cause to adhere. To act in agreement. To share a common opinion, attitude.

It is an ungodly linking between two people linked through following:

- Sex (outside God's will and plan) (1 Corinthian 6:16)
- Idols (Hosea 4:17)
- Bad company (1 Corinthian 15:33)
- Bestiality (Leviticus 18:23)
- Emotional (family, friends, church, coworker, and even animals)
- Blood/organ transplants (Leviticus 17:11)
- Sin
- Witchcraft
- Generational sexual sin

An ungodly soul tie can also be as follows:

- Any illicit relationship
- One person puts another into unclean or inappropriate control or bondage
- Someone promises something they can't righteously fulfill
- Over control or dominance
- Maternal domination
- Domination of husband over wife or the opposite
- One person controls others by moods or threats, etc.
- Illegitimate sexual partners (both pre-marriage and during marriage)
- Sexual hurt or abuse, even rejection
- Creates fear and control

Ungodly soul ties can be demonic in nature through idolatry. Hosea 4:17 (NKJV) says, "Ephraim is joined to idols."

Godly Soul Ties

- Marriage:

    For this reason a man will leave his father and mother and be united to his wife, and the two will become one flesh. (Ephesians 5:31)

    Through covenant of marriage, a husband and wife are "joined" unity and become one in flesh and spirit.

- Friendships:

    Jonathan became one in spirit with David and he loved him as he loved himself. (1 Samuel 18:1)

A man who has friends must himself be friendly, but there is a friend who sticks closer than a brother. (Proverbs 18:24)

- Parents and children:
  Souls of parents and children are "joined" together.

  Israel (Jacob) loved Joseph more than any of his other children. (Genesis 37:3)

  One translation says "bound up in the boy's life."

Breaking of Soul Ties

Always in the name of Jesus Christ... First, repentance of any sin that allowed the ungodly soul tie (see chapter 4). Second, repentance for allowing the soul tie to exist. Third, renounce the soul ties. This is *breaking* all agreement you have given to any demonic associated with the soul tie. Fourth, take the sword of the Spirit.

For the word of God is alive and active. Sharper than any double-edged sword, it penetrates even to dividing soul and spirit, joints and marrow; It judges the thoughts and attitudes of the heart. Nothing in all creation is hidden from God's sight. Everything is uncovered and laid bare before the eyes of him to whom we must give an account. (Hebrews 4:12–13)

Cut yourself or the person you are praying over free from every ungodly soul ties. In case of abuse-illicit relationships, bestiality, controlling relationships, you may want to cut all soul ties, not just ungodly.

(This is where I will usually ask the person to repeat after me and walk them through this cutting away prayer. The reason for doing this is to have their will engaged and activating the authority power of their words.)

Fifth, give back to the other party every or *all* ungodly things that belong to them. It is important to remember that it is the Holy Spirit has instructed you to cut *all* soul ties or only the ungodly ones. You will want to make that application here also as well as in the next step.

Sixth, take back *all* ungodly soul ties or *all* depending on situation that belong to me (self/prayer). Seventh, thank Jesus.

Now if this is all you are doing, you can now command any demonic associated with any ungodly soul tie to go *right now in Jesus's name*.

Sexual Sin

Open doors can come through our own beliefs about sex and those ideas are usually taught to us by our parents, grandparents, siblings, and peers. We will learn from one source or another, and our sexual appetites will be driven by what we are taught is normal and socially acceptable. Satan cannot create, so he perverts the way God created a husband and wife to develop intimacy and life. Satan uses sex to destroy the temples of God through sexual defilement.

Sexual perversion creates death instead of life. It leads to sexual abuses of adults and children. It defiles sexual identities. It creates false identities such as homosexuality and lesbianism, dominating sexual partners within the marriage, and it even says that oral and anal sex is acceptable—all of which are lies of Satan. When we believe these lies, we are not in alignment with the word of God and are giving Satan and his demons rule over our lives.

Deliverance and Inner Healing

The bondage of abuse steals our identity and keeps a person bound to sin through fear and rejection, the fear of man and even suicide, death, and murder. Oftentimes with children who have been abused, Satan will send a demon dressed as an angel of light to befriend the child as his or her imaginary friend. Satan is no respecter of mankind and will seek to demonize a child at the earliest possible age. He knows the younger a child is when a demonic stronghold are established, the more difficult it will be for the child to come to personal faith in Christ, and the harder it will be for them to be set free from darkness.

Trauma and Accidents

Fear is always the result of trauma and accidents. Fear induces open doors for sickness and disease. It causes depression, anxiety, and panic—all of which demonic thrive on to find entry into our lives. Satan is again no respecter of persons and will look for anything to gain entry, and fear is a great motivator for him and his demons.

Post-Traumatic Stress Disorder (PTSD) is a remembered trauma which has damaged the nervous system and the physical, emotional, and spiritual wellness of a person. It is an anxiety disorder that may develop after exposure to a terrifying event or ordeal (Hutchings 2014). In extreme PTSD, everything is overwhelming, painful, and remembered. I am not a doctor, but it looks to me like PTSD is very much demonically influenced and controls a person through *remembered fear*! (This is my own personal observation and that of no one else.) Watch for my next book that will cover PTSD in greater detail.

Fatherlessness is a trauma... It is a spiritual trauma! Let's look at some statistics about fatherlessness. According to the US Census Bureau, twenty-four million children in America—one out of every three—live in biological father-absent homes. Nine in ten American parents agree that this is a "crisis."

US Fatherless Statistics/Fatherless Stats (http://fatherhood-factor.com/us-fatherless-statistics) are as follows:

1. Forty-three percent of US children live without their father (US Department of Census).
2. Ninety percent of homeless and runaway children are from fatherless homes (US DHHS, Bureau of the Census).

3. Eighty percent of rapists motivated with displaced anger come from fatherless homes (*Criminal Justice and Behavior*, Vol 14, pp. 403–26, 1978).

4. Seventy-one percent of pregnant teenagers lack a father (US Department of Health and Human Services press release, Friday, March 26, 1999).

5. Sixty-three percent of youth suicides are from fatherless homes (US DHHS, Bureau of the Census).

6. Eighty-five percent of children who exhibit behavioral disorders come from fatherless homes (Center for Disease Control).

7. Ninety percent of adolescent repeat arsonists live with only their mother (Wray Herbert, "Dousing the Kindlers," Psychology Today, January 1985, p. 28).

8. Seventy-one percent of high school dropouts come from fatherless homes (National Principals Association Report on the State of High Schools).

9. Seventy-five percent of adolescent patients in chemical abuse centers come from fatherless homes (Rainbows for all God's Children).

10. Seventy percent of juveniles in state-operated institutions have no father (US Department of Justice, Special Report, September 1988).

11. Eighty-five percent of youths in prisons grew up in a fatherless home (Fulton County Georgia jail populations, Texas Department of Corrections, 1992).

12. Fatherless boys and girls are twice as likely to drop out of high school, twice as likely to end up in jail, and four times more likely to need help for emotional or behavioral problems (US DHHS news release, March 26, 1999).

Yes, fatherlessness is an open door to orphan heart and spirit, lawlessness, anger, rage, violence, addiction, poverty, lack, sexual perversion, and the list goes on and on.

Death

Death is certainly an open door for the demonic. A spirit of death will feed off the fears of a person. Death is also a familiar spirit. It will follow a family's bloodline and latch on to a person who is vulnerable, self-loathing, struggling with lack of self-esteem, unworthiness, depression, and paranoia. One who has had an abortion or whose mother had contemplated abortion while pregnant with them can have this spirit. The spirit of death or any other spirit can find a vulnerable (meaning with deep sin or other open doors) host at a funeral home or at the bedside of a dying family member or friend. Other areas associated with death can also be entry points for demonic access, such as grief or shock with an unexpected death and loneliness.

Curses, Inner Vows, and Wrongful Praying

A curse is an invocation or prayer for harm or injury to come upon someone. Today, we see that curses are often released through jokes or taunting a person in a setting that is one of playfulness. The world will tell you that this is harmless, "It was just a joke," or someone will say, "I was only messing around. I really didn't mean it." I want to remind you that no words curses can fall unless they are undeserved. Playing around or joking would indicate that there is a gray area in which we can safely speak these curses and no harm be done. I am here to say that this is wrong; we cannot dabble in anything that is not ordained by God!

Curses are often considered superstitious in society and are dismissed without further thought, but the fruit of the curse continues to produce in people and their descendants. For instance, someone who is accident prone is usually under a curse. A family member's early or premature death is most likely under a curse or that of a vow or oath associated with Freemasonry. Heart disease and other heart issues are sometimes associated with this secret society as is autoimmune diseases.

A curse can be generational, one that a former family member may have made against another member of the family or one that was made upon the family bloodline by another. It can also be a vow or oath that was made by a past member of one's family that involved the family and future generations. Sometimes, we can trace the curse or vow, and other times we cannot; however, a curse always leaves clues.

We often curse ourselves with things like, "I will never be like… (fill in the blank). I am so stupid… I will never find anyone to love me." We also curse others without realizing it with things like (this was my dad's favorite)… "I hope your kids grow up to be worse than you!" Yes, just in case you're wondering, I did renounce that curse and break the power it had over me and my children.

Our words carry power of life and death.

> The tongue has the power of life and death, and those who love it will eat its fruit. (Proverbs 18:21)

> The soothing tongue is a tree of life, but a perverse tongue crushes the spirit. (Proverbs 15:4)

> Those who guard their mouths and their tongues keep themselves from calamity. (Proverbs 21:23)

> A lying tongue hates those it hurts, and a flattering mouth works ruin. (Proverbs 26:28)

> Their throats are open graves; their tongues practice deceit. The poison of vipers is on their lips. (Romans 3:13)

James teaches us that we must tame our tongues. Look at chapter 3 of James starting at verse 1…

Not many of you should become teachers, my fellow believers; because you know that we who teach will be judged more strictly. We all stumble in many ways. Anyone who is never at fault in what they say is perfect, able to keep their whole body in check. When we put bits into the mouths of horses to make them obey us, we can turn the whole animal. Or take ships as an example. Although they are so large and are driven by strong winds, they are steered by a very small rudder wherever the pilot wants to go. Likewise, the tongue is a small part of the body, but it makes great boasts. Consider what a great forest is set on fire by a small spark. The tongue also is a fire, a world of evil among the parts of the body. It corrupts the whole body, sets the whole course of one's life on fire, and is itself set on fire by hell. All kinds of animals, birds, reptiles and sea creatures are being tamed and have been tamed by mankind, but no human being can tame the tongue. It is a restless evil, full of deadly poison. With the tongue we praise our Lord and Father, and with it we curse human beings, who have been made in God's likeness. Out of the same mouth come praise and cursing. My brothers and sisters, this should not be. Can both fresh water and salt water flow from the same spring? My brothers and sisters, can a fig tree bear olive, or a grapevine bear figs? Neither can a salt spring produce fresh water. (James 3:12)

With our tongues, we can bless or curse, so we must take captive of every thought so that no unclean word will pass over our tongues. We are usually products of what people speak over us as children. Satan is waiting to ride out on these curses to see them fulfilled, and

God is waiting for us to confess and renounce these curses so that he can fulfill our blessing!

I have included the following teaching from the International Society of Deliverance Ministers (ISDM) Conference 2015 on September 15, 2015, by Selwyn Stevens (jubileeresources.org) because it is a clear biblical reference to the effects of curses and blessings!

Selwyn says and I quote, "Inner healing and deliverance ministry is a place and time of divine appointments."

It is…

Spiritual-Chain Cutting Prayer

Blessings is for wholeness.
Goal number 1: understand the power it has.
Goal number 2: recover missed blessings.
Goal number 3: learn how to bless others.

The Power in Blessings

Praise be to the God and Father of our Lord Jesus Christ, *who has blessed us* in the heavenly realms with every spiritual blessing in Christ. (Ephesians 1:3)

Will make you into a great nation, and I will bless you; I will make your name great, and you will be a blessing. *I will bless those who bless you*, and whoever curses you I will curse; and all peoples on earth will be blessed through you. (Genesis 12:2–3)

When Isaac was old and his eyes were so weak that he could no longer see, he called for Esau his older son and said to him, "My son." "Here I am," he answered. Isaac said, "I am now an old man and don't know the day of my death. Now then, get your equipment-your quiver and bow-and go out to the open country to hunt some wild game for me. Prepare me the kind of tasty food I like and bring it to me to eat, so that I may give you my blessing before I die."

Now Rebekah was listening as Isaac spoke to his son Esau. When Esau left for the open country to hunt game and bring it back, Rebekah said to her son Jacob, "Look, I overheard our father say to your brother Esau, 'Bring me some game and prepare me some tasty food to eat so that I may give you my blessing in the presence of the Lord before I die.' Now, my son, listen carefully and do what I tell you: Go out to the flock and bring me two choice young goats, so I can prepare some tasty food for your father, just the way he likes it. Then take it to your father to eat, so that he may give you his blessing before he dies."

Jacob said to Rebekah his mother, "But my brother Esau is a hairy man while I have smooth skin. What if my father touches me? I would appear to be tricking him and would bring down a curse on myself rather than a blessing."

His mother said to him, "My son, let the curse fall on me. Just do what I say; go and get them for me."

So, he went and got them and brought them to his mother, and she prepared some tasty food, just the way his father liked it. Then Rebekah took the best clothes of Esau her older son, which she had in the house, and put them on her younger son Jacob.

She also covered his hands and the smooth part of his neck with the goatskins. Then she handed to her son Jacob the tasty food and the bread she had made.

He went to his father and said, "My father."

"Yes, my son," he answered. "Who is it?"

Jacob said to his father, "I am Esau your firstborn. I have done as you told me. Please sit up and eat some of my game, so that you may give me your blessing."

Isaac asked his son, "How did you find it so quickly, my son?"

"The Lord your God gave me success," he replied.

Then Isaac said to Jacob, "Come near so I can touch you, my son, to know whether you really are my son Esau or not."

Jacob went close to his father Isaac, who touched him and said, "The voice is the voice of Jacob, but the hands are the hands of Esau." He did not recognize him, for his hands were hairy like those of his brother Esau; so he proceeded to bless him. "Are you really my son Esau?" he asked.

"I am," he replied.

Then he said, "My son, bring me some of your game to eat, so that I may give you my blessing."

Jacob brought it to him and he ate; and he brought some wine and he drank. Then his father Isaac said to him, "Come here, my son, and kiss me."

So, he went to him and kissed him. When Isaac caught the smell of his clothes, *he blessed him and said,*

"Ah, the smell of my son is like the smell of a field that the Lord has blessed. May God give you heaven's dew and earth's richness-an abundance of

grain and new wine. May nations serve you and peoples bow down to you. Be lord over your brothers and may the sons of your mother bow down to you. May those who curse you be cursed and those who bless you be blessed."

After Isaac finished blessing him, and Jacob had scarcely left his father's presence, his brother Esau came in from hunting. He, too, prepared some tasty food and brought it to his father. Then he said to him, "My father, please sit up and eat some of my game, so that you may give me your blessing."

His father Isaac asks him, "Who are you?"

"I am your son," he answered, "your first-born, Esau."

Isaac trembled violently and said, "Who was it, then, that hunted game and brought it to me? I ate it just before you came, and *I blessed him and indeed he will be blessed!*

When Esau heard his father's words, he burst out with a loud and bitter cry and said to his father, "Bless me-me too, my father!"

But he said, *"Your brother came deceitfully and took your blessing."*

Esau said, "Isn't he rightly named Jacob? This is the second time he has taken advantage of me: He took my birthright, and now he's taken my blessing!" Then he asked, "Haven't you reserved any blessing for me?"

Isaac answered Esau, *"I have made him lord over you and have made all his relatives his servants, and I have sustained him with grain and new wine.* So, what can I possibly do for you, my son?"

Esau said to his father, "Do you have only one blessing, my father? *Bless me too, my father!"*

Then Esau wept aloud. His father Isaac answered him,

"Your dwelling will be away from the earth's richness, away from the dew of heaven above. You will live by the sword and you will serve your brother. But when you grow restless, you will throw his yoke from off your neck" [Isaac curses Esau].

Esau held a grudge against Jacob because of *the blessing his father had given him.* He said to himself, "The days of mourning for my father are near; then *I will kill my brother Jacob.*"

When Rebekah was told what her older son Esau had said, she sent for her younger son Jacob and said to him, "Your brother Esau is planning to avenge himself by killing you. Now then, my son, do what I say: Flee at once to my brother Laban in Harran. Stay with him for a while until your brother's fury subsides. When your brother is no longer angry with you and forgets what you did to him, I'll send word for you to come back from there. Why should I lose both of you in one day?" Then Rebekah said to Isaac, *"I'm disgusted with living because of these Hittite women. If Jacob takes a wife from among the women of this land, from Hittite women like these, my life will not be worth living"* [Rebecca curses herself]. (Genesis 27:1–46)

All these are the twelve tribes of Israel, and this is what *their father said to them when he blessed then, giving each the blessing appropriate to him.* (Genesis 49:28)

Busy means buried under Satan's yoke. These are the seven areas of a individual's developmental stages that can be blessed or cursed. As ministers, we must look at each of these stages of the person's life and break any curses that will not release the fruit of blessing. We must bless them if necessary!

1. Conception. Am I welcome? How was I conceived, and the news taken?
2. Pregnancy. Safe Place (Psalm22). How was pregnancy experience?
3. Birth. Will my needs be met? Dedication, naming.
4. Early childhood. Who can I trust without blessing?
5. Puberty. Do I have what it takes? Leading role in shaping mentally preparing emotion, socially.
6. Emerging adulthood.
7. Senior years. Honored with age.

A curse is empowered to bring failure. Blessings are empowered to bring success.

Deception brings a curse and can include Freemasonry, Islam, Mormonism, and Jehovah's Witness. Children are taught about the Easter Bunny, Santa, and Jesus, and we wonder why they don't believe in Jesus. When we dabble or practice in counterfeit religious systems this also brings curses upon us and our bloodline.

We need to learn about our past to release the blessing.

Fruit of curses are as follows:

- Shame
- Pain
- Lies
- Unfulfilled dreams
- Dishonor—to make light

The original blessing was blocked by curse.

God blessed them and said to them, "Be fruitful and increase in number; fill the earth and subdue it. Rule over the fish in the sea and the birds in the sky and over every living creature that moves on the ground." (Genesis 1:20)

The divine order is to first bless Hebrew for blessing, transmittal of blessing.

Transmit the favor and power of God and how blessings work. To honor and instill value:

- words say it,
- deeds show it, and
- ceremonies seal it

[We have blessings stored up] Praise be to the *God and Father* of our Lord Jesus Christ, *who has blessed us* in heavenly realms *with every spiritual blessing* in Christ. (Ephesians 1:3)

Then Melchizedek king of Salem brought out bread and wine. He was priest of God Most High, and he blessed Abram, saying, "*Blessed be Abram* by God Most High, Creator of heaven and earth. And praise be to God Most High, who delivered your enemies into your hand." Then Abram gave him a tenth of everything. (Genesis 14:18–20)

Genesis 27, the story of Jacob stealing Esau's blessing (see above).

"They are the sons God has given me here," Joseph said to his father. Then Israel said, "Bring them to me so I may bless them." Now Israel's eyes were failing because of old age, and he could hardly see. So, Joseph brought his sons close to him, and his father kissed them and embraced the. Israel said to Joseph, "I never expected to see your face again, and now God has allowed me to see your children too." Then Joseph removed them from Israel's knees and bowed down with his face to the ground. And Joseph took both of them, Ephraim on his right toward Israel's left hand and Manasseh on his left toward Israel's right hand, and brought them close to him. But Israel reached out his right hand and put it on Ephraim's head, thought he was the younger, and crossing his arms, he put his left hand on Manasseh's head, even though Manasseh was the first born. Then he blessed Joseph and said, May the God before whom my father's Abraham and Isaac walked faithfully, the God who has been my shepherd all my life to this day, the Angel who has delivered me from all harm—may he bless these boys. May they be called by my name and the names of my father's Abraham and Isaac, ad may they increase greatly on the earth.

When Joseph saw his father placing his right hand on Ephraim's head he was displeased; so he took hold of his father's hand to move it from Ephraim's head to Manasseh's head. Joseph said to him, "No, my father, this one is the first born; put your right hand on his head."

But his father refused and said, "I know my son, I know. He too will become a people, and he too will become great. Nevertheless, his younger brother will be greater than he, and his descendants will become a group of nations." He blessed them that day and said, "In your name will Israel pronounce this blessing: May God make you like Ephraim and Manasseh." So, he put Ephraim ahead of Manasseh.

Then Israel said to Joseph, "I am about to die, but God will be with you and take you back to the land of your fathers. And to you I give one more ridge of land than to your brother, the ridge I took from the Amorites with my sword and my bow."

Then Jacob called for his sons and said; "Gather around so I can tell you what will happen to you in days to come. Assemble and listen, sons of Jacob; listen to your father Israel."

"Reuben, you are my firstborn, my might, the first sign of my strength, excelling in honor, excelling in power. Turbulent as the waters, you will no longer excel, for you went up onto your father's bed onto my couch and defiled it."

Simeon and Levi are brothers-their swords are weapons of violence. Let me not enter their council, let me not join their assembly, for they have killed men in their anger and hamstrung oxen as they pleased. Cursed be their anger, so fierce, and their fury, so cruel! I will scatter them in Jacob and disperse them in Israel. Judah, your brothers will praise you; your hand will be on the neck of your enemies; your father's sons will bow down to you. You are a lion's cub, Judah; your return from the prey, my son. Like a lion he crouches and lies down, like a lioness-who dares to rouse him? The scepter will not depart from Judah, nor the ruler's staff from between his feet, until he to whom it belongs shall come and the obedience of the nations shall be his. He will tether his donkey to a vine, his cold to the choicest branch; he will wash his garments in wine, his robes in the blood of grapes. His eyes will be darker than wine, his teeth whiter than milk.

Zebulun will live by the seashore and become a haven for ships; his border will extend toward Sidon. Issachar is a rawboned donkey lying down among the sheep pens. When he sees how good is his resting place and how pleasant is his land, he will bend his shoulder to the burden and submit to forced labor. Dan will provide justice for his people as one of the tribe of Israel. Dan will be a snake by the roadside, a viper along the path that bites the horse's heels so that its rider tumbles backward.

I look for your deliverance, Lord.

Gad will be attacked by a band of raiders, but he will attack them at their heels. Asher's food will be rich; he will provide delicacies fit for a king. Naphtali is a doe set free that bears beautiful fawns. Joseph is a fruitful vine, a fruitful vine near a spring, whose branches climb over a wall. With bitterness archers attacked him; they shot at him with hostility. But his bow remained steady, his strong arms stayed limber, because of the hand of the Mighty One of Jacob, because of the Shepherd, the Rock of Israel, because of our father's God, who helps you, because of the Almighty, who blessed you with blessings of the skies above, blessings of the deep springs below, blessings of the breast and womb. Your father's blessings are greater than the blessings of the ancient mountains, than the bounty of the age-old hills. Let all these rest on the head of Joseph, on the brow of the prince among his brothers.

Benjamin is a ravenous wolf; in the morning he devours the prey, in the evening he divides the plunder.

All these are the twelve tribes of Israel, and this is what their father said to them when he blessed them, giving each the blessing appropriate to him.

Then he gave them these instructions: "I am about to be gathered to my people. Bury me with my fathers in the cave in the field of Ephron the Hittite, the cave in the field of Machpelah, near Mamre in Canaan, which Abraham bought along with the field as a burial place from Ephron the Hittite. There Abraham and his wife Sarah were buried, there Isaac and his wife Rebekah and buried, and there I buried Leah. The field and the cave in it were bought from Hittites."

When Jacob had finished giving instructions to his sons, he drew his feet up into the bed, breathed his last and was gathered to his people. (Genesis 48:9–22, 49:1–33)

Tell Aaron and his sons, "This is how you are to bless the Israelites. Say to them: *'The Lord bless you and keep you; the Lord make his face shine on you and be gracious to you; the Lord turn his face toward you and give you peace.'*

"So they will put my name on the Israelites, and I will bless them." (Numbers 6:23–27)

The Command

This is how you will bless:

- biblical promises,
- family genealogy,
- ethnic background,
- church promises (what's the history),
- geographic regions (city state, nations),

- the meaning of names (the meaning of the name of my city), and
- personal prophet life

A curse or blessing spoken according to Dereck Prince:

- usually expressed in words, either written or spoken;
- enforced/charged with power;
- from God or Satan;
- meant to determine destiny;
- usually continue from generation to generation;
- discerning where it came from or began can be difficult;
- origin could be hundreds or thousands of years past; and
- *God has a solution for curses!*

Blessings

I swear by myself, declares the Lord that because you have done this and have not withheld your son, your only son, *I will surely bless you and make your descendants as numerous as the stars in the sky and as the sand on the seashore. Your descendants will take possession of the cities of their enemies, and through your offspring all nations on earth will be blessed,* because you have obeyed me [Blessing of Obedience]. (Genesis 22:16–18)

Jacob went close to his father Isaac, who touched him and said, "The voice is the voice of Jacob, but the hands are the hands of Esau." He did not recognize him, for his hands were hairy like those of his brother Esau; so he proceeded to bless him.

"Are you really my son Esau?" he asked. "I am," he replied. Then he said, "My son, bring me some of your game to eat, so that I may give you my blessing."

Jacob brought it to him and he ate; and he brought some wine and he drank. Then his father Isaac said to him, "Come here, my son, and kiss me."

So he went to him and kissed him. When Isaac caught the smell of his clothes, he blessed him and said, "Ah, the smell of my son is like the smell of a field that the Lord has blessed. *May God give you heaven's dew and earth's richness— an abundance of grain and new wine. May nations serve you and peoples bow down to you. Be lord over your brothers and may the sons of your mother bow down to you. May those who curse you be cursed and those who bless you be blessed"* [Blessing That Was Stolen but God Honors the Blessing]. (Genesis 27:22–29)

Isaac trembled violently and said, "Who was it, then, that hunted game and brought it to me? I ate it just before you came, and I blessed him—and indeed he will be blessed!" [Power in the Blessing—Blessing Are Prophetic— Supernaturally Empowering and Determines One Destiny]. (Genesis 27:33)

Curses

Like a fluttering sparrow or a darting swallow, an undeserved curse does not come to rest. (Proverbs 26:2)

A curse must have a cause; therefore, to be released from a curse, it is important to discover the cause... God Himself has spoken a curse over a person and nations as a form of judgment.

Look at the call of Abram/Abraham (Genesis 12:1–3). There was seven specific points the Lord made here...

The Lord had said to Abram, "Go from your country, your people, and your father's household to the land I will show you..."

- I will make you into a great nation,
- I will bless you,
- I will make your name great,
- you will be a blessing,
- I will bless those who bless you,
- whoever curses you I will curse, and
- all people on earth will be blessed through you.

God built in this blessing a protection of descendants of Abraham... "A cursing by God of those whom curses Abraham and or his descendants." Derrick Prince refers to this as anti-Semitism which curses Abraham's descendants therefore anti-Semitism is cursed...

These are the lists of twelve curses that the Israelites were instructed to agree to if they disobeyed the laws (Deuteronomy 27:11–25).

- Cursed is anyone who makes an idol—a thing detestable to the Lord, the work of skilled hands—and sets it up in secret.
- Cursed is anyone who dishonors their father or mother.
- Cursed is anyone who moves their neighbor's boundary stone.
- Cursed is anyone who leads the blind astray on the road.
- Cursed is anyone who withholds justice from the foreigner, the fatherless, or the widow.
- Cursed is anyone who sleeps with his father's wife for he dishonors his father's bed.
- Cursed is anyone who has sexual relations with any animal.
- Cursed is anyone who sleeps with his sister, the daughter of his father or the daughter of his mother.
- Cursed is anyone who sleeps with his mother-in-law.
- Cursed is anyone who kills their neighbor secretly.

- Cursed is anyone who accepts a bribe to kill an innocent person.
- Cursed is anyone who does not uphold the words of this law by carrying them out.

A curse that is over many Christians churches because our trust is in man.

> This is what the Lord says, "Cursed is the one who trusts in man who draws strength from mere flesh and whose heart turns away from the Lord."
>
> That person will be like a bush in the wastelands; they will not see prosperity when it comes. They will dwell in the parched places of the desert, in a salt land where no one lives. (Jeremiah 17:5–6)

> I looked again, and there before me was a flying scroll.
>
> He asked me, "What do you see?" I answered, "I see a flying scroll, twenty cubits long and ten cubits wide" And he said to me, "This is the curse that is going out over the whole land; for according to what it says on one side, every thief will be banished, and according to what it says on the other, everyone who swears falsely will be banished. The Lord Almighty declares, 'I will send it out, and it will enter the house of the thief and the house of anyone who swears falsely by my name. It will remain in that house and destroy it completely, both its timbers and its stones.'" (Zechariah 5:1–4)

How Do We Get Rid of Block Blessings?

But if they will confess their sins and the sins of their ancestors-their unfaithfulness and their hostility toward me. (Leviticus 26:40)

The curse of Jeremiah 17:5–6 goes on to tell us what we are to do to be blessed...

> But blessed is the one who trusts in the Lord, whose confidence is in him. They will be like a tree planted by the water that sends out its roots by the stream. It does not fear when heat comes; its leaves are always green. It has no worries in a year of drought and never fails to bear fruit. (Jeremiah 17:7–8)

Sample Prayer for Breaking Curses (from Derek Prince)

Lord Jesus Christ, I believe that You are the Son of God and the only way to God. I believe that You died on the cross for my sins and rose again from the dead. I *renounce* all my sins, and I turn to You, Lord Jesus, for mercy and for forgiveness. I do believe that You forgive me.

From now on, I want to live for You... I want to hear Your voice and do what You tell me in order to be released from any curse over my life.

First, I *confess* any known sin committed by me, my ancestors, or any other related to me...

(Please take a minute between you and God to *confess* these sins.)

Lord, I thank You and believe You have forgiven me. Lord... now I want to say that I also forgive all other persons whom ever has wronged me or hurt me. I forgive them all right now as I would have God the Father forgave me. I choose to forgive _____ (now silently name those people between you and God).

Furthermore, Lord, I renounce any contact by myself or any related to me with Satan with occult power in any and all forms or any kind of secret society. Lord, I commit myself to remove my house of any kind of occult objects that honor Satan and dishonor Jesus Christ.

With Your help, Lord, I will remove them all...

Now Lord Jesus, I thank You further that on the cross You were made a curse so I could receive the blessing and because of what You have done for me on the cross I release myself from every curse and every evil influence, ever dark shadow, and every evil source unmentioned...over me, my family, and all future generations of my bloodline. I release myself and my bloodline now in the name of Jesus!

Now Lord as Your representative... I now break every curse over these people. I revoke those curses, and I release them from them.

In the name of Jesus, the Son of God, His all prevailing name... I *declare* these people released.

Satan, I *declare* you have no more claims, no more access to plunder their families, their businesses, in their ministries, in their finances, and anything else that they lay claim too. They have been lifted out of the domain of darkness and translated into the kingdom of the Son of God's love and blessing!

Thank You, Jesus!

Now Praise Jesus... Confess to one another that Jesus is Lord!

Cursed Objects, Building, or Land

Yes, it is true that objects, building, and even land can be cursed. They can be cursed the same ways and for the same reasons as a person is cursed, which is to bring forth harm or injury. If we know the curse spoken or the cause of the curse, we can break agreement with those curses or repent on behalf of the mankind sin in order to break those agreements and bless the land, buildings, or even objects. Remember objects are sometimes just meant to be destroyed and not blessed at all. But keep in mind that destroying an object doesn't mean tossing it into the trash. Why? Because we are responsible for what happens to that cursed object. It must be destroyed, and burning it is the best way!

Example: After the Temple in Jerusalem had been defiled by the occult in 2 Chronicles 29, King Hezekiah had to clean up the defilement. Everything in that temple including the priests had to be ritually cleaned.

It is not unusual for an occultist or Satanist to steal religious objects and use them to yield demonic powers through the misuse of such objects. We must be wise to use our discernment of spiritual nature when purchasing objects. We need to rely on the gifts that God has given us to discern good from evil. Learn the history of the land you are purchasing. What spiritual curses or blessings may be in that land?

Addictions

No one chooses to become addicted to something; it is actually a compulsive behavior or reaction to some underlying issue. For instance, someone who is a compulsive eater will usually eat to fill a void, eat to cover a wound, or eat to substitute for a feeling or emotion. It is actually to cover up or mask the real problem. Fear of something…so putting something else (eating) in its place gives a temporary sense of control.

Those who are compulsive about porn are looking for a desire to be fulfilled in fantasy. They are looking for a need to be met.

Any addictive patterns are almost always a reaction to gaping holes that are not being filled in a rightful or healthy way. Feelings of deep rejection craves acceptance, so drug addicts always are accepting of each other.

The root of addiction must be found and dealt with before one can begin to cast out any demons associated with addictions and compulsive behaviors. Otherwise, the addict will be like a dog who returns to his own vomit, and it will get worse, seven times worse.

I will return to the house I left. When it
arrives, it finds the house unoccupied, swept clean

and put in order. Then it goes and takes with it seven other spirits more wicked than itself, and they go in and live there. And the final condition of that person is worse than the first. That is how it will be with this wicked generation. (Matthew 12:44–45)

Fears and Phobias

Fears can actually enter a person at conception or during pregnancy. This was my personal experience which I shared in the "Inner Healing" chapter. Not all fear is demonic. Fear is also a God-given gift to keep us tucked under the shelter of our God! "There is no fear in Love. But perfect Love cast out all fear" (1 John 4:18).

Rodney Hogue says that demons smell fear and that the enemy will try to disable us with fear.

Fatigue and Tiredness

There is a saying in the Recovery Community that "one should not get too hungry, angry, lonely, or tired." All of these things lead to temptation, and if not dealt with, will lead to relapse (sin). We tend to push ourselves beyond our limits. When we do, we get angry, and anger unresolved can lead to our acting out in our flesh, the loss of self-control, and we usually end up hurting someone. We should always find rest in the presence of God and sometimes that just requires sleep or soaking.

Diagnosis

We often do not think of the power of agreement when we go to the doctor and he or she says to us, "I am sorry but what you have is _____ (fill in the blank)! For now, let's just say it is the flu. We all know that the flu is viral and often times causes us to feel as though we might die. Some people fight it off really well. We are going to talk about that agreement that comes as soon as the doctor says those words, "You have…" Okay, some of you are thinking that this is about naming it and claiming it. Well, maybe it is!

So why is it when we are sick and the doctor tells us what our diagnosis is, we always manifest the symptoms with a greater intensity? In October 2012, I had a two-year-old in my home, and he was just susceptible to everything. I was his primary caregiver, and I caught everything he had but worse. My mindset was, *Oh my, I know I am going to be sick next.* Then I got sick, only much worse than he did every single time. That particular fall and winter, I was sick more than I was well. My physical body had been so worn down that it was really hard for me to fight off anything.

Funny thing was I am a person who rarely gets sick, but this was the worst winter I had experienced since about 1990. I had been asking God to teach me in this and to show me what it was He wanted me to see in this totally miserable season. He said nothing until the fall of 2013.

As the flu season was growing closer, I found myself becoming anxious about it. I said to our Lord, "Oh, Lord, please don't let me get sick again all winter!"

I once again thought I heard Him chuckle and instead of correcting me, He said, "Take authority over it!"

Oh, okay, I thought. "Over what?" I asked Him. Again, He said nothing! So I started taking authority over sickness in my home. I began to use the tools that I had, the blood of Jesus to cover us, our home. I began asking the Lord to send His angels into our house and clean out all sickness and disease. I began to bind all sickness both viral and bacterial over my family and my home. I began to speak life and health over each one of us! Guess what? The fear and anxiety of getting sick just fled! It ran away, and we had only colds that winter.

The Lord showed me that the year before, I had come into agreement with the sickness; and therefore, the sickness had power over me. I was not reigning over sickness. It was a hard lesson but a deep one. I believe that our Lord is calling all of His children to walk in the fullness of who we are as His children. After all, we are created in His image and likeness; we are to be walking in our fullness in

Christ! What is bound on earth will be bound in heaven, so let's start practicing at home!

My example was one of the flu, but Jesus has authority and has given us authority over all sickness and disease. My question to you is why aren't we using it? Each one of us has to submit to God and allow Him to search us on this question!

What is it that allows the roots and seeds of disease and sickness to remain fruitful?

- Was there a trauma, accident, a wounding, *or* entanglement within a year of the diagnosis? This is the best place to start.
- What is the medical history of the family. Is there generational disease on either paternal or maternal side?
- Is there any history back as far as third and fourth generations with Freemasons, Knights of Columbus, Knights of Malta, Shriners, KKK, Brotherhoods, or any other secret society? Secret societies are those that vows and oaths are kept in secret. Many are public societies, but the vows and oaths are kept in secret.
- All of these other open doors mentioned in this chapter can be roots and seeds to disease.

CHAPTER 7

Exposing New Age Healing Models

*When you enter the land the Lord your God is
giving you, do not learn to imitate the detestable
ways of the nations there. Let no one be found
among you who sacrifice their son or daughter
in the fire, who practices divination or sorcery,
interprets omens, engages in witchcraft, or
casts spells, or who is a medium or spiritist or
who consults the dead. Anyone who does these
things is detestable to the Lord; because of these
same detestable practices the Lord your God
will drive out those nations before you. You
must be blameless before the Lord your God.*
—Deuteronomy 18:9–13

New Age Healing Models

My heart became more intertwined with Jesus and with learning more about the New Age Movement in 2010 when I first began to study at the Wilmington School of the Spirit. I became fascinated with the supernatural from a Christian perspective because I was learning the truth for the first time. Oh, I knew the supernatural really well; it was a lifelong acquaintance of mine after all. It was not the first time I had been deceived. Having learned that all I had experienced since childhood was in fact real and not just an illusion, I then had the freedom to share my experiences with instructors that I had come to trust in Jesus's kingdom.

Since this revelation of truth, I have been given a new heart for healing in the name of Jesus. Jesus had brought me out of the darkness and into the light, His light, in 1992. I believe it was then that I first realized He had a specific purpose for me. But I did not yet have the revelation of what that plan was or that I had the ability in Christ Jesus to fulfill my calling.

Since my childhood, I have had a total fascination with the outdoors. I loved trees and flowers, and I especially loved to lay in my yard and chew on a blade of sweet grass and stare at the clouds and just feel the warmth of the sun on my face. At night, I would lay there and watch the stars and take in all the sweet smells of the night and the cool dampening the air. I would be in a supernatural place of peace when I would rest in the presence of all that God had created. I was so fascinated that I would spend every moment I had exploring all that I could in the great outdoors, the smells, the sounds, the tastes, and sensations to my touch. I loved to sleep outside in my homemade tents and just be close to heaven. However, I had no clue how this would open me to the vulnerability of the spiritual realms.

As I grew, I sought after that sensation, that feeling of belonging and that place of peace. I tried so many different things to experience that passion for "oneness." I got into herbal healing, the all-natural methods especially when my mother was diagnosed with breast cancer in 1992 at the age of forty-six. Ironically, I was saved that same year. I was determined I would not see her die, but I would see her healed, and she would live to see her great grandchildren.

I researched and treated her with every herbal remedy, crystals, and music therapy I could find. These things did help her, but they did not heal her. Since I was spiritually born again during this year, I prayed and prayed, and I just knew that Jesus would answer me and help her, after all these things were His, right? I did not know until much later that He was her healer. I was still praying with the mind-set that Jesus was still under that angry ole God that I knew from my childhood. I had just met Jesus, and I was learning about Him every day but still not recognizing Him as the Healer. I looked at the world as though Jesus Himself had given all this knowledge to different people to use for His good so I had all this "stuff" at my disposal.

I believed at one point in my life that all religions were just a deeper revelation of the identity of the Trinity—the Father, the Son, and the Holy Spirit—after all, they all taught about "God." They also seemed to desire and bare positive fruit like peace, love, kindness, gentleness, faithfulness, and compassion, and I knew very little about the occult and the mysterious power that lay behind it. I did not know anything about spiritual warfare, but I was about to begin to learn and learn swiftly...

Introduction to New Age

"He who does not love does not know God,
for God is love" (1 John 4:8, NKJV).

What is John saying to us here? God is concerned for His creatures and especially His people. He is tender toward them and does not take pleasure in their suffering or condemnation. He seeks the best for us, and He offered up His Son in love as a substitution for sin, our sin. He loves to love people through His Son. We, as His children, know this from our relationship with our Father, Abba! This is the one most important fact that I can give you as we go through this teaching. And here are three facts about the New Age:

First, New Age is a *love* movement. Second, it is a *oneness* movement. Third, it is a *spiritual* movement.

One of the most important facts that I will share with you throughout this teaching is the deception used within the New Age Movement claiming they stand on "Love, Love for All Things, Universal Love." They center on unity and peace, but love is the key that draws all this together. You will hear about "oneness," a unity of all being of the same. Not the "Oneness" of the Trinity, the Father, Son, and Holy Spirit.

> Remain in me, as I also remain in you. No branch can bear fruit by itself; it must remain in the vine. Neither can you bear fruit unless you remain in me. I am the vine; you are the branches. If you remain in me and I in you, you will bear much fruit; apart from me you can do nothing. (John 15:4–5)

> My prayer is not for them alone. I pray also for those who will believe in Me through their message, that all of them may be one, Father, just as you are in Me and I am in you. May they also be in us so that the world may believe that you have sent Me. I have given them the glory that you gave Me, that they may be one as We are one I in them and you in Me—so that they may be brought to complete unity. Then the world will know that you sent Me and have loved them even as you have loved Me. (John 17:20–23)

The deception of new age...the lie...its core...is not Jesus Christ.

Jesus Christ, the Bearer of the Water of Life: A Christian Reflection on the "New Age" asks this question...why now?

The beginning of the Third Millennium comes not only two thousand years after the birth of Christ but also at a time when astrologers believe that the Age of Pisces—known to them as the Christian age—is drawing to a close. These reflections are about the New Age, which takes its name from the imminent astrological Age of Aquarius. The New Age is one of many explanations of the significance of this moment in history which are bombarding contemporary (particularly western) culture, and it is hard to see clearly what is and what is not consistent with the Christian message.

People hover between certainty and uncertainty these days, particularly in questions relating to their identity. New Age is attractive mainly because so much of what it offers answers to hungers often left unsatisfied by the established institutions, especially Christian religion.

Creation of Self-Centered Thinking

People feel the need to "belong" to institutions less and less (and yet loneliness is very much a scourge of modern life) and are not inclined to rank "official" judgments above their own. With this cult of humanity, religion is internalized in a way which prepares the ground for a celebration of the sacredness of the self.

New Age influence is clear from the rapidly-growing numbers of people who claim that it is possible to blend Christianity and New Age by taking what strikes them as the best of both. New Age imports Eastern religious practices and reinterprets them to suit Westerners—this involves a rejection of the language of sin and salvation. New Age is unity through fusion. It claims to reconcile soul and body, female and male, spirit and matter, human and divine, earth and cosmos, transcendent and immanent, religion and science, differences between religions, and yin and yang.

Some of the traditions which flow into New Age are ancient Egyptian occult practices, Cabbalism, early Christian Gnosticism, Sufism, the lore of the Druids, Celtic Christianity, mediaeval alchemy, Renaissance Hermeticism, Zen Buddhism, Yoga, and so on.

Let's talk for a few minutes about the occult…*what does occult mean?*

Occult is the phenomenon, events, and religious practices engaging a practitioner in a realm of the supernatural that is rooted in things secret or hidden.

It comes from the Latin word *occultus* which means "things hidden." The study of the occult is usually classified into three different areas: (1) spiritualism, (2) fortune-telling, and (3) magic which includes Satanism, witchcraft, and gothic witchcraft. Many other groups practice the occult or have influences and have historical roots in the occul, to name one specific that we will look at in detail later is *theosophy*!

Because so many different religions, groups, and practices have sprung from occult origins, the history of occult itself is varied, depending on each group.

You will recognize games like Dungeons and Dragons, the Ouija board, and tarot cards. Each has their origins in the occult. The reading of horoscopes and widespread interest in divination, palmistry, and others are also rooted in the occult (Larry Nichols 2006).

Let's look at what the Word of God has to say about this, in Deuteronomy 18: 9–13 (NIV):

> When you enter the land the Lord your God is giving you, do not learn to imitate the detestable ways of the nation's there. Let no one be found among you who sacrifices their son or daughter in the fire, who practices divination or sorcery, interprets omens, engages in witchcraft, or casts spells, or who is a medium or Spiritists or who consults the dead. Anyone who does these things is detestable to the Lord; because of these same detestable practices the Lord your God will drive out those nations before you. You must be blameless before the Lord your God.

Verse 12 says these things are *detestable* to the Lord, depending on your translation others say *abomination* to the Lord.

I want you to get a picture and understanding of how the Lord thinks of these occult practices... Let's look for a minute at what the word *detestable*. It means:

- to regard with extreme repugnance or dislike, detest utterly, loathe, abominate;
- highly offensive, disgusting;
- deserving or causing hatred; and
- utter loathing, abomination.

Abomination means:

- a person or thing that is disgusting;
- an action that is vicious, vile, etc.;
- intense loathing; and
- wretchedly bad, foul, filthy.

I believe God's Word is clear about how the Almighty God, Creator of all, feels about the occult!

> Do not practice Divination or Sorcery. (Leviticus 19:26)

> They (Israelites) sacrificed their sons and daughters in the fire. They practiced divination and sorcery also sold them to do evil in the eyes of the Lord, provoking him to anger. (2 Kings 17:17)

In 2 Kings 21, it tells us that Manasseh, the son of Hezekiah, reined in Jerusalem for fifty-five years destroying everything that his father had restored. Verse 6 says that Manasseh did much evil in the eyes of the Lord, provoking Him to anger.

Manasseh built High Places (H1116) high place, ridge, height, bamah (technical name for cultic platform (a) high place, mountain; (b) high places, battlefields; (c) high places [as places of worship]) (Strong 1990).

Leviticus 26:30, Numbers 33:52, Deuteronomy 12:2, 1 Kings 3:2–3, 1 Kings 12:31–33, 2 Kings 21 in the King James Version, there are ninety-one references to high places. In the New International Version, there are fifty-nine references. High places were referred to in almost all instances for worship of celestial hosts (moon, stars, sun, etc.) also known for worship of idols, false gods, sacrifices to false gods (included their children to Molech), obelisks called Asherah poles, prostitution, and much more.

Altars to Baal and starry hosts: a raised place or structure where sacrifices are offered and religious rites performed.

Baal—the god Baal, chief god of the Canaanites. Baal epic is that Baal was the principle figure of the whole god system. They believed Baal was killed and resurrected. Pictures of how Satan counterfeits what God is all about. Baal is the son of El. His father's name was El, a false, phony god. Also, the name of the one true god, god of fertility, nature, reproduction, and connected to controlling the rain and storms. Sun god (sun worship). A drought indicated that Baal was either dead, inactive, or captured by another god (Dutch Sheets 2011).

Starry hosts—sun, moon, stars, and constellations. Everything in the day and night sky! Also called *aeromancy* is divination.

Asherah pole—the obelisk in the Bible is called *Asherah* in Hebrew. The King James Version uses the word *groves*!

The *Strong's Concordance* defines it as Asherah, ash-ay-raw or asheyrah, ash-ay-raw (Strong's 842); from Hebrew 833 (Asher), happy, Asherah (or Astarte) a Phoenician goddess. Also, an image of the same grove. Compare Hebrew 6253 (Ashtoreth). The word *Asherah* is from the root Asher which means to be straight, erect, or upright.

Asherah (in KJV uses groves) is found in the scriptures forty times, always referring to idol worship.

The Companion Bible, appendix 42, defines *Asherah* as follows: It was an upright pillar connected with Baal worship and is associated with the goddess Ashtoreth, being the representation of the productive principal of life and Baal being the representative of the generative principal. The image, which represents the Phoenician Ashtoreth of Pathos as the sole object of worship in her temple, was an upright block of stone, anointed with oil, and covered with an embroidered cloth. Sacrificed his own son in the fire (to Molech). Molech was the god of the Amorites (1 Kings 11:5, 33 and Leviticus 20:1–5). There was a detestable practice of sacrificing children to Molech in Phoenicia and other surrounding countries. Manasseh even sacrificed his sons to Molech (2 Chronicles 33:6; 2 Kings 23:10).

Practiced sorcery—the term used in the occult world that refers to the practice of manipulating or controlling supernatural spirits, often through black magic. This magic is used to bring evil, cursing, or negative effects on the person(s) to whom it is directed. It applies to Satanism, some witchcraft groups, sorcerers, or magicians. The goal is to conjure up evil spirits and invoke them to carry out intended harm (Larry Nichols 2006).

> So I will come to put you on trial. I will be quick to testify against sorcerers, adulterers and perjurers, against those who defraud laborers of their wages, who oppress the widows and the fatherless, and deprive the foreigners among you of justice, but do not fear me, says the Lord Almighty. (Malachi 3:5)

On the Day of Judgment, the Lord will testify against those who practice magic.

> The acts of the flesh are obvious: sexual immorality, impurity and debauchery; idolatry and witchcraft; hatred, discord, jealousy, fits of rage, selfish ambition, dissensions, factions and envy; drunkenness, orgies, and the like. I warn you, as I did before, that those who live like this will not inherit the kingdom of God. (Galatians 5:19–21)

Those who practice witchcraft will not possess the kingdom of God.

Divination—the attempt to foretell and/or explore the future. The most common means of divination are astrology, tarot cards, crystals balls, numerology, palmistry, random symbols, and various omens (Larry Nichols 2006).

I will destroy your witchcraft and you will no longer cast spells. (Micah 5:12)

All because of the wanton lust of a prostitute, alluring, the mistress of sorceries, who enslaved nations by her prostitution and peoples by her witchcraft. (Nahum 3:4)

The idols speak deceitfully, diviners see visions that lie; they tell dreams that are false, they give comfort in vain. Therefore, the people wander like sheep oppressed for lack of a shepherd. (Zechariah 10:2)

Consulted mediums—one who acts as an intermediary between the spirit world and the physical world. They make use of various objects to convey a message from spirits to the living. Mediums will serve as spokesperson (Larry Nichols 2006).

Saul died because he was unfaithful to the Lord; he did not keep the word of the Lord and even consulted a medium for guidance, (14) and did not inquire of the Lord. So, the Lord put him to death and turned the kingdom over to David son of Jesse. (1 Chronicles 10:13–14)

Spiritists—a person who practices Spiritism, the esoteric belief that says the human personality exists after death and that it can communicate with the living through a medium of psychics. Believers in this phenomenon say this communication comes from the spirit world and is commonly conveyed through apparitions, clairaudience, clairvoyance, the Ouija board, poltergeist, séances, telepathy and telekinesis, etc., (Larry Nichols 2006).

> A man or woman who is a medium or Spiritists among you must be put to death. You are to stone them; their blood will be on their own heads. (Leviticus 20:27)

Look at Isaiah 57:1–13:

1. "The righteous perish, and no one takes it to heart; the devout are taken away, and no one understands that the righteous are taken away to be spared from evil."
2. "Those that walk uprightly enter into peace; they find rest as they lie in death."
3. "But you—come here, you children of a sorceress, your offspring of adulterers and prostitutes!"
4. "Who are you mocking? At whom do you sneer and stick out your tongue? Are you not a brood of rebels, the offspring of liars?"
5. "You burn with lust among the oaks and under every spreading tree; you sacrifice your children in the ravines and under the overhanging crags."
6. "The idols among the smooth stones of the ravines are your portion; indeed, they are your lot. Yes, to them you have poured out drink offerings and offered grain offerings. In view of all this, should I relent?"
7. "You have made your bed on a high and lofty hill; there you went up to offer your sacrifices."
8. "Behind your doors and your doorposts you have put your pagan symbols. Forsaking me, you uncovered your bed, you climbed into it and opened it wide; you made a pact

with those whose beds you love, and you looked with lust on their naked bodies."

9. "You went to Molech with olive oil and increased your perfumes. You sent your ambassadors far away; you descended to the very realm of the dead!"

10. "You wearied yourself by such going about, but you would not say, 'It is hopeless.' You found renewal of your strength, and so you did not faint."

11. "Whom have you so dreaded and feared that you have not been true to me, and have neither remembered me nor taken this to heart? Is it not because I have long been silent that you do not fear me?"

12. "I will expose your righteousness and your works, and they will not benefit you."

13. "When you cry out for help, let your collection of idols save you! The wind will carry all of them off, a mere breath will blow them away. But whoever takes refuge in me will inherit the land and possess my holy mountain."

New Age Beliefs Compared to Christian Beliefs

Christian Doctrines Challenged by New Age Healing Modalities, Reiki, and Therapeutic Touch Christian beliefs will be detailed followed by New Age beliefs.

1. *Doctrine of Creation*
    God created out of nothing. God created creation by speaking. God permeates and sustains His creation. God is separate and different from creation (Genesis 1:1–2; Psalm 90:2; Acts 17:24; Revelations 10:6). New Agers believe that there was no creation. Matter itself is eternal. Universe is matter, and eternal matter has always existed, and God is as matter.

2. *Doctrine of God's Nature*

God is personal and the Father. God is the creator of all things. God is Love. He is just, kind, and peaceful. He is very patient and understanding. The Father communicates with His children.

New Agers believe that God is matter. Matter is not personal; therefore, they do not pray to a personal god. Its nature is a force; god just in nature. It cannot be grieved, love, quenched. It just remains. Good and evil coexist; therefore, the god of nature is "God's" nature.

3. *Doctrine of Time*

Christians, we believe in linear time, a beginning and an end before moving into eternity. Linear has history of His story and has meaning. God started it. He is in complete control of time, and there is purpose and destiny—moving in time to His purpose (Revelation 21:6, 22:13; Psalm 119:112).

New Agers believe that time is *circular* = O. It "cycles" around with no beginning or end. Hinduism is circular. Reincarnation is moving toward *no* ultimate destination.

4. *Doctrine of Human Beings*

We believe in free will. We can choose to sin because God gives us free will. God created man and woman to fellowship with Him. God created man to have dominion over all other living things and to subdue the earth (Genesis 1:26–28, 2:7; Psalm 8:6–8, 115:14–16).

New Agers believe that man and woman evolved from matter (Darwinism and evolution). All acts, words, and thoughts determine a person's fate in his next stage of existence. This is called *karma*. Karma works against Christian compassion.

5. *Doctrine of Sin*

We believe there are "absolute" things that we cannot do and that we can be captive to sin and we need to be saved from sin… *Sin is real* and often related to disease (Genesis 4:7; 1 Kings 8:46; Jeremiah 31:30; Romans 6:23).

New Agers believe that there are "no absolutes." Sin *is not* an act but a thought or an understanding that you are not part of the "one" or "oneness." Sin is an illusion, and there is no sickness in oneness.

6. *Doctrine of Salvation*

Salvation is forgiveness of sin, healing, restoration of life, escape from hell, and deliverance from demonic (John 14:6; Acts 2:21, 15:11; Hebrews 10:39; Psalm 34:4, 79:9, 80:3, 116:8; Romans 1:16; Titus 2:11).

New Agers believe that salvation is only an illusion that humanity is separate from all that is because salvation is knowledge. Gnosticism is a secret knowledge of knowing how things are! Salvation for New Age followers is when they become gods.

7. *Doctrine of Jesus's Incarnation*

We believe historically (1 Corinthians 15) that God became flesh in Jesus (John 1:1–14). The word became flesh and made His dwelling among us. We have seen His glory, the glory of the One and Only who came from the Father, full of grace and truth.

New Age believes that Jesus is a cosmic spirit that came upon men and will continue to come upon men. Nonhistorical and Jesus is among many spirits. "Cults will use our language and terms and give a very different meaning to our stuff."

8. *Doctrine of Jesus's Lordship*

Jesus is the *only* way (John 14:6; Romans 6:4; 2 Corinthians 5:17; John 1:12–13, 3:1–7; 1 Peter 1:22–25; Galatians 3:26–27)!

New Agers believe that Jesus is one of the many ways and there are many (Muhammad, Dalai Lama, Buddha, and many others). Some believe that Jesus is one of the ascended masters (believed to be spiritually enlightened beings who in past incarnations were ordinary humans but who have undergone a series of spiritual transformations originally called initiations).

9. *Doctrine of Resurrection*

We believe that Jesus rose from the dead and ascended into heaven and is now seated at the right hand of the Father (Romans 1:4, 6:5).

Jesus said to her, "I am the resurrection and the life. The one who believes in me will live, even though they die; and whoever lives by believing in me will never die. Do you believe this?" "Yes, Lord," she replied, "I believe that you are the Messiah, the Son of God, who is to come into the world." (John 11:25–27)

New Agers do not believe in resurrection but reincarnation, the cycle of life over and over again. Hindus believe in hell as being a holding place between life and reincarnation. *Reincarnation* is the belief that the soul, upon death of the body, comes back to earth in another body or form. It's a rebirth of the soul in a new body, a new incarnation or embodiment as of a person.

10. *Doctrine of Second Coming*

We believe Jesus Christ will return (Revelations 19:11). The rider on the white horse, his name was "Word of God" (Revelations 22:7–21). "Behold I am coming soon" (Acts 1:11). We are told He will come back the same way the disciples watched Him go into heaven (Titus 2:13; 1 Corinthians 1:8; Philippians 1:6; 1 Thessalonians 4:16, 5:2; Matthew 24:30–31).

New Agers believe that some do not believe that Jesus Christ is God's Son because the god that they believe in is a spiritual force not a personal God (impersonal indweller that is compatible with science). Some believe that a messianic figure is coming, but it will be his first not his last.

11. *Doctrine of Heaven*

God's dwelling place (1 Kings 8:30; Matthew 6:9) His Sanctuary (Psalm 102:19, 2:4; Isaiah 63:15) tells us where His throne is. Where Jesus ascended is recorded in *Luke 24:51* and *Hebrews 9:24*. We believe that we will remain individuals. We will know each other and family members, and we will continue to exist in a glorified body (1 Corinthians 15:50–54).

New Age believes that in Nirvana, final place of oneness in all things.

12. *Doctrine of Judgment*

We will be judged by God on the day of the Lord (Revelation 20:11–14). God has brought temporal judgment historically such as:

- The flood (Genesis 7:17–23)
- Plagues (2 Samuel 24:15–16)
- Exile (2 Chronicles 36:20)

The purpose was to punish sin.

New Agers believe that karma is the natural judgment. Repetitive reincarnation is the judgment until perfection is complete, and they become part of the one. In Hinduism, a person can come back as an animal. Therefore, in some cultures, they do not eat animals because they are afraid that they may be eating a relative.

13. *Doctrine of Justice*

God is just… (2 Thessalonians 1:6–12). Justice is getting what you deserve. Mercy is not getting what I deserve. Grace is getting what I do not deserve. It is a gift! Believers have grace (Ephesians 2:8; Psalm 84:11; James 1:17; John 1:17; 1 Corinthians 1:4; Zechariah 12:10; Hebrews 10:29).

New Agers believe karma—Hinduism, Buddhism. Action, seen as bringing upon oneself inevitable results, good or bad, either in this life or in a reincarnation. In Hinduism, one of the means of reaching Brahman. Theosophy, the cosmic principle according to which each person is rewarded or punished in one incarnation according to that person's deeds in the previous incarnation. It's fate, destiny. What goes around comes around. A person gets what they deserve.

14. *Doctrine of Impartation*

Therefore I remind you to stir up the gift of God which is in you through the laying on of my hands (2

Timothy 1:6). This is the power of God coming upon us by the Holy Spirit through the laying on of hands through a blessing:

- Imparting of spiritual gifts (Romans 1:11–12)
- Christ's power is made perfect in our weakness (2 Corinthians 12:9)
- I will pour out my Spirit (Joel 2:28–29; Acts 2:17–18, 2:38–39; Romans 8:9–17)
- Laying on of hands in the New Testament was an act to impart healing (Mark 16:18, NKJV)

> "They will lay hands on the sick, and they will recover." *Anointing is transferred* (imparted). *Straight from heaven's outpouring.*
>
> And suddenly there came a sound from heaven as of a rushing mighty wind, and it filled the entire house where they were sitting. (Acts 2:2, KJV)

New Agers believe that since they are part of the "One" (humans are gods), they have the energy in them or within themselves, and one must learn to channel god's energy. *Channel* means to convey through or as through a channel (He channeled the information to us) to direct toward or into some particular course (to channel one's interests). Reiki practitioners must receive an impartation called an attunement from a Reiki master, which is very dangerous! (I will talk about this later.)

15. *Doctrine of Healing*

We are deeply dependent on God, who is working in our lives through the Holy Spirit. Jesus said that He could do nothing without the Father. We believe in the great commissioning; we are all called to do as Jesus did (Matthew 28:18–20; Mark 16:15–18).

In New Age, there is no personal God or Holy Spirit to help you. It is just an understanding that God is in everything and everything is in you, and you just need to channel the healing energy within you. If someone needs help, there are spirit guides that can come and help them.

This section is taken from a teaching of Randy Clark, Christian Healing Certification Program (CHCP).

The founder of therapeutic touch, Dora Kuntz, says this, "Whether or not a person gets healed depends upon their karma. Worst case they must ask their spirit guide..."

This is a direct quote from Sedona New Age Center, titled "New Age Enlightenment,"

> The New Age is a free-flowing spiritual movement comprised of believers and practitioners who share beliefs integrating mind, spirit, and body. It is the reemergence of earliest esoteric knowledge coupled with contemporary scientific advances... New Age covers a wide variety of disciplines from alternative medicine to goddess worship.
>
> In fact, New Age incorporates any pursuit which allows individuals to express themselves in terms of self, the Creation and individual freedom.
>
> To participate, one merely has to have an interest and a desire to know more about the subject.
>
> There is neither gospel nor dogma in the New Age. All that is necessary for one to be attuned is an open mind and a positive attitude.
>
> This combination allows someone to examine universal truths independent of religion and these truths, this New Age, may very well lead to a more satisfying life on this plane and in other dimensions.
>
> New Age is a spirituality that searches for the truth. Though the truth may be different for every seeker, the philosophy recognizes that the basis for that truth is love, goodness, integrity and sincerity.

The New Age person focuses on the elimination of ego; developing unconditional love for mankind regardless of religious preference or geographical origin; and achieving a close union with the "real" psychic self.

History of New Age and Theosophical Society

Worldview of New Age Major Influences on Our World

- A religious and social movement, spiritualism is characterized by a pronounced scientific attitude combined with a bohemian opposition to institutionalize Christianity.
- Other names you may recognize are Age of Aquarius, Holistic Health, Ancient Wisdom, Eastern Spirituality, Higher Consciousness Movement, Occultism, and Eastern Mysticism.

Here are some organizations you may know…

- *Share International (Benjamin Crème).* Share international's publications claim that the coming of Maitreyan (meaning "friendly" in Sanskrit) fulfills not only Buddhist prophecies about the appearance of a future great teacher named Maitreya but also the prophecies of a number of other world religions—including Christianity (the second coming of Christ), Hinduism (the Kalki avatar of Vishnu), Islam (the Imam Mahdi), and Judaism (the Jewish Messiah). Crème claims that Maitreya manifested himself through (or overshadowed) Jesus two thousand years ago.
- *The Peace Alliance (Marianne Williamson).* Founder of and author of the best-selling book, *A Return to Love*, says that we have "a natural tendency to focus on love."

Only love is real. All that is negative is illusion. It simply does not exist. If anything, negative is in your consciousness, it is real only because you give it reality by holding it in your mind. According to The Course, sickness, hate, pain, fear, guilt, and sin are all illusions. The Cyclopedia in a Course in Miracles states that "illusions are investments. They will last as long as you value them." The Cyclopedia continues, "The only way to dispel illusions is to withdraw all investment from them, and they will have no life for you because you will have put them out of your mind."

The Course sums it up this way, "There is no life outside of heaven. Where God created life, there life must be. In any state, apart from heaven, life is illusion." There you have it! It is perfectly clear—murder, rape, and other forms of evil do not exist because they do not come from "love." Try explaining to a mother who has lost a son or daughter that their loss is the result of an illusion.

- *The Lucis Trust (Alice Bailey)*. Formerly named The Lucifer Trust. The activities of the Lucis Trust promote the education of the human mind toward recognition and practice of the spiritual principles and values upon which a stable and interdependent world society may be based. The activities of the Lucis Trust include the worldwide financial support of the Arcane School, the Lucis Publishing Companies, World Goodwill, Triangles, Lucis Trust Libraries, and Lucis Productions. The Lucis Trust maintains lending libraries of esoteric and occult books covering a wide variety of classifications. The libraries are maintained by voluntary donations only; books may be borrowed by mail. *The Beacon* magazine is published bimonthly by the Lucis Press. This is a magazine of esoteric philosophy presenting the principles of the Ageless Wisdom teaching as a contemporary way of life.

- *Triangles (Alice Bailey)*. Triangles aids the divine plan by establishing right human relations and to spread goodwill and understanding (light) amongst all peoples through the power of constructive thought. This power can be employed on a worldwide scale for spiritual purposes if each one tries to understand the spiritual need of the world. A triangle is a group of three people who link each day in thought for a few minutes of creative meditation. They invoke the energies of light and goodwill, visualizing these energies as circulating through the three focal points of each triangle and pouring out through the network of triangles surrounding the planet. At the same time, they sound the Great Invocation and so help to form a channel for the down pouring of light and love into the consciousness of humanity.

- *Arcane School (Alice Bailey).* The Arcane School was established by Alice A. Bailey in 1923 to help meet an obvious and growing demand for further teaching and training in the science of the soul. The purpose of the esoteric training given in the Arcane School is to help the student grow spiritually toward acceptance of discipleship responsibility and to serve the plan by serving humanity. Esotericism is a practical way of life. The function of the school is to assist those at the end of the probationary path to move forward on to the path of discipleship and to assist those already on that path to move on more quickly and to achieve greater effectiveness in service.
- *World Goodwill (Alice Bailey).* World Goodwill is an accredited nongovernmental organization with the Department of Public Information of the United Nations. It maintains informal relations with certain of the specialized agencies and with a wide range of national and international nongovernmental organizations. World Goodwill is an activity of the Lucis Trust, which is on the Roster of the United Nations Economic and Social Council.
- *Amnesty International.* Receives funding from Lucis trust (occult tie).
- *Green Peace.* Receives funding from Lucis Trust.

- *New Earth (Oprah Winfrey and Eckhart Tolle)*. It is multi-faceted in varying degrees of far eastern mystical religions, mainly in the following:

  o *Hinduism*—the third largest religion in the world (Christianity and Islam). The complex of beliefs, values, and customs comprising the dominant religion of India, characterized by the worship of many gods, including Brahma as supreme being, a caste system (social position), belief in reincarnation, etc. Having an extremely diversified character with many schools of philosophy and theology, many popular cults, and a large pantheon symbolizing the many attributes of a single god. Buddhism and Jainism are outside the Hindu tradition but are regarded as related religions.

  o *Buddhism*—a religion originated in India by Buddha (Gautama) and later spreading to China, Burma, Japan, Tibet, and parts of southeast Asia, holding that life is full of suffering caused by desire and that the way to end this suffering is through enlightenment that enables one to halt the endless sequence of births and deaths to which one is otherwise subject.

  o *Taoism*—also known as Hsüan Chiao (shawn jowl), a popular Chinese system of religion and philosophy claiming to be teachings of Laozi but also incorporating pantheism and sorcery. The philosophy of Lao Zi (sixth century BC Chinese philosopher) that advocates a simple honest life and noninterference with the course of natural events. Its followers attempt to live according to the Tao—the "Way," which they believe governs the universe.

  o *Western occultism*—occult of or pertaining to magic, astrology, or any system claiming use or knowledge of secret or supernatural powers or agencies...beyond the range of ordinary knowledge or understanding. It's mysterious...secret, disclosed, or communicated only to the initiated. It's hidden from view...

not apparent on mere inspection but discoverable by experimentation.

- Its organized religious forms are New Thought, Christian Science, Unity School of Christianity, Life Spring, and even forms of witchcraft—all of which provides an eclectic blend of New Age ideology with psychology, mind dynamic, and religious ideas.

- New Age is open to all ways to Nirvana or heaven except Christianity. It is the fastest growing religion in the United States. The goal is to establish a "One World Religion."

- The majority of people in New Age are Evangelical Christians who grew up in cessations churches who are looking for real power. (These Christians are our Methodist, Lutheran, Protestant, Baptist, and even Catholic friends, neighbors, and for some of us family, who grew up listening to moralistic sermons with no real power manifestations in their churches. New Age religion offers them real power manifestations.)

- New Age despises two things—rational science and Christianity. *Why?* Because rational science can disprove them and looks at the human body as a machine and Christianity holds the key to the truth and can expose their deceit.

- New Ages tells us that they believe a messianic figure is coming to bring us into the Age of Aquarius. They also blame Christianity for standing in the way.

- New Age takes on an appearance of scientific teaching and/or Christian practice and twists it to something that is not truth but makes it sound as though it is the truth or scientific—much like Satan did in Genesis when he took on the appearance of the serpent to cause doubt in God's word and alienate God's people from Him.

- New Age Religion doesn't come from the east; it started in America. It came out of New England; the roots of it came from esoteric religions of "New Thought" and Theosophical Society of the nineteenth century. Satan's plan, to be more specific, the plan of one religion, began in Genesis 3.

Theosophical Society and How It Influenced Society[2]

- The Theosophical Society was developed by three people. Its founder, Henry Steel Olcott, was born in New Jersey into an English Puritan family in 1832. Mr. Olcott became Colonel Olcott and special commissioner of the war department.
- The cofounder, Helena Petrovna Blavatsky, was born in Southern Russia on the 12 of August 1831.
- Here are some interesting quotes, "Madame Blavatsky stands out as the fountainhead of modern occult thought and was either the originator and/or popularize of many of the ideas and terms which have a century later been assembled within the New Age Movement. The Theosophical Society, which she cofounded, has been the major advocate of occult philosophy in the West and the single most important avenue of Eastern teaching to the West" (Melton, Clark, and Kelly 1991, p. 16).

"Helena Petrovna Blavatsky is surely among the most original and perceptive minds of her time. Buried in the sprawling bulk of her two major books...there lies, in rudimentary form,

---

[2] www.ts-adyar.org & www.blavatskyarchives.com

the first philosophy of psychic and spiritual evolution to appear in the modern West. With all criticisms weighed up against her, HPB stands forth as a seminal talent of our time. Above all, she is among the modern world's trailblazing psychologists of the visionary mind. At the same historical moment that Freud, Pavlov, and James had begun to formulate the secularized and materialist theory of mind that has so far dominated modern Western thought. HPB and her fellow theosophists were rescuing from occult tradition and exotic religion a forgotten psychology of the super conscious and the extrasensory. Madame Blavatsky may be credited with having set the style for modern occult literature" (Roszak 1975, pp. 118, 124–125).

- Third, William Judge (1851–1896) was born in Ireland but became a naturalized citizen of US at twenty-one years old. Passed bar and practiced commercial law. He was a pupil of HPB and believed in her vision; he would eventually split from Olcott and Besant in India and take over the TS in America after HPB's death. He was editor of the TS magazine *The Path*.
- Here is an interesting quote from his first Publication, "The Christian nations have dazzled themselves with a baneful glitter of material progress. They are not the peoples who will furnish the clearest clues to the Path… The Grand Clock of the Universe points to another hour, and now man must seize the key in his hands and himself—as a whole—open the gate… Our practice consists in a disregard of any authority in matters of religion and philosophy except such propositions as from their innate quality we feel to be true."
- The Theosophical Society, founded in 1875, is a worldwide body whose primary object is universal brotherhood

without distinction based on the realization that life and all its diverse forms, human and nonhuman, is indivisibly one.

- Theosophy is the wisdom underlying all religions. It offers a philosophy which renders life intelligible and demonstrates that justice and love guide the cosmos. Its teachings aid the unfolding of the latent spiritual nature in the human being without dependence.

The Emblem of the Theosophical Society

It is composed of several symbols, all of which have been used from very ancient times to express profound spiritual and philosophical concepts about the human being and the universe. They are found in a variety of forms in the great religions of the world and their universality is further shown by their appearance in widely separated cultures. Each symbol studied separately will yield a wealth of understanding. Taken together, as in this emblem, they suggest a vast evolutionary process embracing the whole of nature, physical, and spiritual, and their study may lead the serious inquirer to contemplate some of the deepest mysteries of existence. Partly because of their antiquity and partly because of the difficulty of establishing their origin, the symbols cannot be interpreted with a narrow precision.

The Motto

Surrounding the emblem runs the motto of the Theosophical Society, "There is no religion higher than truth." Truth is the quest of every theosophist, whatever their faith, and every great religion reflects in some measure the light of the one eternal and spiritual wisdom.

The chief cause of nearly two-thirds of the evils that pursue humanity...is religion under whatever form and in whatsoever nation. It is the sacerdotal caste (priestly class), the priesthood and the churches; it is in those illusions that man looks upon as sacred, that he has to search out the source of that multitude of evils which is the great curse of humanity and that almost overwhelms mankind. Ignorance created God and cunning took advantage of the opportunity. It is priestly imposture that rendered these gods so terrible to man; it is religion that makes of him the selfish bigot, the fanatic that hates all mankind out of his own sect without rendering him any better or more moral for it. It is belief in God and gods that makes two-thirds of humanity the slaves of a handful of those who deceive them under the false presence of saving them. Is not man ever ready to commit any kind of evil if told that his god or gods demand the crime?... For two thousand years India groaned under the weight of caste, Brahmins alone feeding on the fat of the land, and today the followers of Christ and those of Muhammad are cutting each other's throats in the name of and for the greater glory of their respective myths. Remember the sum of human misery will never be diminished until the day when the better portion of humanity destroys in the name of truth, morality and universal charity, the altars of their false gods. (Mahatma Letters, p. 57)

The Ankh

In the center of the two interlaced triangles is what is known as the ankh (or the Crux Ansata). This comprises a circle surmounting the Tau Cross (the type of cross which follows the shape of the letter *T*). The ankh is an Egyptian symbol of great antiquity, and it portrays the resurrection of the spirit out of its encasement of matter, otherwise expressed as the triumph of life over death, of spirit over matter, of good over evil. This concept of the "resurrection" is found in all the great religions.

The Interlaced Triangles

These are often called the Double Triangle, viewed by the Jewish Cabalists as the Seal of Solomon and known as Sri Yantra and Satkona Chakram in the Indian tradition. They are surrounded by a serpent. This combination of the triangle and the surrounding serpent symbolizes the created universe through which creation is limited in time and space. The triangles, looked at separately, symbolize the three facets of the manifestation which is known as the Trinity in various religions and personified in Christianity as Father, Son, and Holy Ghost and in Hinduism as Shiva, Vishnu, and Brahma. The darker of the two triangles, which is downward pointing; and the lighter triangle, which is upward pointing, symbolize respectively the descent of the life of Spirit into matter and the ascent of that life out of matter into Spirit—the perpetual opposition between the light and dark forces in nature and in man.

The Serpent

Apart from the significance of its surrounding the triangles as mentioned above, the serpent itself has always been a symbol of wisdom. The Hindus call their wise men "Nagas" (a word meaning serpent). Christ adjured His disciples to be as "wise as serpents." What is known as the *Uraeus* (or sacred Cobra) seen on the forehead of a Pharaoh of Egypt denoted his initiation into the sacred rites where knowledge was gained of the hidden wisdom. The serpent swallowing its tail represents the "circle of the universe," the endlessness of the cyclic process of manifestation.

The Swastika

This is another of the numerous forms in which the cross is found. It is the Fiery Cross with arms of whirling flame revolving (clockwise) to represent the tremendous energies of nature incessantly creating and dissolving the forms through which the evolutionary process takes place. In religions which recognize three aspects of deity, the swastika is associated with the third aspect, the Third Person of the Trinity, who is the Creator—Brahma in Hinduism and the Holy Ghost in Christianity.

The Aum

Surmounting the emblem is the sacred word *om* of Hinduism in Sanskrit characters, the three letters representing the Trinity. There is also the idea of the creative word or *logos* sounding throughout and sustaining the universe. In the prologue of the Gospel according to John in the Holy Bible, we read, "In the beginning was the Word, and the Word was with God, and the Word was God."

- The Theosophical Society emblem symbolizes the Absolute God, both transcendent and immanent. God transcendent—that is, in and beyond creation (the sacred word *aum*)—overshadows the cycle of manifestation (serpent), energized by divine activity (swastika), and within this field of manifestation, the linked triangles of spirit and matter enshrine the symbol of immortality (the ankh). God immanent—that is, indwelling in all created forms.
- The emblem and all that each symbol represents and speaks volumes about the occult backgrounds of the Theosophical Society and that any practice, teaching, or impartation that traces back to this society is that of occult background and clearly no good can come from it.
- H. P. Blavatsky was established in the occult and studied for years under an occult master. It is the purposes of the occult to undermine established Christianity. Her major

area of study was in Esoteric doctrine such as channeling, ESP, contacting the dead, all which *Deuteronomy 18:9–12* warns us about.

Theosophy was considered by Blavatsky to be "the underlying basis of all the world religions and philosophies." In her book *The Key to Theosophy*, she stated the following about the meaning and origin of the term:

ENQUIRER. Theosophy and its doctrines are often referred to as a new-fangled religion. Is it a religion?

THEOSOPHIST. It is not. Theosophy is divine knowledge or science.

ENQUIRER. What is the real meaning of the term?

THEOSOPHIST. "Divine Wisdom" (Theosophia) or Wisdom of the gods, as (theogonia), genealogy of the gods. The word *theos* means a god in Greek, one of the divine beings, certainly not "God" in the sense attached in our day to the term. Therefore, it is not "wisdom of God," as translated by some, but divine wisdom such as that possessed by the gods. The term is many thousand years old.

ENQUIRER. What is the origin of the name?

THEOSOPHIST. It comes to us from the Alexandrian philosophers called lovers of truth, Philaletheians, from *phil* (loving) and *aletheia* (truth.) The name Theosophy dates from the third century of our era and began with Ammonius Saccas and his disciples, who started the Eclectic Theosophical system (http://en.wikipedia.org/wiki/Secret_Doctrine#Theosophy).

Last fact is that most members of TS are also members of Freemasonry…

Theosophical Society and Its Role in New Age

- Therapeutic touch is accepted worldwide by Christians, but its cofounder, Dora Kuntz, was at one time a president of the Theosophical Society.
- Theosophical Society and therapeutic touch share the same office in Craryville, New York.
- Theosophical Society is one of the most anti-Christian organizations in the world, outside communism, deeply rooted in New Thought also transmigration of the soul, reincarnation, and karma.
- Dora Kuntz is a self-proclaimed psychic. She was born with the ability to see subtle energies around people and other living beings. From childhood, she studied how to control these energies under Charles Webster Leadbeater from Australia, who was a seer occultist of the twentieth century and a high ranking official of the Theosophical Society. Dora fine-tuned this knowledge as a fine instrument in her hand that she can turn on or off at her will. Dora was very good at moving in and out of the occult realm.
- Dora teams up with Delores Krieger while a student at New York University. She took special courses on kinesis, clairvoyance, and fourth dimension as an aura around our bodies. This same aura is the "white" aura referred to in the advanced spirituality of the Masters of Ancient Wisdom known as "The Great White Brotherhood."
- Here are some other keys names and their associations with Theosophical Society that influence New Age:

1. *Alice A. Bailey.* Founder of the Lucis Trust in New York City (www.lucistrust.org) *Beacon Magazine* (1922 to present). The Arcane School (founded in 1923) which graduated over twenty thousand students by 1954. She authored many books such as *Discipleship in the New Age, The Externalization of Hierarchy,* and *The Treatise on Cosmic Fire.*

2. *Annie Wood Besant (1847–1933).* Was responsible for founding the British Federation of the International Order of Co-Freemasonry. Besant was intimately involved with Fabian socialism and was a member of the Fabian Society. Having been converted to the teachings of the Theosophical Society after a review of Madame Blavatsky's *The Secret Doctrine,* she joined the organization, rose in the ranks, becoming its head, first in Europe then the world. She was also one of the leaders of the Feminist movement.

3. *C. W. Leadbeater (1847–1934).* A 33o Freemason, a prolific author and teacher on occult subjects and Masonic history, an adept theosophist and prelate in the Liberal Catholic Church. He was a mystic and clairvoyant widely regarded by both his masonic brothers and other occultists of his time. His works on the occult origins of the craft are still widely read and printed, *Freemasonry and Its Ancient Mystic Rites and Hidden Life of Freemasonry,* being the most sought after. His greatest contributions to the world of the occult were by association with the Theosophical Society. He joined Theosophy in 1883 and traveled with its founder, Madame Helena Blavatsky, to India in 1884. He helped spread the teachings of Theosophy to a wide audience through "his ability to write and speak in a direct, convincing, simple popular style." Obscure concepts such as the "aura, reincarnation, vegetarianism, long hair, bare feet, the spiritual life as practiced in India and the bioenergetic field surrounding the human body" were easily grasped through his accessible exposition of the material.

4. *Manly Hall (1901–1990).* Unequaled, he is the most prolific occult philosopher of all time. No one in history has even come close to matching his literary output on the subject. Hall authored over two hundred books on occult subjects ranging from works on

astrology, the Bible, tarot, dreams, mysticism, Eastern and Western philosophy, religion, psychology, symbology, and reincarnation plus hundreds of essays and a monthly magazine published called the *PRS Journal*. From an early age, he was interested in occult matters and subsequently joined several societies: Theosophy, Freemasonry, the Societas Rosicruciana in Civitatibus Foederatis, and the American Federation of Astrologers.

5. *L. Frank Baum.* Author of children's fantasy novels, most famous for Wizard of Oz series.

6. *Paul Gauguin.* Celebrated French painter known for his warm paintings of Polynesian people.

7. *William Butler Yeats.* W. B. Yeats was an influential Irish poet. He received Novel Prize for Literature.

8. *Ruth Crawford-Seeger.* Composer.

9. *Dane Rudhyar.* Composer.

10. *Alexander Scriabin.* Composer.

11. *Sir Arthur Conan Doyle.* Writer of *Sherlock Holmes.*

12. *Lewis Carroll.* Author of *Alice in Wonderland.*

13. *Shirley MacLaine.* Actress and New Age activist.

14. *T. S. Eliot.* Poet and playwright.

15. *Carl Gustav Jung.* Swiss psychologist.

16. *Jack London.* Writer, rancher, and sailor.

17. *Thornton Wilder.* American playwright and novelist. He won three Pulitzer Prizes.

18. *Thomas Edison.* Inventor.

19. *Abner Doubleday.* Founder of baseball.

Nineteenth century esotericism is seen by some as completely secularized. Alchemy, magic, astrology, and other elements of traditional esotericism had been thoroughly integrated with aspects of modern culture, including the search for causal laws, evolutionism, psychology, and the study of religions. It reached its clearest form in the ideas of Helena Blavatsky.

What Does New Age Claim to Offer?

- *Spirituality, as it is referred to, however it should be called spiritualism* because it is a fascination with extraordinary manifestations and with paranormal entities. People recognized as "mediums" claim that their personality is taken over by another entity during trances in a New Age phenomenon known as "channeling" during which the medium may lose control over his or her body and faculties. These manifestations are indeed spiritual but are not from God, despite the language of love and light which is almost always used.

- *Angels are known as spirit guides.* There are many levels of guides, entities, energies, and beings in every octave of the universe. They are all there to pick and choose from in relation to your own attraction/repulsion mechanisms. These spiritual entities are often invoked "non-religiously" to help in relaxation aimed at better decision-making and control of one's life and career. Fusion with some spirits who teach through people is another New Age experience claimed by people who refer to themselves as "mystics." Some nature spirits are described as powerful energies existing in the natural world and on the "inner planes": i.e., those which are accessible using rituals, drugs, and other techniques for reaching altered states of consciousness. In theory at least, the New Age often recognizes no spiritual authority higher than personal inner experience.

- *Harmony and peace.* There is no distinction between good and evil. Human actions are the fruit of either illumination or ignorance. Hence, we cannot condemn anyone and nobody needs forgiveness. Believing in the existence of evil can create only negativity and fear. The answer to negativity is love. But it is not the sort which has to be translated into deeds; it is more a question of attitudes of mind. Love is energy, a high-frequency vibration, and the secret to happiness and health and success is being able to tune in to find one's place in the great chain of being. New Age teachers and

221

therapies claim to offer the key to finding the correspondences between all the elements of the universe so that people may modulate the tone of their lives and be in absolute harmony with each other and with everything around them.

- *Health and healing.* Alternative therapies have gained enormously in popularity because they claim to look at the whole person and are about healing rather than curing. Holistic health, as it is known, concentrates on the important role that the mind plays in physical healing. The connection between the spiritual and the physical aspects of the person is said to be in the immune system or the Indian chakra system. In a New Age perspective, illness and suffering came from working against nature. When one is in tune with nature, one can expect a much healthier life and even material prosperity. For some New Age healers, there should be no need for us to die.

There is a remarkable variety of approaches for promoting holistic health, some derived from ancient cultural traditions, whether religious or esoteric, others connected with the psychological theories developed in Esalen during the years 1960–1970. Advertising connected with New Age covers a wide range of practices as acupuncture, biofeedback, chiropractic, kinesiology, homeopathy, iridology, massage and various kinds of "bodywork" (such as orgonomy, Feldenkrais, reflexology, Rolfing, polarity massage, therapeutic touch, etc.), meditation and visualization, nutritional therapies, psychic healing, various kinds of herbal medicine, healing by crystals, metals, music or colors, reincarnation therapies, and finally, twelve-step programs and self-help groups. The source of healing is said to be within ourselves. Something we reach when we are in touch with our inner energy or cosmic energy.

Energy Healing Modalities

The move from a mechanistic model of classical physics to the "holistic" one of modern atomic and subatomic physics based on the concept of matter as waves or energy rather than particles is central to much New Age thinking. The universe is an ocean of energy, which is a single whole or a network of links. The energy animating the single organism which is the universe is "spirit." There is no difference between God and the world. The world itself is divine, and it undergoes an evolutionary process which leads from inert matter to "higher and perfect consciousness." The world is uncreated, eternal, and self-sufficient the future of the world is based on an inner dynamism which is necessarily positive and leads to the reconciled (divine) unity of all that exists. God and the world, soul and body, intelligence and feeling, and heaven and earth are one immense vibration of energy (Jesus the Bearer, p. 18).

Let's look at chakras *for a minute* because they are the central channels for all energy healing modalities.

The chakras are described as being aligned in an ascending column from the base of the spine to the top of the head. New Age practices often associate each chakra with a certain color. In various traditions, chakras are associated with multiple physiological functions—an aspect of consciousness, a classical element, and other distinguishing characteristics. They are visualized as lotuses/flowers with a different number of petals in every chakra.

They are considered loci (locus) of life energy or prana. It's also called Shakti, *qi* (Chinese; *ki* in Japanese), which is thought to flow among them along pathways called *nadis*. *Nāḍi* (literally "river," here in the sense "tube, pipe") are the channels through which, in traditional Indian medicine and spiritual science, the energies of the subtle body are said to flow. They connect at special points of intensity called chakras.

The function of the chakras is to spin and draw in this energy to keep the spiritual, mental, emotional, and physical health of the body in balance. They are said by some to reflect the unified consciousness of humanity.

Kundalini spirit is the one most noted with this healing modality and is described as a sleeping, dormant potential force in the human organism. It is one of the components of an esoteric description of the "subtle body," which consists of nadis (energy channels), chakras (psychic centers), prana (subtle energy), and Bindu (drops of essence).

Kundalini is described as being coiled up at the base of the spine. The description of the location can vary slightly from the rectum to the navel. The Kundalini has been described as "a residual power of pure desire" by Nirmala Srivastava. The image given is that of a serpent coiled three and a half times around a smoky gray lingam. Each coil is said to represent one of the three gunas, with the half coil signifying transcendence.

Typical kundalini symptoms are as follows:

- Burning hot or ice cold streams moving up the spine
- Perhaps a feeling of air bubbles or snake movement up through the body
- Pains in varying locations throughout the body
- Titillation of the genital area, spine, or head
- Tension or stiffness of neck and headaches
- Feeling of overpressure within the head
- Vibrations, unease, or cramps in legs and other parts of the body
- Fast pulse and increased metabolism
- Disturbance in the breathing and/or heart function
- Sensitivity to sound, light, smell, and proximity of other people
- Orgasm sensations different places in the body or total cosmic orgasms
- Mystical/religious experiences, revelations, and/or cosmic glimpses
- Parapsychological abilities, light phenomena in or outside the body
- Problems with finding balance between strong sexual urges and a wish to live in sublime purity

- Persistent anxiety or anxiety attacks due to lack of understanding of what is going on
- Insomnia, manic high spirits, or deep depression, energy loss
- Impaired concentration and memory
- Total isolation due to inability to communicate inner experiences out
- Experiences of possession and poltergeist phenomena

Therapeutic touch is widely accepted in America.

I found it very interesting that on the Therapeutic Touch International website listed under TT facts, it states this, "Anyone can be a TT healer. All it requires is motivation and desire!" There are certain criteria that one must have: compassion, the willingness to learn the process, do the "inner work" that is essential, and continually challenge one's self with the question "Why do I want to be a healer?" It helps to know how the physical body works.

If healing is their practice then why on this "facts" page is there absolutely no mention of healing results, only the fact that "anyone" can be a TT healer?

Therapeutic Touch

Other names are energy field therapy, biofield therapy. Similar practice is called healing touch.

A. *Definition*

The American Cancer Society describes TT as a technique in which the hands are used to direct human energy for healing purposes. There is usually no physical contact. This practice is based on the belief that problems in the patient's energy field that caused the illness and pain can be identified and rebalanced by a healer. Harmful energy is believed to cause blockages and other problems in patients' normal energy flow and TT claims to remove those blockages and bring relief and or healing in conditions such as pain, fever, swelling, infections, wounds, ulcers, thyroid problems, colic, burns, nausea, premenstrual syndrome diarrhea, and headaches. Diseases it is said to treat are measles, Alzheimer's disease, AIDS, asthma, autism, multiple sclerosis, stroke, comas, and cancer. TT is usually used with standard medical treatment.

A session would be between ten to thirty minutes on a clothed patient, sitting or standing or normally lying down.

Step one is "centering." Centering is when the practitioners quits his or herself and makes every effort to clear their mind so that they may communicate with the patient's energy field so they may locate the blockages that are to be the source of the illness or pain.

Step two involves an assessment. This is where the practitioner will hold their hands about two to six inches above the patient's body, palm facing downward, pass their hands over the patient's entire body head to toe. This is done to locate the blockages.

Step three is when the practitioner will then conduct several passes over the patient's body with their hands, and at the end of each pass, the practitioner will then make this flicking motion into the air past the toes which is said to be releasing harmful energy in the patient.

In the last step, the therapists now transfer their own excess of health energy to the patient.

B. *Healing Claims*

TT is effective in decreasing anxiety, decreasing stress, evoking the relaxation response, decreasing pain, and promoting wound healing.

C. *Scientific Evaluation*

ASC says that the scientific evidence does not support many claims made by therapeutic touch or that energy is balanced or transferred using TT. Based on scientific studies, there is no evidence that

226

TT can cure cancer or any other diseases. *This scientific evidence is falling on deaf ears in America* and in the world.

D. *Roots and Fruit*

Somewhat like Reiki also compared to "laying on of hands" in Christianity. There are different Asian cultures that believe life energy flows through invisible pathways in the body. The masters of Qigong, Hinduism, Buddhism, Taoism, Shinto, Munay-Ki, and Shamanic energy healers also share similar beliefs. Energy healing can be traced back almost five thousand years through some of these ancient religions.

E. *Biblical/Christian Evaluation*

It's high level demonic activity.

F. *Potential Dangers*

The energy behind therapeutic touch is not the Holy Spirit, but there is a spirit that is present during these sessions and there is in the spirit realm a real transference of energy called demonic transference. When we come into agreement with such a practice, we are making the agreement with the generational, religious, and territorial spirits already assigned and attached to ritual practice.

Reiki

A. *Definition*

Reiki is a word that is made up of two Japanese words—*rei* which means "supernatural knowledge or spiritual consciousness." This wisdom comes from "god" (oneness) or higher self. The all-knowing "god" consciences understand each person completely.

Ki (chi in Chinese) which means "life force energy." Chi or ki is widely used in martial arts and by shamans in all cultures for "divination" (an act of seeing the future or discovering what is hidden or obscure by supernatural or magical means).

Ki is a nonphysical energy used by all Reiki healers. It is the "god" consciences "Rei" that calls forth the "Ki" life force in the practice of Reiki. Reiki can be defined as spiritually guided life force energy. Reiki guides itself on its own wisdom and is unresponsive to the practitioner.

B. *Healing Claims*

Reiki is a Japanese technique for stress reduction and relaxation that also promotes healing. It is believed that if your "life force energy" is low, then one is susceptible to illness and feels stress. If it is high, then one will be happier, stress free, and healthier.

C. *Scientific Evaluation*

People are experiencing relief of illness and receiving a transference of depression.

D. *Roots and Fruit*

It is traced back past the Ming dynasty; however, in studies, it has similar structure as Hinduism which traces back at least five thousand years. Its means of entering the United States was one of deception. Reiki was repackaged for the Western world in the 1940s. Why? Because it was known that the Western world had a Christian worldview. A myth was created that this Buddhist monk (Mikao Usui or Usui Sensei) was a Christian man who taught the practice of Reiki to Chujiro Hayashi to mislead Americans because this was a Japanese practice and Pearl Harbor had just happened. It was imported by Mrs. Takata, a Hawaiian resident. She embellished the Christian aspect so that Christians would accept Reiki.

E. *Biblical/Christian Evaluation*

This power is aligned with demonic and occult powers but accredits itself to Jesus. Let me remind you of Deuteronomy 18:9–12. God is very clear in His warning against divination, charmers, medium, psychics, etc. Reiki involves mediums and divination and ignores the Bible.

F. *Potential Dangers*

Self-guided energy is not Holy Spirit's; therefore, it is totally demonic! There is absolutely no faith needed to be healed.

Reiki Attunement and Christian Impartation

The Reiki attunement process is how one becomes a Reiki practitioner. Being attuned to Reiki gives one the ability to easily access the Reiki (universal life force) energy, for healing a person or situation. Attunements can be given only by a Reiki master and can be given for either the purpose of training one in Reiki, or for simply giving someone a larger experience of Reiki than usually experienced in treatments.

The attunement procedure is a ceremony of spirit. In this ceremony, the Reiki master uses the Reiki symbols and other gestures in a prescribed way. This ceremony creates an energy pattern around the recipient of the attunement which entrains (or attunes) their energy field to the energies represented by the symbols. The attunement is permanent, thus making the recipient a Reiki practitioner, only if the master uses the symbol for the "subconscious." If this symbol is not used the entrainment is temporary only.

In this ceremony, the master does the following:

Grounds and centers themselves. Instructs the recipient(s) in grounding and centering themselves. Reminds the recipients this is their ceremony and to be open to all experiences which happen. Perhaps puts on some mood setting music, lights incense, etc. The Master starts standing in front of the recipients and it is traditional for him/her to hold their hands up high at shoulder height with palms facing forward. The recipients should be seated in a row with room around them for the Master to walk around them easily.

- Walk around the recipients one full circle and then behind the row again standing behind the first recipient.
- There are two halves to the ceremony, one part done behind the recipient, the other part done in front.
- Hold the left-hand palm up next to the recipient's head. The left hand generally receives energy while the right hand generally gives energy.
- With the right hand, draws the symbols over the crown of the recipient's head.
- When done with their backsides, walk around to the front. At the front take the recipients hands between your own for a moment.
- Draw the symbols over the hand. Drawing each symbol once, and as you draw silently chanting the name of the symbol three times.

- Visualize the master symbol in violet and lightly blow, twice, from the base chakra to the crown chakra.
- Lightly touch the forehead (third eye).
- Draw the symbols over the forehead (third eye). Again, drawing each symbol once, and chanting the name of the symbol three times.
- Gently separate the hands.
- Visualize the master symbol again and gently blow from base to crown.
- Visualize the master symbol in the palm of your right hand and hold it over the recipient's left hand. Lightly slap the palm of your right hand into the palm of their left hand.
- Visualize the master symbol in the palm of your left hand and hold it over the recipient's right hand. Again, lightly slap your palm into theirs.
- Visualize the master symbol and gently blow into the area between their hands while bringing their palms together again.
- Give back their hands and gently touch them in the heart area, visualizing that you've given them back to themselves.
- Step back and bow, honoring them for who they are.
- Once all the recipients have been attuned make another circle around them, ending up in front again. (The Reiki Page)

The Reiki Symbols
Symbol, Symbol Name, Purpose, and Meaning

Body

- Cho-Ku-Rei
  o Increase power
  o "Put the power here" or "*God* is here" (*you will see this capitalized but it is not Our Abba)*
  o Mind
- Sei-He-Ki
  o Emotional, purification, protection, clearing
  o "Key to the universe" or "Man and god becoming one"
  o Spirit
- Hon-Sha-Ze-Sho-Nen
  o Distant healing, *Akashic records*, past-present-future
  o "The Buddha in me reaches out to the Buddha in you to promote enlightenment and peace"
  o Master
  o Dai-Ko-Myo
  o Passing attunements
  o Reiki mastership, "man-woman-universe = whole energy"

The Power Reiki Symbol

Japanese name: Cho Ku Rei, *body symbol*
Intention: Light switch
Purposes: Manifestation, increased power, accelerated healing, healing catalyst. The Cho Ku Rei (power symbol) is used to increase power and decrease power (when used in reverse). This symbol looks like a coil. The coil is meant to expand and retract, regulating the flow of "ki" energies. Sometimes, a subtle energy flow is needed whereas other times, a blast of energy is better. Praised

for its manifestation power. This symbol is a wonderful law of attraction focusing tool.

The Harmony Reiki Symbol

Japanese name: Sei Hei Ki, *mind symbol*
Intention: Purification
Purposes: Cleansing, protection, mental and emotional healing. The Sei Hei Ki symbolizes harmony. Call it peacemaker or harmonizer if you like, but the Sei Hei Ki will refuse to negotiate an unfair outcome. It truly is a protective shield of armor. It gives courage to the disheartened and helps to level the playing field when life's hard knocks is kicking your butt. It scorches addictions and expels negative energies. Make this symbol your best bud, and it will not let you down. Sei Hei Ki is loyal friend, especially whenever you are facing difficulties.

The Connection Reiki Symbol

Japanese name: Hon Sha Ze Sho Nen, *spirit symbol*
Intention: Timelessness
Purposes: Distant healing, past/present/future, healing karma, spiritual connection. Best known for its extension powers, the Hon Sha Ze Sho Nen symbol is used when sending Reiki in a long distance. It symbolizes a shape shifter that can slip through time and space. Another name for this symbol is "Pagoda" (temple or secrete building) because of its tower like appearance. Elastic in texture, it is a fun symbol to play with during your healing visualizations. Hon Sha Ze Sho Nen can also transform itself into a key that will unlock the Akashic records. For this reason, this symbol is an essential tool for the Reiki practitioner when working on inner child or past live issues with their clients.

The Master Reiki Symbol

Japanese name: Dai Ko Myo
Intention: Enlightenment
Purposes: Empowerment, soul healing, oneness. This master symbol
represents all that is Reiki. Dai Ko Myo is the heart of Reiki.
The symbol is seldom used for any particular purpose other
than as a reminder that Reiki is love and available to everyone.

The Completion Reiki Symbol

Japanese name: Raku
Intention: Grounding
Purposes: Kundalini healing, hara connection, chakra alignment.
The Raku symbol is used solely during the final stage of the
Reiki attunement process. Its intention is to ground and seal
the newly awakened Reiki energies. The striking lightning bolt
symbol is drawn downwards from the heavens to the earth.

Akashic (Akasha) records is a recorded philosophies of India. The
ether, regarded as including material and nonmaterial *entities* in a
common medium. The Akashic records are an energetic imprint of
every thought, action, emotion, and experience that has ever occurred
in time and space.

Lie is the system, then, contains the same trinity which appears
in all spiritual systems.

The body/mind/spirit trinity which can be read many ways
(ego/subconscious/super conscious, self/family/all, father/son/Holy
Ghost, etc.).

Energy Psychotherapy

A. *Definition*

Psychotherapy is a general term for treating mental health problems by talking with a psychiatrist, psychologist, or other mental health provider.

During psychotherapy, you learn about your condition and your moods, feelings, thoughts, and behaviors. Psychotherapy helps you learn how to take control of your life and respond to challenging situations with healthy coping skills. There are many specific types of psychotherapy, each with its own approach. The type of psychotherapy that's right for you depends on your individual situation. Psychotherapy is also known as talk therapy, counseling, psychosocial therapy, or simply, therapy (Mayo Clinic).

So what is *energy* psychotherapy? Association for Comprehensive Energy Healing says that energy psychology interventions address the various aspects of the human "subtle energy system" including the following:

- Energy pathways: meridians and acupoints
- Energy centers: chakras and vortices
- Human energy field: the human biofield or "aura"

Energy psychology is used by practitioners for treating and relieving those suffering from emotional challenges such as addictions and compulsions, anxiety, depression, limiting beliefs, personality disorders, phobias, stress, and trauma.

- Maximizing human performance in business, sports, and the arts
- Supporting the healthy development and well-being of individuals and groups
- Increasing compassion, understanding, and peace throughout the world

B. *Healing Claims*

Positive clinical and experimental outcomes have shown EP methods to help alleviate multitude of issues including trauma and PTSD, anxiety and phobias, depression, addictions, weight management, and pain. They have also been found to support improvement in school, sports, and work performance.

C. *Scientific Evaluation*

This approach to mental and physical health is currently being studied by the National Institutes of Health, the Kaiser Foundation, and the Veterans Administration. Though scientific study of energy psychology modalities is in it its early phases, the growing body of clinical research has thus far been very promising. MRI and QEEG results have shown positive brain activity after the use of energy psychology techniques.

D. *Roots and Fruit*

Esoteric philosophies tied to Hinduism and Theosophy through the ancient wisdom techniques.

E. *Various Names*

Emotional Freedom Techniques (EFT), Thought Field Therapy (TFT), Tapas Acupressure Technique (TAT), EDXTM, Comprehensive Energy Psychology (CEP), Matrix Energetics, and Sandplay and HeartMath. (Sandplay Therapy by Dora Kalff, a Jungian therapist, developed sandplay therapy in Switzerland in the 1950s and '60s based on her studies at the C. G. Jung Institute, Zurich, in Tibetan Buddhism and with Margaret Lowenfeld in England.)

Summary

The client is given the possibility by means of figures and the arrangement of the sand in the area bounded by the sandbox to set up a world corresponding to his or her inner state. In this manner, through free, creative play, unconscious processes are made visible in a three-dimensional form and a pictorial world comparable to the dream experience. Through a series of images that take shape in this way, the process of individuation described by C. G. Jung is stimulated and brought to fruition.

Shamanic Energy Medicine

Shamanic energy medicine is a holistic approach of healing based on ancient wisdom and techniques of the shamans from the high mountains of the Andes. The shaman interacts with the spirit world on behalf of another person, providing healing assistance on a physical, mental, emotional, and spiritual level.

Shamanic energy medicine uses the energies of the great archetypes, the organizing principles of the universe. Energy healing techniques work with your body's luminous energy field and energy centers called chakras to gently achieve transformation and balance.

- *The Illumination Process* clears the imprints of karma and disease from the luminous energy field and brings about healing at the source of your being.
- *The Extraction Process* extracts both hardened and intrusive energies. Energies such as fear, envy, and anger can penetrate the luminous energy field which create emotional and physical dysfunction. Extracting intrusive energies can decrease symptoms of anxiety, depression, and other disorders.
- *Soul Retrieval* recovers our essential whole self that has been lost as a result of pain or trauma. The practitioner will journey to retrieve your lost soul part and reclaim your grace. Soul retrieval can accomplish in a few sessions what can sometimes take years to achieve in conventional therapy.

- *Destiny Retrieval* reveals the luminous threads and potential that you have yet to bring into your awareness and finds your destiny. It assists you in stepping into your becoming.
- *Decoupling of the Fight or Flight* is a form of deep relaxation which creates a safe and sacred space to assists an individual to relieve the brain and disengage the body from their fight or flight response. The decoupling process releases anxiety, stress, and fear, allowing one to attain calmness and peacefulness.
- *Munay-Ki Rites* are the nine great rites of initiation of the Inka medicine way. The rites of the Munay-Ki are experienced in the form of energetic transmissions that heal our wounds and transform our luminous energy field. These sacred rites bring us back into "Ayni," a balanced relationship with nature and with each other. The Munay-Ki rites help us to embrace the fullness of our becoming (munay-ki.org). The Four Winds Society is approved with the California Board of Registered Nursing and CA Board of Behavioral Sciences (as a continuing education). National Certification Board for Therapeutic Massage and Bodywork as well as National Association for Social Workers.
- *Despacho Ceremony* is an Andean practice of making offerings of gratitude to Pachamama (mother earth) and the Apus (mountain spirits). A Despacho is an act of love and an opportunity to create a sacred connection with all beings, elements, spirits, and sacred places. A Despacho ceremony brings us into harmony with ourselves and with all of creation. The offerings are composed of a variety of items, each with its own symbolic meaning. The items are arranged on a piece of white paper infused with prayers of gratitude and intentions for manifestation. These prayers are then "dispatched" to the spirits by burning the Despacho in a sacred fire ceremony.
- *Dying Consciously and Final Death Rites* are the great rites of passage. The death rites assist the person who is making

the journey beyond death by allowing their soul to rest in a peaceful manner. The dying process guides the individual and family members to find emotional resolution and how to make the transition of this life with grace and dignity (www.luminoushealing.ca/energy.html).

- *Qigong or Qi Revolution* is a five thousand-year-old energy art for strengthening the flow of life force and improving health. Two hundred million people are practicing Qigong worldwide. A long-kept secret it was seldom taught outside family bloodlines and royalty in China. Qigong was passed down from father to son and used in the military to build the bodies endurance. It enhances energy rather than depletes it, and it is said to increase sex drive and healing energy. Arteries pulse with great vigor and at the same time remain calm, focused, and in a relaxed state. It is said to be the most significant self-empowerment technique on earth. No matter a person's culture or beliefs, the results are the same with a clearer relationship to the "True Source."

In April of 2010 on the fortieth anniversary of Earth Day in Los Angeles, there was a coming together of Supreme Science of Qigong foundation, James Cameron and the cast of the film *Avatar*. In partnership with the mayor of Los Angeles and Los Angeles partnership schools, they brought in six thousand "at-risk" students for a special screening of *Avatar* and the first ever ECO warrior training with a level 3 SSQF trainer. The event coordinators were so impressed with the response of the students that they decided to implement Supreme Science Qi into their curriculum in the fall (2010).

Our next generation is being invaded!

Energy Healing Modalities and Our Children

Children are exposed to a variety of stressful situations with their family, friends, school, and bullies. Some children experiencing feelings of stress, frustration, helplessness, and anger can be overwhelmed. They often do not recognize and express their emotions or release their feelings. They can become depressed and restless. These emotions lead to behaviors that may be misdiagnosed with disorders.

These children are suffering in silence, troubled by issues that adults do not recognize. Often when things go wrong, children blame themselves. They feel ashamed, embarrassed, or angry and hold themselves responsible for the situation.

Most children are very sensitive and aware of their surroundings. They carry the energy of the stories and wounds of their loved ones, eventually becoming their own stories and wounds. These energies do not belong to them.

Shamanic energy medicine is promoted to be effective in working with children that do not feel like talking about what is bothering them. In contrast to conventional therapy, this work takes place in a purely energetic environment using crystals and tools found in nature. Practitioners SEM say children can relate to this environment which helps to decrease their anxiety. Children are very accepting of different approaches, and they welcome new and fun experiences. They truly do not want to be stuck in their story, and they can transform their negative experiences into positive ones. Healing becomes a gentle and empowering experience for them.

All children are light beings; they carry within them the source of light. They are the new evolution of our human species. They are here to show us the way to remind us that we once had that light within us.

Children with Special Needs

Although spectrums of learning disorders, autism, Asperger's, and ADHD are considered disabilities. Perhaps we can view them in a new light and start to consider them as gifts and divine purpose.

We are all spiritual beings here on earth with a unique and special purpose. Our children are born with the gifts and talents to remind us of that purpose. All children are gifted with immeasurable potential to heal our world, perhaps better entrusted are children with spectrums of autism and ADHD. Many of these children are also considered to be star children. They hold the wisdom and awareness of the consciousness shift that is presently taking place. They hold a sacred space for our evolution. Each spectrum is described as a very distinct condition with a long list of symptoms.

These special children vibrate with a different frequency due to their direct connection to spirit. These sensitive and gentle beings perceive our seen and unseen world at the deepest levels. They are angels on earth radiating divine light naturally with a supernatural intensity to inspire us to find our higher selves.

They have a deep appreciation for beauty and nature with a genuine connection with animals and all living creatures. They are highly sensitive to our environment and can sense the world of energy.

They struggle with academics, constant sense of failure, low self-esteem, rejection, lack of supportive relationships, anxiety and depression—only to name a few. They learned at a very young age that they are different, and their disabilities separate them from the rest. Unfortunately, some grow up desensitizing their pain through drugs and alcohol, and sadly, some attempt to end their own existence on this earth. We must recognize their spiritual intelligence and unlimited possibilities so we can support their journey. We all are divine beings with extraordinary abilities to demonstrate compassion, sensitivity, patience, and unconditional love to all who have chosen to come into our lives. This is our divine purpose.

This is being taught to our Children in different healing therapies.

Star Children

Star children are also known as the rainbow, crystal, and indigo children. Star children come from all corners of the universe. They are star beings who have been sent to earth to assist humanity with the evolution and rebirth of our new world. Their divine presence alone can assist others in the transformation to their higher selves. Through their vibrations of peace and unconditional love, they will shift our old paradigm and cocreate with us a new dimension of consciousness.

Star children may appear like ordinary human beings; however, they possess extraordinary human potential. These human angels have direct access to spiritual realms. Star children are exceptionally creative, sensitive, and clairvoyant. These star spirits have come to remind us that we are all spirits in human bodies vibrating as one. Their purpose is to bring heaven to earth.

The following extract comes from Doreen Virtue's article "Indigo, Crystal, and Rainbow Children."

Indigo, Crystal and Rainbow Children

Meet the Rainbow Children! They are the embodiment of our divinity and the example of our potential. The Rainbow Children have never lived on this planet before, and they're going straight to the Crystal Children as their moms and dads. These children are entirely fearless of everybody. They're little avatars who are all about service. These are children who are only here to give—Rainbow Children are already at their spiritual peak.

Then, there's the Crystal Children. The first thing that most people notice about them is their eyes--large, penetrating and wise beyond their years. The Crystal Children's eyes lock on and hypnotize you, while you realize your soul is being laid bare for these children to see. Perhaps you've noticed this special new "breed" of children rapidly populating our planet. They are happy, delightful and forgiving. This generation of new light workers, roughly ages 0 through 7, is like no previous generation. Ideal in many ways, Crystal Children are the pointers for where humanity is headed…and it's a good direction!

The older children (approximately ages 7 through 25), are called "Indigo Children".

They share some characteristics with the Crystal Children. Both generations are highly sensitive and psychic and have important life purposes. The main difference is their temperament. Indigos have a warrior spirit, because their collective purpose is to mash down old systems that no longer serve us. They are here to quash government, educational and legal systems that lack integrity. To accomplish this end, they need tempers and fiery determination.

Those adults who resist change and who value conformity may misunderstand the Indigos. They are often mislabeled with the psychiatric diagnoses of Attention Deficit with Hyperactivity Disorder (ADHD) or Attention Deficit Disorder (ADD). Sadly, when they're medicated, The Indigos often lose their beautiful sensitivity, spiritual gifts and warrior energy.

In contrast, the Crystal Children are blissful and even-tempered. Sure, they may have tantrums occasionally, but these children are largely forgiving and easy-going. The Crystals are the generation who benefit from the Indigos' trailblazing. First, the Indigo Children lead with a machete, cutting down anything that lacks integrity. Then the Crystal Children follow the cleared path, into a safer and more secure world. And now, the fearless Rainbow Children are pure givers ready to fulfill our needs.

The terms "Indigo", "Crystal" and "Rainbow" were given to these three generations, because they most accurately describe their aura colors and energy patterns. Indigo Children have a lot of indigo blue in their auras. This is the color of the "third eye chakra," which is an energy center inside the head located between the two eyebrows. This chakra regulates clairvoyance, or the ability to see energy, visions and spirits

Many of the Indigo Children are clairvoyant. The Crystal Children have opalescent auras, with beautiful multicolor in pastel hues. This generation also shows a fascination for crystals and rocks. The Rainbow Children radiate rainbow energy, the kind that we were created with, to instill within us health and balance.

Indigo Children can sense dishonesty, like a dog can sense fear. Indigos know when they're being lied to, patronized, or manipulated. And since their collective purpose is to usher us into a new world of integrity, the Indigos' inner lie detectors are integral. As mentioned before, this warrior spirit is threatening to some adults. And the Indigos are unable to conform to dysfunctional situations at home, work, or school.

They don't have the ability to dissociate from their feelings and pretend like everything's okay…unless they're medicated or sedated.

Crystal Children's innate spiritual gifts are also misunderstood. Specifically, Crystal Children have telepathic abilities that lead them to talk later in life. In the new world, we will all be much more aware of our intuitive thoughts and feelings. We won't rely so much upon the spoken or written word. Communication will be faster, more direct and more honest, because it will be mind-to-mind. Already, increasing numbers of us are getting in touch with our psychic abilities. Our interest in the paranormal is at an all-time high, accompanied by books, television shows and movies on the topic.

The parents engage in mind-to-mind communication with their Crystal Children. And the

Crystals use a combination of telepathy, self-fashioned sign language and sounds (including song) to get their point across.

The diagnostic criterion for autism is quite clear. It states that the autistic person lives in his or her own world and is disconnected from other people. The autistic person doesn't talk because of an indifference to communicating with others.

Crystal Children are quite the opposite. They're among the most connected, communicative, caring and cuddly of any generation. They are also quite philosophical and spiritually gifted. And they display an unprecedented level of kindness and sensitivity to this world. Crystal Children spontaneously hug and care for people in need. An autistic person wouldn't do that!

ADHD should stand for Attention Dialed into a Higher Dimension. This would more accurately describe that generation. In the same vein, Crystal Children don't warrant a label of autism. They aren't autistic, they're AWE-tistic!

These children are worthy of awe, not labels of dysfunction. If anything is dysfunctional, it's the systems that aren't accommodating the continuing evolution of the human species. If we shame these children with labels, or medicate them into submission, we will have undermined a heaven-sent gift. We will crush a civilization before it has time to take roots. Fortunately, there are many positive solutions and alternatives. And the same heaven that sent us the Crystal Children can assist those of us who are advocates for these children. (www.luminoushealing.ca/energy.html)

Acupuncture and Acupressure

A. *Definition*

It used the belief that "energy flow" can be redirected to balance healing energies by inserting needles or by applying pressure to specific points on the body.

B. *Healing Claims*

It is centered on the supposed ability to stimulate the flow of cosmic life energy through alleged invisible channels or meridians in the body, meridian points on the surface of the body which supposedly refer to internal organs functions, cannot actually be seen or measured. It is believed that this stimulation can benefit organs and return their functions to normal.

C. *Scientific Evaluation*

Acupuncture has become a respectable research topic in universities and medical centers. Research has failed over the last twenty years to demonstrate that these two methods are altering any diseases.

D. *Roots and Fruit*

It is based in the occult religion of Taoism, an ancient Chinese healing incorporating pantheism and sorcery.

E. *Potential Dangers*

Sterilization of needles and potential nerve damage (natural dangers). Spiritual dangers are the same as all other energy healing modalities.

Hypnosis

A. *Definition*

Mesmerize or animal magnetism (Franz Mesmer, 1734–1815) a German physician with an interest in astrology theorized that there was a natural energetic transference that occurred between all animated and inanimate objects that he called animal magnetism and other spiritual forces often grouped together as mesmerism. This is considered vitalism and emphasizes the movement of life "energy" through distinct channels in the body. In 1843, a Scottish physician named James Braid coined the name *hypnosis*. The earliest definition of hypnosis was given by Braid, who coined the term *hypnotism* as an abbreviation for "neuro-hypnotism," or nervous sleep, which he opposed to normal sleep, and defined as "a peculiar condition of the nervous system, induced by a fixed and abstracted attention of the mental and visual eye, on one object, not of an exciting nature."

"The hypnotist does not hypnotize the individual. Rather, the hypnotist serves as a sort of coach or tutor whose job is to help the person become hypnotized." While hypnosis is often described as a sleep-like trance state, it is better expressed as a state characterized by focused attention, heightened suggestibility, and vivid fantasies.

B. *Healing Claims*

- The treatment of chronic pain conditions such as rheumatoid arthritis.
- The treatment and reduction of pain during childbirth.
- The reduction of the symptoms of dementia.
- Hypnotherapy may be helpful for certain symptoms of ADHD.
- The reduction of nausea and vomiting in cancer patients undergoing chemotherapy.
- Control of pain during dental procedures.
- Elimination or reduction of skin conditions including warts and psoriasis.

- Alleviation of symptoms association with irritable bowel syndrome.

C. *Scientific Evaluation*

The American Psychology Association (APA) website has declared most clinicians now agree hypnotherapy can be a powerful, effective therapeutic technique for a wide variety of conditions.

D. *Roots and Fruit*

Its roots are in vitalism, channeling of energy and subliminal suggestions (occult).

E. *Biblical/Christian Evaluation*

Children tend to be more susceptible to hypnosis and people who can become easily absorbed in fantasies are much more responsive to hypnosis. Mind control and altered state of conscienceless.

F. *Potential Dangers*

Occult bondage and spirit possession, some hypnotists view suggestion as a means of communicating with the "unconscious" or "subconscious" mind. These concepts were introduced into hypnotism at the end of nineteenth century by Sigmund Freud. The concept of subliminal suggestion.

Chiropractic

A. *Healing Claims*

Some chiropractors claim that all diseases stem from the spine, such as pinched nerves and cut off blood flow.

B. *Scientific Evaluation*

"With this business of 'all disease stemming from spine,' there's no evidence to support that," said chiropractic physician Jim Winterstein, president of the National University of Health Sciences in Lombard, one of eighteen accredited chiropractic schools in the country. "And I'd never suggest the adjustment of spine is the answer to human ailments. It plays a role like exercise and nutrition and lifestyle changes. All are tools." Winterstein also disputes claims that regular adjustments can help improve overall health, again citing a lack of science (Deardorff 2009).

C. *Roots and Fruit*

It was practiced by priest healers in ancient Egypt and for centuries by Asian healers. Modern chiropractic was founded by Daniel D. Palmer, a grocer and magnetic healer. D. D. Palmer was influenced by the metaphysical movement that emerged during the 1830s. Two groups that came out of that movement that influenced Palmers beliefs were spiritualism and Theosophy.

Palmer was greatly involved with spiritualism, and this is what leads him into magnetic healing. Palmer was extremely attracted to influence by the theosophists and its society. It may not be an over statement to say the metaphysical influence is far more important than the osteopathic influence so often referred to by various writers. So what was the metaphysical movement? J. Stillson Judea said this and I quote, "Spiritualism, which developed in this country in the 1840s, came to spawn a large array of interrelated religious, healing, and paranormal investigative groups. Much of their foundation was the extreme liberalism of American transcendentalism, which first began in the 1830s and produced the influential philosophy of Ralph Waldo Emerson. Their goals sometime different. They exhibit a common philosophical core with individualistic variations that spread rapidly in increase of sects. Still they are like branches of a single tree growing out of the cultural soil that produced American *transcendentalism.*"

- Palmer did believe in the ability to beneficially communicate with the spirit world.
- Palmer came to be a magnetic healer via his spiritual investigations.
- Palmer was arrested three separate times of practicing medicine without a license—twice acquitted and third time convicted.
- Theosophical influence was especially strong as Palmer effort to reconcile orthodox religion with the rapid advance of science in that time. He eventually studied both, and then he tried to blend these two belief systems.
- Palmer believed that the phenomena of nature both physical and spiritual are expressions of infinite intelligence.
- That communications with the dead is a fact scientifically proven by the phenomena of spiritualism.
- Palmer believed that "man as uncreated spirit has always been in existence and that after death only eternal progression of the spirit."
- On display at Palmer College is a collection of what is called the Traveling Library. The Traveling Library contains a collection of metaphysical topics including magnetism, torrential philosophy, spiritual evolution, and occult philosophy about the nature of disease. Among these books is one that is coauthored by Theosophy leader Anne Beasant. Another contains a large ad for a book on Theosophy by D. D.'s friend W. J. Colville (old friend of D. D.'s).
- Colville lectured and authored on occult subjects and Theosophy.
- Taken from D. D. Palmer own writing on page 12 of *Chiropractor's Adjuster*, he states the he received from his friend Colville a typewritten information "concerning centuries of old cult practicing a form of spinal manipulation."
- Theosophists and Palmer held to more modern version of the centuries old universal ether theory. This theory sup-

posedly accounted for the fact that natural forces such as light propagation, gravity, and magnetic forces had to work through some real although invisible medium.

- His son, BJ Palmer, whom eventually bought the college from his father, would put a different twist on the religious philosophies. Nonetheless, he filled the college with ornaments, statues, and idols from various religions and cultures all over the world from his travels. BJ's stance was one of all religions have some basis of truth.

- Here is one *epigram* that rests on the campus walls at Palmer College... *There is power within... A fountainhead of unlimited resource... And he who controls it controls circumstances instead of it controlling him.*

- Read the World Chiropractic Alliance...

D. *Biblical/Christian Evaluation*

Be wary of those who say spinal manipulation can cure whatever ails you. "Look for a chiropractor who uses an evidence-based approach and is willing to work with other medical professionals," said Scott Fonda, a chiropractor at the Rehabilitation Institute of Chicago. Ask whether exercise is part of the program. "Evidence suggests the best approach to spinal problems is a short series of treatments followed by a gradual transition to taking care of your own spine and using exercise on a regular basis to prevent future problems," said chiropractic physician Donald Murphy of Rhode Island (Deardorff 2009).

You have the right to ask your Christian chiropractor if he or she is aware of the occult foundation of this practice. If not, ask them to research it for themselves. *Ask* them if they have renounced all connections with the roots of this practice. We are responsible for what we know. Be aware of how your doctor is treating you. Ask questions and look at the books on their shelf. Just because they say they are Christian, does not mean they have the same revelation that you have been given. The term *Christian* has a wide range of beliefs. Believing in Jesus Christ is not enough. Are they living like they know him? Do you know the fruit of their life? If you do understand what they are saying, then ask them to test it—in prayer and *in* the Word.

E. *Potential Dangers*

A 2010 review of prior medical publications identified twenty-six cases of death following chiropractic manipulation of the neck, which the researcher interpreted as resulting from damage to arteries that supply blood to the brain. There have also been reports of misdiagnoses of patients' conditions, resulting in delayed medical care and worse outcomes. In several people with cancer, paralysis of the legs and full-body paralysis developed after manipulation of the spine when cancer had spread to and weakened the bones.

People with bleeding problems or those taking blood-thinning medications may have a higher risk of stroke caused by manipulation of the spine. People with cancer and chronic conditions such as arthritis, heart disease, and weakened bones should talk to their doctors before having any type of therapy that involves manipulation of joints and muscles.

Relying on this treatment alone and delaying or avoiding conventional medical care for cancer may have serious health consequences.

Spiritually, the dangers are other holistic influences coming into play, such as muscle testing.

Iridology

A. *Definition*

It is the study of the iris of the human eye to diagnose present and future illnesses and disease.

B. *Healing Claims*

The eye can mirror the health condition of the body because the iris displays in detail the status of every organ system.

C. *Scientific Evaluation*

Discredited with numerous testing. In a study published in the journal of the American Medical Association (1979, vol. 242, 1385–1387), three iridologists incorrectly identified nearly all of the study slides of the irises of 143 healthy and diseased people. "In fact, they often read the irises of the sickest people as being healthy and vice versa. They did not even agree with each other." Similar results involving five Dutch iridologists were published in the *British Medical Journal* (1988, vol. 297, 1578-1581) (Niebergall n.d.).

D. *Roots and Fruit*

Similar practices trace back to ancient Chinese practices that are related to astrology. Sympathetic magic is a specific magical paranormal belief that similar objects affect each other. (This concept is often phrased as "like affects like," as in homeopathy.) Anthropologically speaking, this is apparently one of the most common and most primitive forms of magical belief found in communities and cultures all over the world. It was known to the sorcerers of ancient India, Babylon, and Egypt, as well as Greece and Rome. An easily understandable example of sympathetic magic is the Haitian tradition of the voodoo doll.

E. *Biblical/Christian Evaluation*

Medical doctors and optometrists recognize that certain symptoms of monocular disease can be detected by examining the eye.

F. *Potential Dangers*

The roots of this practice were used by ancient sorcerers in India (Hinduism), Babylonian (occult, Baal, and Asherah worship), and Haitian (voodoo witchcraft).

Crystal Healing

A. *Definition*

It is a form of vibrational medicine in which subtle energy given off by the crystal(s) is used to treat the body, the mind, and the spirit.

B. *Healing Claims*

Because crystals can absorb and transmit light, they are able to transmit universal energy, reflecting it among their internal crystalline structures and transmitting it to a receiving source—any being that will accept the crystals generous healing energy. Crystals act as conduits of the universal healing energy of light. Key element is the important fact that the healing energy must be intentionally directed. Sedona New Age Center, *Crystal Healing Newsletter* says this, and I quote, "It is not the crystal that possesses healing energy; it is one's intent to heal by way of the crystal, which can, when properly used, manifest results. Crystal healing is not meant to replace congenital medicine but only to enhance it. Crystal healing is an independent therapy, one that is part of a holistic healing approach. Not every cure can be explained by conventional wisdom and some are, indeed, closer to the 'magical' realm than to the disciplines of contemporize thought!"

C. *Scientific Evaluation*

It's completely discredited by scientific community.

D. *Roots and Fruit*

Adoration of crystals by human beings connects all cultures and civilizations throughout the history of the earth, dating back thousands of years ago. Crystals are also used for developing psychic abilities, spirit contact.

E. *Biblical/Christian Evaluation*

It's forbidden based on the occult, witchcraft, and Satanism usage.

F. *Potential Dangers*

It's opening up doors into demonic realm, occult influence. Crystal healing is being used in psychotherapy in our very own Social Services System to treat adults and children who have suffered trauma and abuse.

Homeopathy

A. *Definition*

It came from the Greek word *homeo* which means "similar" or "like" and *pathy* also a Greek word which means "suffering." A nontraditional system for treating and preventing disease, in which minute amounts of a substance, that in large amounts causes disease symptoms are given to healthy individuals. This is thought to enhance the body's natural defenses. Sedona New Age Center interprets diseases and sickness as caused by disturbances in the life force and sees these disturbances as manifesting themselves in unique symptoms. Homeopathy maintains that the vital force can react and adapt to internal and external causes. Homeopaths refer to this as the "law of susceptibility" which states that a negative state of mind can attract disease entities called miasma to invade the body and produce symptoms of diseases.

B. *Healing Claims*

Its founder, Dr. Samuel Hahnemann, believed that by inducing a disease using his remedies, the artificial symptoms empowered the vital force to neutralize and expel the original disease and that the artificial disturbance would naturally subside when dosing ceased.

C. *Scientific Evaluation*

Despite its widespread acceptance in some countries, most modern scientific authorities do not take homeopathy seriously, putting it in the same category as perpetual motion machines, ghosts, and ESP. There are several reasons for this intense skepticism, but the most important focuses on a basic fact of chemistry. Simply put, there is absolutely nothing material in a "high-potency" homeopathic remedy. Some force of nature unknown to modern science would have to be involved if homeopathy is effective.

D. *Roots and Fruit*

Dr. Hahnemann also was known for his interest in paranormal. Notable Names Database (NNDB) also lists his occupation as doctor and paranormal.

E. *Biblical/Christian Evaluation*

All potential occult practices should be avoided.

F. *Potential Dangers*

History and roots of its founder does suggest that there is psychic healing, spiritism, and astrology as well as other occult philosophies, the use of pendulums, radionics instruments, and other occult devices. Also incorrect and or harmful diagnosis and treatment.

Naturopathy

A. *Definition*

A system of therapeutics in which neither surgical nor medicinal agents are used with dependence being placed only on natural remedies. Also called nature cure, a method of treating disorders involving the use of herbs and other naturally grown foods, sunlight, fresh air, etc.

B. *Healing Claims*

Naturopathy is based on the idea that illness is due to a buildup of toxins in the body and the symptoms of illness are the body's way of attempting to heal itself. The belief is that the body will heal itself when natural methods are the treatment. One can maintain health by changing their lifestyle to one that will better harmonize with nature and its healing elements.

C. *Methods*

Naturopath varies with training and scope of practice. It includes acupuncture, applied kinesiology, botanical medicine, brainwave entrainment, colonic enemas, color therapy, cranial osteopathy, hair analysis, homeopathy, iridology, live blood analysis, nature cures (i.e., a range of therapies based upon exposure to natural elements such as sunshine, fresh air, heat, or cold, nutrition, examples include vegetarian and wholefood diet, fasting, and abstention from alcohol and sugar), meditation, relaxation, and other methods of stress management, public health measures and hygiene, reflexology, Rolfing, and traditional Chinese medicine.

D. *Scientific Evaluation*

In 1968, the United States Department of Health, Education, and Welfare issued a report on naturopathy concluding that naturopathy was not grounded in medical science and that naturopathic education was inadequate to prepare graduates to make appropriate diagnosis and provide treatment. The report recommends against expanding Medicare coverage to include naturopathic treatments. According to the American Cancer Society, "Scientific evidence does not support claims that naturopathic medicine can cure cancer or any other disease since virtually no studies on naturopathy as a whole have been published and no evidence to support its claims."

E. *Roots and Fruit*

Some would say that Hippocrates, ancient Greek "Father of Medicine," was the first advocate of naturopathic medicine, but the modern practice has its roots in the Nature Cure Movement of Europe in the nineteenth century. German born, Benedict Lust is responsible for bringing naturopathy to the United States. Lust defined naturopathy as a broad discipline rather than a particular method and included such techniques as hydrotherapy, herbal medicine, and homeopathy, as well as eliminating overeating, tea, coffee, and alcohol. He described the body in spiritual and ritualistic terms with "absolute reliance upon the cosmic forces of man's nature."

F. *Biblical/Christian Evaluation*

Natural treatments can function as a commendable model for preventative health care and treatment of minor ailments. Christians should exercise extreme cautions due to the roots of New Age cosmic reliance and various technics that could lead to other New Age and occult alternative treatments.

G. *Potential Dangers*

Naturopathy could hinder a correct diagnosis of a problem permitting a curable illness to assume a serious or incurable state, and it could interfere with treatments that could otherwise be effective. Some methods rely on immaterial "vital energy fields." Lastly, it could open up clients to other occultus practices.

H. *Other Names*

Hygienic medicine.

Overview

Summary of New Age Worldview and Belief Systems (Common Points)

1. Cosmos is seen as an organic whole.
2. It is imitated by an energy which is also identified as the divine soul or spirit.
3. Much reliance is given to the mediation of various spiritual entries (spirit guides or demons).
4. Humans are capable of ascending to invisible high spheres and controlling their own lives beyond death.
5. There is held to be a "perennial knowledge" which predates and is superior to all religions and cultures (not the Father, Son, and Holy Spirit).
6. People follow enlightened "ascended masters."

Five Groups that Make Up Western Esotericism

1. Theosophy
2. New Thought
    a. History and development of New Thought
    b. Infinite tenets of New Thought are as follows:
        *   Infinite intelligence
        *   Spirit is the ultimate reality
        *   True human selfhood is divine (themselves are gods)
        *   Divinely attuned thought is a force for good

- All disease is mental in origin
- Right thinking has healing effect

3. American Transcendentalism
4. Neo-paganism
5. Occult
   a. The relationship between the occult and esotericism
   b. Esotericism in the mirror of secular thought
   c. Jungian psychology and its relationship to the occult (did you know that Hitler studied Jung's Philosophy?)
   d. Western esotericism's understanding of Hinduisms concepts of reincarnation and karma

It has become secularized that reincarnation doesn't always mean you're going to come back as something better. Hinduism has also been perverted by Blavatsky (Theosophical Society) to be accepted in society to influence cultures.

You can recognize New Age by what it rejects (Clark n.d.)!

1. Is God a being with whom we have relationship or something to be used or a force to be harnessed?
2. Is there one Jesus Christ or thousands of Christs? (They believe the word *Christ* meaning "ascended master.")
3. The human being—is the one universal being or are there many individuals?
4. Do we save ourselves, or is salvation a free gift from God?
5. Do we invent truth, or do we embrace it?
6. Are we tempted to deny sin, or do we accept that there is such a thing?
7. Are we encouraged to reject death or accept suffering and death? (NA views suffering as self-imposed, bad karma, or at least a failure to harness one's own resources.)
8. Is social commitment something shirked (avoided) or positively sought after? (NA is all about self-promotion.)

9. Prayer and meditation—are we talking to ourselves or God, as in the creator of all things (biblical)?

10. Is our future in the stars, or do we help construct it? (Christians are partnered with the Father, Son, and Holy Spirit. New Agers are waiting for the Age of Aquarius, looking to the stars.)

CHAPTER 8

Prayer Models

This, then, is how you should pray:
Our Father in heaven, hallowed be your
name, your kingdom come, your will be done,
on earth as it is in heaven. Give us today our
daily bread.¹² And forgive us our debts, as we also
have forgiven our debtors. And lead us not into
temptation, but deliver us from the evil one.
For if you forgive other people when they sin
against you, your heavenly Father will also
forgive you. But if you do not forgive others their
sins, your Father will not forgive your sins.
—Matthew 6:9–15

In training for the healing ministry, the most asked question is, "What is the best way to do ministry?" The best and only way to minister to someone is out of our overflow of love of the Father!

I can tell you that there are many ministry session models for anyone to follow, and they will work because God works in our systematic beliefs.

The following models are those of Randy Clark, the founder of Global Awakening and the Apostolic Network of Global Awakening. I have included them because these are models which are used all over the world. As a certified master equipper under the Christian Healing Certification Program (CHCP), I have been released to teach and train these models as guidelines.

Five-Step Prayer Model for Healing

Step 1: The Interview

The purpose for the interview is to determine the root cause(s) of the infirmity or sickness. Possible roots—an afflicting spirt, sickness rooted in the soul (psychosomatic), or natural causes such as accident, injury, or disease. Ask probing questions such as:

- What's your name? (asking for a person's name creates relationship)
- How can I pray for you?
- How long have you had this condition?
- Do you know the cause?
- Why do you think you have this problem? (you would be surprised what a person already knows about the root cause)
- Do you have a doctor's diagnosis?
- Did someone cause the condition?
- Have you forgiven him or her? (unforgiveness can a major hindrance healing)

- Did any event significant traumatic event happen to you when this condition started? Or within six months to a year before?

Note that before you begin to pray for healing, you may need to help the person with unforgiveness or emotional wounds such as fear, shame, and rejection.

Always depend on the Holy Spirit—quietly ask Him if He has anything to show you about the condition or its cause. *Listen to Him!*

Step 2: Prayer Selection

- *Petition.* Father, in Jesus's name, I ask you to heal the _____ (inflammation in Joe's knee and take out the swelling and pain).
- *Command.* In the name of Jesus, I command the _____ (inflammation in Joe's knee to be healed and all swelling and pain to leave).
  Use commands when...
  o breaking a curse or a vow,
  o casting out an afflicting spirit or other spirit,
  o you have used petition prayer and progress has stopped,
  o when you are led by Holy Spirit; and
  o a word of knowledge or other circumstance indicates that God wants to heal the person immediately.

Step 3: Prayer Ministry (Praying for Effect)

- Audibly ask the Holy Spirit to be present with His guidance and His healing power!
- Ask the person not to pray but instead to close his eyes and focus on his body. It is their time to just receive the work of the Holy Spirit.
- Let the person know that they should interrupt you if they feel anything in their body—heat, electricity, trem-

bling, etc. (about 50 percent of people being healed feel something).

- If indicated, have the person confess any sin (unforgiveness, anger, etc.) and/or pray for the person's emotional healing before praying for physical healing.
  Tips for you, the minister:
  o Keep your eyes open to see God's touch!
  o Use short specific prayers.
  o Try different kinds of prayers.
  o Be loving! Be persistent!
  o Follow any leading of Holy Spirit!
  o *Always* pray in the name of Jesus!
  o *Do not* preach or give advice!
  o If a specific prayer brings improvement, keep using it immediately!
  o Pray for symptoms and cause, if the cause is known.
  o Periodically *ask*, "What is going on?"
  o Remember, trust the Holy Spirit, *not* the method!
  o *Thank God* for whatever He does… You cannot thank Him too much!

Step 4: Stop and Reinterview

Keep listening to Holy Spirit and stop to reinterview. If the pain moves around or increases during prayer or if a condition has existed a long time, consider casting out an afflicting spirit. If you are not making progress, consider interviewing the person further:

- Would you try again to remember any significant event that may have occurred around the time of or caused the onset?
- Have any other of your family members had this condition?
- Do you have a strong fear of anything?
- Has anyone ever pronounced a curse over or your family?
- Do you know anyone who is very angry at you?
- Have you ever participated in any satanic or occult activity?

- Has any member of your family been a member of the Freemasons?
- Have you had any accidents? (e or she may be accident prone.)

Stop praying when:

- The person is healed or the person wants to stop!
- The Holy Spirit tells you to stop!
- You are gaining no ground and receive no other way to pray!

Step 5: Post-Prayer Suggestions

After praying, it is beneficial to give helpful follow-up instructions or exhortations.

- Encourage the prayee with scripture.
- Share appropriate lifestyle changes for maintaining healing and preventing problem reoccurrence.
- If someone is not healed or is partially healed, *do not* accuse the person of a lack of faith or of a sin in his or her life as the cause.
- Prepare the person to resist any further attack after healing.

Prayer Model for Deliverance

The objective is to expel any demons, close their avenues of access to the person, and enable them to keep those avenues closed in the future. It is most effective to work as a team. One person is in charge, he or she does all the talking and in steps 2, 6, 7 and 8, all the touching. Others pray silently and talk with the leader quietly. Leadership can rotate during ministry. Step 6 and 7 can be very painful. Don't hesitate to stop, provide comfort, and pray for healing. If the person can't remember important details or identify the cause of feelings, you can interrupt the ministry time and have him go home and ask the Holy Spirit!

1. *Give the individual priority!* Maintain a loving attitude. Be encouraging. Move to a quiet place if possible. Invite the Holy Spirit to be present.

2. *If a spirit manifests, make it be quiet!* Repeat, "Submit in the name of Jesus!" Be persistent. This may take time! Remember, only the leader touches the person!

3. *Establish and maintain communication with the person.* You must have the person's cooperation! ("Joe, can you hear me? Please look at me.")

4. *Ask the person what he or she wants freedom from!* Make sure he or she really wants freedom from bondage(s).

5. *Make sure that the person has received Jesus Christ as their Lord and Savior.* If not, lead him in prayer for salvation. If you can't, bless him but do not do deliverance!

6. *Interview the person to discover the events(s) or relationship(s) that have led to the bondages(s).* Expose where forgiveness is required and where healing, repentance, and breaking bondage are needed. Find all open doors. If there is no obvious place to start, begin with his or her paternal relationships then move to other areas.

7. *Be thorough, don't rush.* Do not stir up any demons, keep them quiet. List the spirits encountered and areas requiring forgiveness of others and repentance. Consider a curse if the person has persistent difficulty in an area of life. Fear in an entry point for different spirits and a problem in many illnesses (in body, soul, spirit) such as:
   • Sexual sin of any kind
   • Uninvited sexual relationship
   • Long illness
   • General weakness
   • Addictions
   • Cutting
   • Tattoos

- Resentment/anger
- Trauma and its effect
- Rejections/loneliness
- Unforgiveness/bitterness
- Despair/hopelessness
- Pride/arrogance
- Rebellion/vengeance
- Fear in all forms
- Hatred (all forms)
- Criticism/gossip
- Envy in all forms
- Greed
- Any occult experiences
- Witchcraft/manipulation
- Satanism/Freemasonry
- Curses/inner vows

8. *Lead the person in closing the door(s) through which the spirit(s) entered.* If there is no one to forgive, go to steps B through D. He or she should:

   A. *Forgive* whoever caused the hurt or led him or her into wrong conduct. Be specific, item by item. The seeker should release the offender to God and commit to take his or her hands off—to not try to change the offender and ask God to bless him or her in every way. If the seeker is unable to forgive, explain the scripture to him or her. You quietly bind any spirit of unforgiveness. If he or she is still unable to forgive, pray for healing and blessing but not deliverance.

   B. *Repent* of his or her specific sins in the situation(s). ("Father forgive me for ___ (hate, bitterness, sharing my body with___, reading horoscopes, etc.)

   C. *Renounce* audibly and firmly all spirits involved in the name of Jesus. In case of sex outside marriage, the person should renounce spirits taken in from every partner he or she can recall, individually by first names.

    D. Pacts with Satan and inner vows must be renounced and curses broken. ("In the name of Jesus, I renounce the spirits of ___ and ___." "In the name of Jesus, I renounce the vow I made (never too/to always___.")

    E. *Break* the bondage(s) caused by the sin, attitude, conduct, vow, spirit, curse, etc., in the name of Jesus. This closes the door. You or the seeker can do this. ("In the name of Jesus, I break the power of the ___ spirit(s) of ___ and ___ over (Tom) so that when they are cast out the will not come back." "In the name of Jesus, I break the power of every curse over (Tom) from ___ (the father's careless critical words, the father's Freemasonry, etc.)"

9. *Cast out the unclean spirit(s) in the name of Jesus.* Some people cast out spirits one by one; some cast them out by groups. Do what works for you. With all doors closed, the spirits will leave quickly and quietly. If they don't leave promptly, go back to step 6. Tell the person that there may be other spirits to deal with. Reinterview. Ask the Holy Spirit to show you or the seeker or a team member what He wants to do next. He is very willing to help!

10. *Have the person thank Jesus for his or her deliverance!* If he or she cannot or if spirits manifest more doors need to be closed (same for step 10).

11. *Have the person ask the Holy Spirit to fill him or her and all places formerly occupied by evil spirits.*

PTSD Prayer Model

    The following is a healing prayer model for Post-Traumatic Stress Disorder. This model was actually given to Dr. Mike Hutchings from the Holy Spirit. Dr. Mike Hutchings is the Director of Global Awakenings, Christian Healing Certification Program, and Global School of Supernatural Ministry.

Eight-Step Prayer Model for Post-Traumatic Stress Disorder

- *Ask.* Interview the person. What experience or action resulted in PTSD?
- *Explain.* Tell the person what you will do and ask permission to do it!
  - o Keep eye contact during the prayer time.
  - o Explain that you will be taking authority and commanding out all effects the mentioned experiences/actions have over their being.
- *Forgive.* Declare the forgiveness of God to them by the power of the blood of Jesus Christ!
  - o Work through the prayers of repentances as needed to access this forgiveness.
  - o If PTSD stems from experiences/actions coming from military involvement, thank them for their service!
- *Declare.* Welcome the presence of Holy Spirit and the empowering presence of God to fulfill the mission of Jesus according to Isaiah 61:1–3.
  - o Speak through declaration to break off any feelings of shame, guilt, condemnation, etc., for anything the person has done, been ordered, or have had done to them.
  - o Break off the *responsibility* of their experiences or actions.
- *Cancel.* Cancel every assignment of the powers of darkness against the person's mind, body, and spirit that cause fear, anxiety, worry, etc.
  - o Command all afflicting and tormenting spirits associated with the experiences/actions to leave and never return.
- *Heal.* Heal through declaration prayer the wounds of their soul that were caused by traumatic experiences/actions.
  - o Destroy strongholds of thoughts and beliefs that they have built up around their wounds.
  - o Speak faith, trust, peace, and the promise of protection according to Psalm 91.

o Heal through declaration prayer the physical healing over any wound or injury associated with the trauma, disconnect triggers of five senses that bring back memories or images.

- *Pray.* Pray that the Lord releases the person from imprisonment or captivity associated with experiences/actions.
  o Speak healing over the systems of their bodies that have been affected (nervous, lymphatic, muscular, and immune).
  o Declare freedom to the mind, body, and spirit.
  o Ask Holy Spirit for reintegration of their brain, restoring healthy connections.
- *Release.* If they are military, thank them again for service to our country and release them from the vows and oaths they spoke when they entered the service.
  o If they are Vietnam veterans, then welcome them home. Break any curses that were spoken over them.
  o Declare God's blessing of their faithfulness.
  o Identify the person as a royal son or daughter of a loving Father and speak a blessing. Their experiences/actions no longer have a hold over them.

Step 8 New Creation Declaration Blessing (have the person receiving prayer repeat this after you).

This is who my Father says I am...

I am a child of the King. I am a coheir with Jesus. All Jesus bought and paid for is my inheritance. I am loved. I am forgiven. I am cleansed by the blood of Jesus. I am accepted in the Beloved. I am filled with His Spirit. I have angels protecting me and assisting me in the ministry of Jesus. I am united with Jesus. I have been crucified with Christ. I died with Him. I was buried with Him. I was raised with Him. I am seated with Him in the heavenlies far above all rule, all power, all authority, and above every name that is named, not only in this age, but also in the age to come. Therefore, I carry the authority of Christ. I have authority over sickness, over sin, over demons, and over the world. I am the salt of the earth. I am the light of the world. All things work together for my good because I love God, and I am called according to His purpose, which is for me to be conformed to the image and likeness of Christ. I can do all things through Christ because greater is He who is in me than he who is in the world.

CHAPTER 9

Aftercare and Keys to Maintaining Your Freedom

It is God's will that you should be sanctified: that
you should avoid sexual immorality; that each of
you should learn to control your own body in a way
that is holy and honorable, not in passionate lust
like the pagans, who do not know God; and that in
this matter no one should wrong or take advantage
of a brother or sister. The Lord will punish all those
who commit such sins, as we told you and warned
you before. For God did not call us to be impure,
but to live a holy life. Therefore, anyone who rejects
this instruction does not reject a human being but
God, the very God who gives you his Holy Spirit.
—1 Thessalonians 4:3–8

Some will ask, "Why do we need aftercare?" Let me give you a good example of why we need an aftercare program in ministry.

Let's say that we were talking about a man who just moved to a new town with no family near to take care of him if something were to happen. For the sake of this example, let's say he has no family at all. He is utterly alone in a new town.

One day while driving home from grocery store, he is in a terrible automobile accident, hospitalized. He has no health insurance. This accident has cost him his ability to work, and he has no automobile and absolutely no means to take care of himself.

His physical outcome is as follows. He has had surgery on both legs as a result of two broken femurs with steel rods attached to both damaged knees. He will be without the use of his legs for minimum of six weeks. He is totally restricted to a wheelchair, not allowed to put any pressure on his legs at all.

During his two-week hospital stay, he had the care of doctors and nurses to help with everything. They got him to the restroom, bathed him daily, and meals were delivered to him. He had people to clean his room and wash his clothes and his care was good while in that hospital. No needs to worry, right?

Wrong! The fear of what will happen to him afterward crept in with every breath he took. Who will help him? How will his rent be paid? How will he get to his doctor's appointments? The lists of concerns are turning into panic and torment! The hospital social workers are telling the man that they are releasing him from the hospital, but the man is terrified. *I have no way to get to my rental room. I have no wheelchair ramp. I have no one to get me food and no means to pay. Who will help me to the restroom? What is going to happen to me after I am released from this place?*

He was placed in a hotel that had handicap access and was paid for ten days. End of story!

Now I know you are wondering what happened to this man, right? Do you ask the same questions for those that you are ministering to? The ones that you are leading to their salvation and afterward from whom you just walk away? I hope you are concerned because we do this every day; we somehow have come to believe that it is enough just to get people saved. In churches, we plug people into programs and groups and never really get too intimate with others. In doing so means that we have to expose our inner selves, and we certainly do not want people to see our dirty laundry and skeletons in the closet. God forbid should we allow them to see our hidden brokenness. All too often, we are too busy putting people out of our sight and mind and then somehow we rationalize that it is no longer our responsibility after we have completed our mission.

I would like to disagree. The body of Christ is not to function without all parts. Each part is essential to function properly in kingdom alignment. The simple but hard to swallow truth is that we need each other. Every church body, ministry, every skilled leader, all gifting and talents, every single person, no matter their race, creed, color, size, shape, denomination, and belief, we need each other in order to function.

One definition of *aftercare* is the medical meaning—the care before and after discharge from hospital of a patient recovering from an illness or operation. I find it interesting that Jesus came into this world as flesh and bone so that He could take on our sickness, diseases, our sins, and transgressions so we could be healed and reconciled to the Father. We lead people in prayers of salvation and tell them to trust in the Lord and everything will be okay. I am sorry, but that's a lie. We have to teach people why they should trust in the Lord. We must be there for them like Christ is here for us. We have to guide them through the hard times, pray with them, encourage them, just plain love them with all of our life, just as Jesus did. You and I both know that when we received Jesus Christ as our Lord, we had just enlisted in the army of the Lord. Sometimes that enlistment takes place in the middle of the battlefield in the dark of night with the enemy prowling around ready to kill at a glance.

It is our responsibility to rescue and restore to health all those enlisted and non-enlisted. I like to think of us as "Special Forces—Team Jesus!"

A part of the Special Forces Team is the next definition of *aftercare*—support services. These should be by a kingdom agency for a person discharged from an institution, such as hospital or prison.

Support Services do things like rehabilitation, group support, biblical instruction, and prayer support. In the case of the injured man from the beginning of this chapter, it was a phone contact person who located others to help him. They were kingdom men who assisted in building him a ramp on his home so he could return. It was the food pantry ministries that brought him food. It was the women's ministry who once a week would gather his clothes and wash them for him. It was the men in the church who gave up a golf game to go drive him to the doctors for his scheduled appointments. I wish I could say that all these things happened for this man. Some of these things did happen, but the ball still got dropped. It is the vision of the Wilmington Healing Center to see every piece working together for the one. We should be with people until they become a part of the team in helping others. Sounds like God to me!

Aftercare also means any system of maintenance or upkeep after one's deliverance, and the following is a handout that Wilmington Healing Center provides to each client. We do believe that each person is responsible to act in their situation.

Maintaining Your Freedom

1. *"Go, and sin no more"* (John 8:11). Being repentant means that we have sorrow for wrongdoing and a desire to live in the Lord's righteousness. *We choose* to stop doing what we understand is wrong before God, and *we choose to do that which is right in His sight*. As Colossians 3:2 advises, "Set your affection on things above, not on things on the earth." We take a new path, and we remember our former sins (and way of life) no more (as Paul also determined in Philippians 3:13–14). We remember and value the fact that God has forgiven us. We become, "Rooted and built up in him, and established in the faith ..." (as counseled in Colossians 2:7).

2. *Keep short accounts of sin.* We are to be obedient and not sin, but if we do sin, we need to bring that sin immediately

before the Lord in confession and repentance. Even if you stumble, don't stay down. Get right back up and continue to walk in the Lord (1 John 1:5, 9 and 2:1). Following Christ means choosing to be obedient to His teachings.

3. *Share your testimony of healing.* Sharing your testimony of healing will help your faith grow and will keep you focused on Jesus. You will be a blessing and witness to others.

4. *Be aware of your thought life.* The battle between good and evil begins in the mind. You do not have to accept evil or wrong thoughts. "And be not conformed to this world: but be ye transformed by the renewing of your mind, that ye may prove what is that good, and acceptable, and perfect, will of God" (Romans 12:2). If the onslaught of evil thoughts continues to be a problem, it is better to say, "God, I don't want this thought," than it is to rebuke the devil and give him any attention. Remember, "Resist the devil, and he will flee from you" (James 4:7). Just because a delivery man (Satan) brings a package to the door (of your mind) with your name on it, doesn't mean you have to accept it. Keep your eyes and ears open for all the sneaky (little and big) traps the devil will be leaving around for you. Then cast "all your care upon him..." (1 Peter 5:7), your Heavenly Father, and He will immediately answer to give you victory.

5. *Fill your mind and spirit with positive thoughts of Jesus.* Philippians 2:5 admonishes us, "Let this mind be in you, which was also in Christ Jesus..." In prayer, gratefully confess the positive areas in which you have received freedom. Listen to nurturing Christian music and hymns. Be reminded, "Finally, brethren, whatsoever things are true, whatsoever things are honest, ...just, ...pure, ...lovely, ... of good report; if there be any virtue, and if there be any praise, *think on these things*" (Philippians 4:8).

6. *Pray every day.* Prayer is the best defense against darkness. At all times, maintain open communication with God.

Allow for quiet time (to *"be still"*) to listen for His voice (John 15:7, 1 Corinthians 14:14, 1 Thessalonians 5:17).

7. *Read the Bible and daily devotionals.* The good spirit in you needs daily spiritual nourishment. If you don't feed your spirit appropriately, it will get sick. If you were physically sick but were not hungry for physical food, a doctor would force-feed you, if necessary, to save your life. Although you may not be hungry for spiritual food, you must also "force-feed" yourself with nourishing spiritual food to save your spiritual life. Read the encouraging testimonies of others and the uplifting biographies of the lives of former heroes of the faith, engage in activities that build up and stimulate growth and development.

8. *Praise the Lord in all circumstances.* "Rejoice in the Lord always, again I say rejoice." Embody the law of gratitude (Philippians. 4:6–7). The words of our mouth invite either Jesus or darkness. Refrain from complaining, murmuring, muttering, grumbling, finding fault, or making judgments—all of which sow seeds of darkness. Paul recommends and informs us, "In everything give thanks: for this is the will of God in Christ Jesus concerning you" (1 Thessalonians 5:18).

9. *Learn to stand firm (by faith) on the promises of Jesus Christ.* Read and study the Bible to discover what His promises are—*appropriate and proclaim them* as your own.

10. *Find a church fellowship and become involved.* Attend regularly. Develop or join a support group that will hold you accountable and will pray with and for you. Beware of thinking that you don't need others and can make it on your own.

11. *Participate in the sacraments as often as possible.* In preparation for communion, follow the scriptural admonition to *examine yourself* (1 Corinthians 11:27–32). If you falter, confess and repent then go to the communion table in celebration. Call for the elders when you are sick, "Is any sick among you? Let him call for the elders of the church; and

let them pray over him, anointing him with oil in the name of the Lord" (James. 5:14).

12. *Find a Christian spiritual mentor.* Ask an experienced mentor to guide you (as a spiritual director) in your spiritual walk and submit to their leadership and counsel.

13. *Seek to be filled with the Holy Spirit.* Yield to the Holy Spirit. You have heard Him speak to you as you received healing. He will speak to you again on a regular basis if you ask and prepare.

14. *Discover your spiritual gifts and your place of service within the body.* Ask the Holy Spirit to guide you and to empower you, shaping you for effective service. Then commit to serve.

15. *"Put on the whole armor of God" every day.* As an added covering, clothe yourself with the armor spoken of in Ephesians 6:10–18.

16. *Commit all your thoughts, desires, and plans to the Lord Jesus.* If you do, He will guide you continuously, and you will be humbled by the generous and blessed things He reveals to you and does for you. He has promised to make you like a watered garden and a constant spring of water. In trusting Him, depending upon Him, and acknowledging Him in all things, He shall "direct thy paths" (Proverbs 3:5–6).

17. *Walk in forgiveness as a lifestyle.* Quick forgiveness is important.

18. *Make restitution if you should.* If you cheated some, repay him. If you should apologize to someone, do so. If you need to ask forgiveness, ask it.

19. *Rebuild godly strongholds.* Once demonic strongholds have been removed, encourage the seeker to replace or rebuild godly strongholds in their place. If there has been bitterness, it needs to be replaced with compassion. If there has been fear, it needs to be replaced with trust and peace.

Conclusion

Hope is found here...

We have hope in the one who is our *hope*—Jesus Christ!

We have healing and freedom at our disposal because we are the sons and daughters of El Shaddai!

It is also my hope that people will get a hold of the will of our Great and Mighty God and see things from His glorious perspective.

Jesus Christ was one man who changed the world... Just imagine what we could do together with Him!

CHAPTER 10

Activation Worksheets

This chapter was created as the activation part of this training manual. It is a twelve-week journey of healing and personal activation to help you become more aware of the voice of God. It is a deeper journey into the Word of God and learning more about who God and what He thinks about you!

Each activation sheet is meant to be accomplished in a week. If you have any questions, ask the Holy Spirit! Enjoy the journey!

Week number 1—Activation and Weekly Study

1. Your name. Who am I? Do you know the meaning of your name?
    My first name is _____, and it means _____.
    My middle name is _____, and it means _____.
    My family name (last) is _____, and it means _____.

2. Two-way journaling. Without filtering what the Lord is saying to you as a response to a question you ask Him or discussion you are having with Him in your journal, share your question, His response, and your reaction/response to His answer. *Now*...find a quiet place and ask the Lord this question, "God, what are Your thoughts about me?"

3. Journal...*be honest* with yourself and God... Describe your childhood relationship with your father and mother in one to two paragraphs. How do you see this affecting you and your heavenly Father?

4. Journal...*be honest* with yourself and God... In the garden of Eden, Adam and Eve traded a perfect, unhindered intimacy with one another and hid behind shame and fear. Describe a fear that you have overcome or need to overcome to have greater intimacy with your heavenly Father.

5. This week, complete one random act of kindness such as offering to anonymously pay a waitress for someone else's meal, ask someone at a gas station if you could pay for their fill-up, offer to pay someone's grocery bill at checkout, cut someone's grass, pay for the person behind you in a fast-food drive-through, etc. Report in your journal what you did and how it went. Please use this activity as a simple act(s) of kingdom kindness and not an evangelistic crusade!

6. Practice listening. *Listen* to a friend for at least fifteen minutes *without* offering any commentaries, answers, or insights. You do not have to be completely silent, but you

want to encourage them to keep talking. Journal... How did you feel as you listened quietly? What was your body language? What was their body language? What did you hear Holy Spirit saying to you as you listened?

Week number 2—Activation and Weekly Study

1. Two-way journaling. Find a quiet place and ask the Lord this question, "God, what is the purpose that You created me?" Share His response without filtering it.
2. Read and journal... *Read* Hebrews 12:2... *Ask* the Lord this question, "Jesus, what was the joy set before You, causing You to endure the cross?" *Share* His response without filtering it.
3. Read the Gospel of Matthew...
   - *Underline* every passage that deals with healing and/ or deliverance.
   - *Highlight* every passage that has a promise that could relate to sozo (salvation, healing, and deliverance). Colored pencils prevents bleed through on pages.
   - *Select* one of those passages and provide "Your Personalized Observation Summary."
4. Two-way journaling. Find a quiet place and ask the Lord this question, "God, what does the praise of man have in my heart?" Share His response without filtering it.
5. Practice listening... *Listen* to a friend, family member, coworker, or stranger for at least fifteen minutes *without* offering any commentaries, answers, or insights. You do not have to be completely silent, but you want to encourage them to keep talking. Journal... How did you feel as you listened quietly? What was your body language? What was their body language? What did you hear Holy Spirit saying to you as you listened?
6. In weeks at end, of course, we will be presenting a case study... Begin to discuss with friends, family members, or coworkers your activation of this course and that you would like an opportunity to minister to at least two different people...

Week number 3—Activation and Weekly Study

1. Read and journal... *Read* Matthew 28... *Ask* the Lord this question, "Jesus, What have I personally been commissioned to 'go' and do for Your kingdom?" *Share* His response without filtering it.

2. Two-way journaling. Find a quiet place and ask the Lord this question, "Jesus, how is fear stopping me from moving forward into Your purpose for my life?" Share His response without filtering it.

3. What is a *worldview*? Study it out and journal your findings...

4. Do you believe that Christians must choose whether character (the fruit of the Spirit) or power (the gifts of the Spirit) is more important to him/her? Please remember that honesty here is important... Please journal your answer and "beliefs" about this question. What scripture backs your belief?

5. Read the Gospel of Acts 1 through 14...
   - *Underline* every passage that mentions *Holy Spirit.*
   - *Highlight* every passage that has that relates to healing and or deliverance. Colored pencils prevents bleed through on pages.
   - *Select* one of those passages and provide a "Your Personalized Observation Summary."

6. Two-way journaling. Find a quiet place and ask the Lord this question, "God, share with me what Acts 2:1–4 actually means to you!" Share His response without filtering it.

7. Practice listening... *Listen* to a friend, family member, coworker, or stranger for at least fifteen minutes *without* offering any commentaries, answers, or insights. You do not have to be completely silent, but you want to encourage them to keep talking. Journal... How did you feel as you listened quietly? What was your body language? What was their body language? What did you hear Holy Spirit saying to you as you listened?

Week number 4—Activation and Weekly Study

1. Two-way journaling. Find a quiet place with the Jesus and ask Him, "Lord, in what areas of my life am I in denial of the finished work of the cross—physically, emotionally, and spiritually?"

2. Read and journal... *Read* Hebrews 12:14. Ask the Lord this question, "Is there anything else You can help me do to live in peace with all men?" As you are comfortable to share, write out His response.

3. Share two or three prophetic words or personal revelations from the Lord that you have received for your destiny. For example, being called to the nations, inventing a world-changing machine, etc.

4. Choose either Moses or David. Write a paragraph or two describing their interaction with God. How does this compare to how you interact with Him?

5. Read the Gospel of Mark...
   - *Underline* every passage that mentions salvation, healing, and deliverance (sozo).
   - *Highlight* every passage that has that relates to healing and or deliverance. Colored pencils prevents bleed through on pages.
   - *Select* one of those passages and provide a "Personalized Observation Summary" (see example from week 2).

6. Two-way journaling. Choose a child between the ages of five to twelve that you have relationship with and ask the Lord how He sees them. It could be a person from the Bible that they are similar to, something that is a destiny word or simply how God loves them. Write this in simple language as a card, sign, and date it and read it to them. Share their relationship to you, the word you gave them, and their reaction.

7. Practice listening... *Listen* to a *family member* (husband, wife, a child, or a grandchild) for at least fifteen minutes *without* offering any commentaries, answers, or insights.

You do not have to be completely silent, but you want to encourage them to keep talking. Journal... How did you feel as you listened quietly? What was your body language? What was their body language? What did you hear Holy Spirit saying to you as you listened?

8. Reminder, you have been asked to present a case study... *Begin* asking the Lord for a word of knowledge (WOK) for someone, preferably someone with whom you are acquainted but not known in a deep way. So the information will be from the Lord and not what you already know about that person. This can be a stranger also!

    Then document your case study... What was the (WOK)? Where were you when you received the WOK? What is your relationship to the person for whom you had a word? How did they receive the word? Were you able to pray for them and what were the results?

Week number 5—Activation and Weekly Home Study

1. Two-way journaling. *Read* Ephesians 2:5–7. Ask the Lord this question, "What does it mean to be seated with You in Heavenly places?" Respond to what you hear. Share both the Lord's reply and your response to His reply—unfiltered.

2. Journal... In two or three paragraphs, share about the legacy that you are building to leave to the next generation. List four or five action steps that you are taking or need to take to accomplish this.

3. What is *honor*? Study it out and journal your findings...

4. This week, perform an act of random "honor." This could involve letting someone else in line before you at the grocery store, giving up your seat in public transportation for someone else, cleaning up garbage in someone else's yard, etc. Share about your experience. Bonus, get someone else to join you.

5. *Read* the book of Acts 15 through 28...
   - *Underline* every passage that mentions Holy Spirit!
   - *Highlight* every passage that has that relates to (sozo) salvation, healing, and or deliverance. Colored pencils prevents bleed through on pages.
   - *Select* one of those passages and provide a "Personalized Observation Summary."

6. Two-way journaling. Ask the Lord if there is someone that you need to ask to forgive you or someone that you need to forgive. Set up an appointment to meet with them. Before you meet with them, ask the Holy Spirit to show you how He sees them. Share this with them and ask them what their response is. You are free to bring up the subject of forgiveness, but it is not required. What were you feeling during this encounter? Share what the Holy Spirit showed you about them and how they responded.

7. Practice listening... *Listen* to a *family member* for at least fifteen minutes *without* offering any commentaries, answers, or insights. You do not have to be completely silent, but

you want to encourage them to keep talking. Journal...
How did you feel as you listened quietly? What was your
body language? What was their body language? What did
you hear Holy Spirit saying to you as you listened?

Week number 6—Activation and Weekly Study

1. Two-way journaling. *Ask* the Lord to show you how He sees your pastor or another leader in your life. Write out a card including a scripture the Lord highlights to you and expound on that scripture in encouragement for them. Hand deliver the card, if possible. Email or domestic mail should be the exception. Journal what you wrote in the card and describe your experience.

2. Read and journal... *Read* Job 22:27–28... *Ask* the Lord this question, "Lord, what would You say to me about this scripture and what should this scripture mean to me?" *Share* His response without filtering it.

3. Write down, type, or record every thought you have about yourself for twenty-four hours (including dreams you remember). Read or listen to this compilation, and for this assignment, share a one-paragraph summary. What surprised you the most? Explain.

4. Read Isaiah 61. Describe how you have seen this fulfilled personally in your own life, how you have already helped fulfill this in other people's lives, and how you would like to see it fulfilled through you to other people in the future.

5. *Read* the Gospel of John...
   - *Underline* every passage that mentions salvation, healing, and deliverance (sozo).
   - *Highlight* every passage that has that relates to healing and or deliverance. Colored pencils prevents bleed through on pages.
   - *Select* one of those passages and provide a "Personalized Observation Summary."

6. Two-way journaling. Find a quiet place and ask the Lord this question, "God, what would You have me do with this training that I am receiving?" Share His response without filtering it.

7. Practice listening... *Listen* to a friend, family member, coworker, or stranger for at least fifteen minutes *without*

offering any commentaries, answers, or insights. You do not have to be completely silent, but you want to encourage them to keep talking. Journal... How did you feel as you listened quietly? What was your body language? What was their body language? What did you hear Holy Spirit saying to you as you listened?

Week number 7—Activation and Weekly Study

1. Two-way journaling. *Ask* the Lord the following question… "Jesus, what areas of my life have I not submitted to Your care and control? What areas of my life do I not trust You, Jesus?" Please be honest with yourself and Jesus and share His response without filtering it.

2. Read and journal… *Read* Romans 8… *Ask* the Lord this question, "Lord, what would You say to me about this scripture and what should this scripture mean to me?" *Share* His response without filtering it.

3. Ask the Lord to Give you an encouraging word for a stranger! You can either write it or speak it. Ask Jesus for the courage to deliver that word and go do it!

4. Ask the Lord for a specific prayer for your class partner… Write it down and pray it all week then give a copy of the prayer and any revelation that you received for them!

5. Read the Gospel of Luke…
   - *Underline* every passage that mentions salvation, healing, and deliverance (sozo).
   - *Highlight* every passage that has that relates to healing and or deliverance. Colored pencils prevents bleed through on pages.
   - *Select* one of those passages and provide a "Personalized Observation Summary."

6. Two-way journaling. Find a quiet place and ask the Lord this question, "God, what are some of the *lies* that I am believing that are keeping me from seeing myself the way You see me?" Share His response without filtering it.

7. Practice listening and releasing what you hear the Lord is saying… *Listen* to a friend, family member, coworker, or stranger for at least fifteen minutes *without* offering any commentaries, answers, or insights. You do not have to be completely silent, but you want to encourage them to keep talking. Then after you have listened, release what you have heard the Lord said to you *for them*…

Journal… How did you feel as you listened quietly? What was your body language? What was their body language? What did you hear Holy Spirit saying to you as you listened?

Week number 8—Activation and Weekly Study

1. Two-way journaling. *Ask* the Lord the following question… "Jesus, show me where I have allowed compromise into my life?" Please be honest with yourself and Jesus and share His response without filtering it.
2. Read and journal… Read Hebrews 11:6… *Ask* the Lord this question, "Lord, what would You say to me about this scripture and where do You see my *faith* and how can my faith increase?" Share His response without filtering it.
3. Ask the Lord to give you an encouraging word for *your class partner!* Please write it and speak it over them next Sunday. (We will make time for this in class.)
4. Please write some of your *personal* prayer requests (at least two but no more than three), and next Sunday, I would like for you to exchange this with your class partner.
5. Read James…
   - *Underline* every passage that are warnings, things to avoid, or renounce and repent of as kingdom children.
   - *Highlight* every passage that has that relates to our identity as *children* of *the one true God.* Colored pencils prevents bleed through on pages.
   - *Select* one of those passages and provide a "Personalized Observation Summary."
6. Two-way journaling. Find a quiet place and ask the Lord this question, "Father, last week I asked You about lies that I am believing about myself that are keeping me from seeing myself the way that You see me… Father, please share with me my kingdom identity as Your child." Share His response without filtering it.
7. Practice listening and releasing what you hear the Lord is saying… *Listen* to a friend, family member, coworker, or stranger for at least fifteen minutes *without* offering any commentaries, answers, or insights. You do not have to be completely silent, but you want to encourage them to keep

talking. Then after you have listened, release what you have heard the Lord said to you *for them*...

Journal... How did you feel as you listened quietly? What was your body language? What was their body language? What did you hear Holy Spirit saying to you as you listened?

8. Finalize your case study this week then document your case study... *Please* keep this as *confidential*, tell us about the event not the name of the person. What was the WOK? Where were you when you received the WOK? What is your relationship to the person whom the word was for? How did they receive the word? Were you able to pray for them, and what were the results?

Week number 9—Activation and Weekly Study

1. Two-way journaling. *Ask* the Lord the following question… "Jesus, in week 8, You showed me areas in my life where I have allowed compromise in my life. Because I was willing to compromise in this or these area(s), have I opened that area up to any demonic influence? If I have, what would You have me do to find freedom from this demonic influence?" Please be honest with yourself and Jesus and share His response without filtering it.

2. Read and journal… *Read* Matthew 12:43–45… *Ask* the Lord this question, "Lord, what would You say to me about this scripture and what should this scripture mean to me?" *Share* His response without filtering it.

3. Word study—*desolation*! Use your Bible, the *Vine's Dictionary*, the *Strong's Concordance*, the *Webster's Dictionary*, and sources to find a complete meaning of this word. After you have done your word study, *ask* the Lord what He would like to show you about this word and how it applies to healing (deliverance) ministry!

4. Word study—*overcomer*! Use your Bible, the *Vine's Dictionary*, the *Strong's Concordance*, the *Webster's Dictionary*, and sources to find a complete meaning of this word. After you have done your word study, *ask* the Lord what He would like to show you about this word and how it applies to healing (deliverance) ministry!

5. Read the Jude and provide a "Personalized Observation Summary."

6. Two-way journaling. Find a quiet place and ask the Lord this question, "God, what are some of the ungodly strongholds [lies, beliefs, and demonic influences] in my life that I have overcome in my relationship with You?" Share His response without filtering it.

7. Practice listening and releasing what you hear the Lord is saying… *Listen* to a friend, family member, coworker, or stranger for at least fifteen minutes *without* offering any

commentaries, answers, or insights. You do not have to be completely silent, but you want to encourage them to keep talking. Then after you have listened, release what you have heard the Lord said to you *for them...*

Journal... How did you feel as you listened quietly? What was your body language? What was their body language? What did you hear Holy Spirit saying to you as you listened?

8. Prepare to write your *testimony...* Talk with the Lord about this writing assignment... When you feel released to begin writing, start to prepare a *draft* of your testimony.

Identify your greatest struggles and where was Jesus during this time. Now *identify* your greatest *victories*, also identify where was Jesus during these times. Remember, *be honest... Hold nothing back from the Lord... Great is His glory revealed through your testimony!*

Week number 10—Activation and Weekly Study

1. Two-way journaling. *Ask* the Lord the following question… "Jesus, do I have a secret sin? Jesus, talk to me about this sin and how it hurts You and me, possibly others!" *Converse* (talk back and forth) with the Lord about this topic. Please be honest with yourself and Jesus and share His response without filtering it.

2. Read and journal… *Read* 2 Peter 3:9… *Ask* the Lord this question, "Lord, what would You say to me about this scripture and what should this scripture mean to me?" *Share* His response without filtering it.

3. Word study—*idolatry*! Use your Bible, the *Vine's Dictionary*, the *Strong's Concordance*, the *Webster's Dictionary*, and sources to find a complete meaning of this word. After you have done your word study, *ask* the Lord what He wants to teach you about idolatry in your own life!

4. Word study—*integrity*! Use your Bible, the *Vine's Dictionary*, the *Strong's Concordance*, the *Webster's Dictionary*, and sources to find a complete meaning of this word. After you have done your word study, *ask* the Lord what He would like to show you about this word and how it applies to you!

5. Read the 1 Peter… *Select* one of those passages and provide a "Personalized Observation Summary."

6. Two-way journaling. Find a quiet place and ask the Lord this question, "God, what are some of the generational curses over my life and over my bloodline that I need to submit to You, God, so the devil can be overthrown in those areas?" Share His response without filtering it.

7. Two-way journaling. Find a quiet place and ask the Lord this question, "Lord Jesus, have I become complacent and comfortable in my way of thinking about who I am and my life with You? What would You, Lord, say to me about this? What do You, Lord, *desire* for me?" Share His response without filtering it.

8. Testimony... Spend this talking with the Lord about this writing assignment... When you feel released to begin writing, start to prepare a *draft* of your testimony.

  Identify your greatest struggles and where was Jesus during this time. Now *identify* your greatest *victories*, also identify where was Jesus during these times. Remember, *be honest... Hold nothing back from the Lord... Great is His glory revealed through your testimony.*

Week number 11—Activation and Home Study

1. Two-way journaling. *Ask* the Lord the following question… "Jesus, do I have a secret sin? Jesus, talk to me about this sin and how it hurts You and me, possibly others!" *Converse* (talk back and forth) with the Lord about this topic. Please be honest with yourself and Jesus and share His response without filtering it.

2. Read and journal… Read 1 Corinthians 13:4–7… *Ask* the Lord this question, "Lord, what would You say to me about this scripture and what should this scripture mean to me?" *Share* His response without filtering it.

3. What did you dream of becoming when you were a child?

4. What was one dream that you accomplished, and how did you feel when you accomplished it?

5. What are ten dreams on your dream list?

6. What do you feel is the next big dream you want to go after?

7. What is one short-term goal you will accomplish in the next month for that dream?

8. Read the 2 Peter… *Select* one of those passages and provide a "Personalized Observation Summary."

9. Two-way journaling. Find a quiet place and ask the Lord this question, "Abba, what is Your dream in me?" Share His response without filtering it.

10. Write your *testimony*… You have spent the last couple weeks preparing to write your testimony. It is time now to follow the guidelines and begin writing… First, a draft and then a final copy!

    Identify your greatest struggles and where was Jesus during this time. Now *identify* your greatest *victories*, also identify where was Jesus during these times. Remember, *be honest… Hold nothing back from the Lord… Great is His glory revealed through your testimony!*

Week number 12—Activation and Weekly Study

1. Two-way journaling. *Ask* the Lord the following question... "Jesus, tell me what doors I have open in my life that are keeping me from fulfilling the plan You have for me?" *Converse* (talk back and forth) with the Lord about this topic. Please be honest with yourself and Jesus and share His response without filtering it.

2. Read and journal... *Read* Psalm 119:68 and 136:1... *Ask* the Lord this question, "Lord, what would You say to me about this scripture and what should this scripture mean to me?" *Share* His response without filtering it.

3. Read and journal... *Read* Ephesians 1:4–6... *Ask* the Lord this question, "Lord, what would You say to me about this scripture and what should this scripture mean to me?" *Share* His response without filtering it.

4. Read and journal... *Read* Isaiah 46:10... *Ask* the Lord this question, "Lord, what would You say to me about this scripture and what should this scripture mean to me?" *Share* His response without filtering it.

5. Read and journal... *Read* 1 Corinthian 6:9–11... *Ask* the Lord this question, "Lord, what would You say to me about this scripture and what should this scripture mean to me?" *Share* His response without filtering it.

6. Read and journal... *Read* Ezekiel 18:19–22 ... *Ask* the Lord this question, "Lord, what would You say to me about this scripture and what should this scripture mean to me?" *Share* His response without filtering it.

7. Two-way journaling. Find a quiet place and ask the Lord this question, "Abba, in all the above scriptures, there are many truth about who You are! Will You share with me something I do not yet know about You that will change my heart forever?" Share His response without filtering it.

8. Finalize writing your *testimony*... Now that you have written your testimony, it is time to finish! Share it to glorify God! Yes, you can read it. Now share it with someone! Remember that your testimony will change as you mature in the Lord.

"SANDY PSALM" (DECEMBER 10, 2010)

My Lord waited patiently upon me and my youth,
He did not grow weary,
He refused to sleep, He just waited quietly.
He knew that the time was approaching,
While waited He stood guard.
I never wondered off too far, He would not let me go.
He allowed me to play with fire so that I would learn His love.
Ever gently, he kissed the pain.
He never grew weary as He waited upon me.
Everywhere I go, He is there, just waiting upon me, his rebellious child.
My Lord continually prayed over me,
Every moment sang over me.
He knew that the time was near.
The many times I cried through my agony,
His tears like a river flowed, washing away my suffering.
Death followed me all my days, but He wanted to die in my place.
My Lord's voice I heard as He screamed out, "No! You can't have her.
    She is mine, not yours."
I ran to him as fast as I could and begged Him not to leave.
He looked into my eyes and then smiled at me.
I love you, my child. I have always loved you!
Leave you…never!
This is the plan… It has always been meant to be.
You are mine, not his!
I will walk with you closer, tucked into My wing,
I have trampled your enemies under My feet.
For this is My love that I offer to you!
The time has come… I've chosen to die for you!
My Lord whispered, "This is how much I love you!"
He breathed His last breath.

His blood ran down and covered me, I turned white as snow.
I swear I heard Him laugh just then,
As His breath brushed my face,
I heard Him say… "I love you now as I loved you then, you are Mine!"
This has been the plan… It has always been meant to be!

GLOSSARY OF NEW AGE WORDS

Atman—the principle of life; (2) the individual self, known after enlightenment to be identical with Brahman; and (3) (initial capital letter) the World Soul from which all individual souls derive and to which they return as the supreme goal of existence.

Bodhisattva—(noun) Buddhism. A person who has attained prajna or enlightenment but who postpones Nirvana to help others to attain enlightenment. Individual Bodhisattvas are the subjects of devotion in certain sects and are often represented in painting and sculpture.

Bohemianism—an unconventional, carefree sort of existence; improper and/or unlawful way of living.

Brahma—(in later Hinduism) "the Creator," the first member of the Trimurti with Vishnu the Preserver and Shiva the Destroyer.

Channel—to convey through or as through a channel (*he channeled the information to us*). To direct toward or into some course (*to channel one's interests*).

Divination—the attempt to foretell and/or explore the future. The most common means of divination are astrology, tarot cards, crystals balls, numerology, palmistry, random symbols, and various omens.

Dualism—good or evil, God or devil are independent and equal forces in the world.

Clairvoyance—the alleged power of perceiving things beyond the natural range of the senses and (2) keen intuitive understanding

Esoteric—understood by or meant for only the select few who have special knowledge or interest, recondite (*poetry full of esoteric allusions*); (2) belonging to the select few; (3) private, secret, confidential; and (4) (of a philosophical doctrine or the like) intended to be revealed only to the initiates of a group.

Extrasensory perception (ESP)—the supposed ability of certain individuals to obtain information about the environment without the use of normal sensory channels.

Evoke—to call upon produce, to elicit or draw forth, cause to appear or summon, to produce or suggest through imagination a vivid impression or reality.

Gnosticism—a religious movement characterized by a belief in gnosis through which the spiritual element in man could be released from its bondage in matter, regarded as a heresy by the Christian church.

Kinesis—the movement of an organism in response to a stimulus, as light.

Orgone energy—"orgonomy" was a hypothetical universal life force originally proposed in the 1930s by Wilhelm Reich. Orgone was a massless, omnipresent substance, similar to luminiferous ether but more closely associated with living energy than inert matter. It could coalesce to create organization on all scales from the smallest microscopic units called bions in orgone theory to macroscopic structures like organisms, clouds, or even galaxies.

Pantheism—the doctrine that God is the transcendent reality of which the material universe and human beings are only manifestations: it involves a denial of God's personality and expresses a tendency to identify God and nature; any religious belief or philosophical doctrine that identifies God with the universe.

Pantheism—is a belief system which posits that God exists and interpenetrates every part of nature and timelessly extends beyond as well. Pantheism is distinguished from pantheism which holds that God is synonymous with the material universe. In pantheism, God is not exactly viewed as the creator or demiurge but the eternal animating force behind the universe, with the universe as nothing more than the manifest part of God. The cosmos exists within God, who in turn "pervades" or is "in" the cosmos. While pantheism asserts that God and the universe are coextensive, pantheism claims that God is greater than the universe and that the universe is contained within God. Pantheism holds that God is the "supreme affect and effect" of the universe.

Medium—one who acts as an intermediary between the spirit world and the physical world. They make use of various objects to convey a message from spirits to the living. Mediums will serve as spokesperson.

Moksha—(noun) Buddhism, Hinduism, Jainism. Freedom from the differentiated, temporal, and mortal world of ordinary experience.

Monism—"Oneness," everything is God. God is everything, and if everything is God, then we are also gods (Genesis 3).

Mysticism—the beliefs, ideas, or mode of thought of mystics. A doctrine of an immediate spiritual intuition of truths believed to transcend ordinary understanding or of a direct, intimate union of the soul with God through contemplation or ecstasy. It's a belief in or experience of a reality surpassing normal human understanding or experience, ESP a reality perceived as essential to the nature of life. A system of contemplative prayer and spirituality aimed at achieving direct intuitive experience of the divine obscure or confused belief or thought, speculation.

Nirvana—Pali, nibbana. *Buddhism.* Freedom from the endless cycle of personal reincarnations with their consequent suffering, as a result of the extinction of individual passion, hatred, and delusion. Attained by the Arhat as his goal but postponed by the Bodhisattva; (2) *Hinduism.* Salvation through the union of Atman with Brahma, moksha; and (3) a place or state characterized by freedom from or oblivion to pain, worry, and the external world. Oneness.

Reincarnation—the belief that the soul, upon death of the body, comes back to earth in another body or form; (2) rebirth of the soul in a new body; and (3) a new incarnation or embodiment, as of a person.

Rolfing—is a therapy system created by the Rolf Institute of Structural Integration (also referred to as "RISI"). It's founded by Ida Pauline Rolf in 1971. The institute states that Rolfing is a "holistic system of soft tissue manipulation and movement education that organize(s) the whole body in gravity." It's manipulation of the muscle fasciae is believed to yield therapeutic benefits, including that clients stand straighter, gain height, and move better through the correction of soft tissue fixations or dystonia. A review found that evidence for clinical effectiveness and hypothesized mechanisms of Rolfing is severely limited by small sample sizes and absence of control arms and that further research is needed, though controlled trials found that a single Rolfing session significantly decreases standing pelvic tilt angle, and that Rolfing caused a lasting decrease in state anxiety when compared to the control group. Only practitioners certified by RISI can use the title "Rolfer" or practice "Rolfing" due to service mark ownership. The Guild for Structural Integration is the other certifying body, whose graduates use the title "practitioners of the Rolf Method of Structural Integration."

Spiritists—a person who practices Spiritism, the esoteric belief that says the human personality exists after death and that it can communicate with the living through a medium of psychics. Believers in this phenomenon say this communication comes from the spirit world and is commonly conveyed through apparitions, clairaudience, clairvoyance, the Ouija board, poltergeist, séances, telepathy, and telekinesis, etc.

Spiritualism—the belief or doctrine that the spirits of the dead, surviving after the mortal life, can and do communicate with the living, especially through a person (a medium) particularly susceptible to their influence; (2) the practices or phenomena associated with this belief; (3) the belief that all reality is spiritual; (4) metaphysics, any of various doctrines maintaining that the ultimate reality is spirit or mind; and (5) spiritual quality or tendency.

Sorcery—the term used in the occult world that refers to the practice of manipulating or controlling supernatural spirits, often through black magic. This magic is used to bring evil, cursing or negative effects on the person(s) to whom it is directed. It applies to Satanism, some witchcraft groups, sorcerers, or magicians. The goal is to conjure up evil spirits and invoke them to carry out intended harm.

Trimurti—a trinity consisting of Brahma the Creator, Vishnu the Preserver, and Shiva the Destroyer.

Vishnu—a deity believed to have descended from heaven to earth in several incarnations or avatars, varying in number from nine to twenty-two but always including animals. His most important human incarnation is the Krishna of the Bhagavad Gita, "the Pervader," one of a half-dozen solar deities in the Rigveda, daily traversing the sky in three strides—morning, afternoon, and night.

RESOURCES

Resources included have been used for my completed study and ongoing study of this New Age topic.

author, unknown. n.d.

Baker, John. *Celebrate Recovery. a Recovery Program Based on Eight Principles from the Beatitudes.* Grand Rapids, MI: Zondervan Pub. House, 2012.

Baker, John. n.d. *Celebrate Recovery Leadership Guide.*

Browne, Rodney Howard. 1999. *Seeing Jesus As He Really Is.* Tampa: Revival Ministries International.

Clark, Randy. n.d. "CHCP New Age Video Teaching 2012." Christian Healing Certification Program.

Clark, Randy, and Bill Johnson. 2011. *The Essential Guide to Healing.* Bloomington: Chosen Books.

Copeland, Kenneth. 1994. *John G. Lake—His Life, His Sermons, His Boldness of Faith.* Fort Worth, Texas: Kenneth Copeland Publications.

CrosswayBibles.org. n.d. Scripture taken from The Holy Bible, English Standard Version. Copyright 2001. A publishing ministry of Good News Publishers. Used by permission. All rights reserved. Accessed December 13, 2013. <a href="http://www.crosswayBibles.org">Crossway Bibles</a>.

Hanegraaff, Wouter J. *New Age Religion and Western Culture: Esotericism in the Mirror of Secular Thought*

Hogue, Rodney. 2012. *Developing Your Equipping Track for Deliverance.* Edited by Global Awakening. Christian Healing Certification Program (CHCP).

Hutchings, Dr. Michael. 2014. *PTSD 8 Step Healing Prayer Model for PTSD.* Global Awakening.

James Strong, LL.D., S.T.D. 1990. *Strong's Exhaustive Concordance.* Nashville, Tennessee: Thomas Nelson, Inc.

Jesus Christ the Bearer of the Water of Life: A Christian reflection on New Age. www.vatican.va

Johnson, Bill, and Randy Clark. 2011. *The Essential Guide to Healing: Equipping all Christians to Pray for the Sick.* Chosen Books.

L3—Video number 7 *Healing & Deception: New Age Models Intro*

L3—Video number 8 *Christian Doctrines Denied by New Age*

L3—Video number 9 *New Age Quotes; Hostility toward Christians*

L3—Video number 10 *Energy Healing—Who's is it?*

L4—Video number 2 *Biblical Basis for Healing*

L4—Video number 3 *Overview of New Age Healing*

Miller, Elliott. *Crash Course on the New Age Movement.*

Nichols, Larry, George Matter, and Alvin Schmidt. 2006. *Encyclopedic Dictionary of Cults, Sects and World Religions.* Zondervan.

Rhodes, Ron. *The Counterfeit Christ of the New Age Movement.*

Weldon, John. *Encyclopedia of New Age Beliefs.*

Wimber, John. 1990. *Equipping the Saints.* Vol. 4.

www.watchman.org

www.sedonanewagecenter.org

www.theosophical.org

www.theraputic-touch.org

www.theosociety.org

www.thetempleofpeople.org

www.thewordfoundation.org

www.ts-adyar.org

www.blavatskyhouse.org

www.cancer.org

ABOUT THE AUTHOR

Sandy Bell is a teacher and minister who is called to train up all generations in the ministry of healing. It is her heart's desire to see the body of Christ walking in the fullness of their identity and stepping into their individual inheritance as a son or daughter of the Most High God. She teaches the biblical basis and practical application of the healing power and authority of Jesus Christ.

Sandy understands the training and sacrifice involved to become a victorious warrior in Christ. Her heart is for the healing of all souls that are hurt, wounded, traumatized, abused, addicted, and just broken into pieces, whether they are saved or unsaved.

Sandy has always served in the domestic frontlines, especially with those battling addiction. She is as transparent as any minister can be with her own personal experiences. She has overcome childhood abuse, domestic violence, sexual assault, addiction, depression, fear, and rebellion. Her testimony is one of the powerful healing and transforming love of Jesus.

Sandy is an ordained minister through the Apostolic Network of Global Awakening. She is a graduate of Christian Healing Certification Program (CHCP) in a school of the Apostolic Network of Global Awakening (ANGA). She is a certified as a master equipper in the ministry of healing and a specialist practitioner in physical healing, inner healing/soul care, and deliverance.

Sandy and her husband, Jimmy, reside in Wilmington, North Carolina. She has served as the founder and director of the Wilmington

Healing Center since 2013. The Wilmington Healing Center is a ministry of Zion under the Glory of Zion International, also a ministry of the Apostolic Network of Global Awakening! There, she is able to minister the love of Jesus Christ to many the physical, emotional, or mentally ill, broken, and addicted in her region.

CPSIA information can be obtained
at www.ICGtesting.com
Printed in the USA
BVHW030436090321
602009BV00002B/236